Robin Hood Marketing

Katya Andresen

Foreword by
Kate Roberts

Robin Hood Marketing

Stealing Corporate Savvy to Sell Just Causes

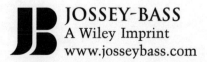

JOSSEY-BASS
A Wiley Imprint
www.josseybass.com

Published by Jossey-Bass
A Wiley Imprint
989 Market Street, San Francisco, CA 94103-1741   www.josseybass.com

Readers should be aware that Internet Web sites offered as citations and/or sources for further information may have changed or disappeared between the time this was written and when it is read.

Jossey-Bass books and products are available through most bookstores. To contact Jossey-Bass directly call our Customer Care Department within the U.S. at 800-956-7739, outside the U.S. at 317-572-3986, or fax 317-572-4002.

Jossey-Bass also publishes its books in a variety of electronic formats. Some content that appears in print may not be available in electronic books.

Library of Congress Cataloging-in-Publication Data

Andresen, Katya, date.
  Robin Hood marketing: stealing corporate savvy to sell just causes/Katya Andresen; foreword by Kate Roberts.
     p. cm.
  Includes bibliographical references.
  ISBN-13: 978-0-7879-8148-8 (cloth)
  ISBN-10: 0-7879-8148-6 (cloth)
  1. Social marketing.   I. Title.
  HF5414.A529 2006
  658.8'02—dc22

                                                     2006004535

Printed in the United States of America
FIRST EDITION
HB Printing 10 9 8 7 6 5 4 3

CONTENTS

FOREWORD

"It's about changing the world . . . wearing shoes!"

When Katya Andresen asked me one day at lunch to write the Foreword to *Robin Hood Marketing,* it took only three spoonfuls of angel hair pasta to agree. Finally, here is a book that all potential "do-gooders" need to read before trying to accomplish good on their own, for their cause, or even for their employer (depending which side of the fence they are on). The principles in these pages make perfect sense to me, as I've experienced them firsthand. I want to tell you my story, because it's further proof of just how powerful it is to engage the private sector and take on its marketing sensibility.

Almost a decade ago, I was a busy executive for an international advertising agency in Romania, marketing soft drinks, cigarettes, and cell phones. I would spend my days plotting the next clever maneuver to get kids to drink more, smoke more, and essentially buy more products that they did not really need. I was a trend-setting machine. But while I was good at what I did, I wasn't sure that I was doing good. That thought started to bother me.

Then a completely different client came through my door. Michael Holscher, the dynamic country director of Population Services International (PSI) in Romania, asked me to help the organization launch a safe-sex campaign called "Do what you want but know what you do." He wanted to protect young people from HIV/AIDS, a problem that had not really hit Romania yet. I jumped at the chance to make it happen, even though it was a pro bono project in my profit-focused world. Here was a chance to throw some creativity into something entirely different, with richer rewards at stake, and it felt like being a kid in a candy store.

Our challenge was to break through the marketing clutter that was already infiltrating the Romanian market. So I asked, What do kids like? Well, they like music, television, sports, fashion—and they like each other! We did nothing different than Coca-Cola would have done: We seized on those likes and developed a brand and positioning, formed key strategic partnerships, established distribution channels for the health products, tapped into the media, and then added sizzle.

The sizzle came in the form of celebrity that courted kids. The most popular music band in Romania at the time, Holograf, offered to write a song about safe sex. This launched the campaign, and the song became a number-one hit. In the band's CDs, we enclosed a condom and other information on how to stay free of HIV and other sexually transmitted diseases. But we also knew that the only truly safe method is abstinence, and we wanted to make that the next big trend. We approached the national TV station to develop a documentary series called *In Bed with You*, which featured various celebrities talking about their experiences and how they wish they had waited. We ran generic TV spots using real kids to talk about the issues they face, along with a series of theme parties. We also pursued kids right into the places they hung out, such as the Black Sea, where we sent "Love Police Cadets" to "arrest" kids if they were not using condoms or abstaining from sex.

The approach was no different from my daytime work with clients, and that got me thinking. Why couldn't I involve all of my other corporate paying clients in this kind of lifesaving work? Why stop at using private-sector approaches? Why not enlist the private sector as partners? Surely this was a win-win. PSI needed funding and the infrastructure of the private sector to reach more kids, and the media and corporations wanted to show customers that they cared. Eventually, some of those clients became sponsors, and PSI was able to expand the campaign and its impact.

Soon after, I took a trip to South Africa to reflect and rest. There I saw with sad clarity that not every country was as fortunate as

Romania, where the destructive HIV pandemic was not yet fully unleashed. In South Africa, I found out that one of every four fourteen-year-old schoolgirls was already infected with HIV. These girls would not live past their twentieth year, and the next generation was at risk. Through sheer poverty, many were driven to take on a "sugar daddy," "teacher," or "rich uncle" to put food on the table or pass their exams in exchange for sex. I could not believe what I saw in this beautiful country: a funeral on every corner. In the townships, every other corrugated iron hut had someone living in it with AIDS. But the stigma of the disease was still so acute that rarely would family members admit to the problem. To do so would mean they would be ostracized from the village.

I looked down at my Gucci shoes and decided I wanted to do something more. That's when the idea of YouthAIDS came to me. Why not do what we were doing in Romania all over the world? Didn't Live Aid raise more than $300 million? The Quincy Jones–led song "We Are the World" raised $90 million overnight. There was more to be done with the power of pop culture and marketing.

Soon after, I founded YouthAIDS, which has since become an initiative of PSI. Based in Washington, D.C., we work in more than sixty countries to educate and protect young people from the horrors of HIV/AIDS. The key ingredients to our success in Romania are all at work on a larger scale: the private-sector marketing approach (including using sports, media, music, fashion, and theater to reach young people with upbeat messages), the role of celebrities (especially our tireless global ambassador, Ashley Judd), and corporate partnerships that present a win-win for everyone involved.

Our key corporate partner is ALDO, which has been involved with the fight against AIDS since 1985, a time when AIDS carried such a stigma that it was extremely difficult to engage companies in AIDS prevention. ALDO decided to take an increasingly vocal role in the cause soon after Robert Hoppenheim, general manager of the shoe giant, was flicking through a copy of the tabloid magazine US

Weekly during one of his many business trips to some of his eight hundred stores. He saw a picture of Kristen Davis, star of the popular TV show *Sex and the City*, wearing a Hello Kitty T-shirt that benefited YouthAIDS. It bore the slogan "Cute outside, angry inside." He picked up the phone and called us, saying, "It's time for us to come out." He was a true risk taker, and his company shared our mission. Aldo Bensadoun, the founder of the ALDO shoe company, looked me straight in the eyes in our initial meeting and said, "Once and for all, we must fight and beat HIV in order to erase it from the face of the earth."

ALDO, together with YouthAIDS, has since developed a true global cause-related marketing campaign that helped us raise millions of dollars, created half a *billion* media impressions in the first three months of the campaign alone, and helped abolish the stigma attached to this silent killer for so many years. The effort combines aggressive marketing with ALDO's huge resources to amplify our message and build visibility. Celebrities popular with youth, including Christina Aguilera, Salma Hayek, Ashley Judd, Penelope Cruz, LL Cool J, Cindy Crawford, and Elijah Wood, play on a popular idiom, posing with duct tape over their eyes and mouth and hands over their ears. The message is designed to seize attention and spur youth to purchase "empowerment tags" with the message "See, Hear, Speak." We were inspired by the yellow band of Lance Armstrong, but we also wanted something that could help us create a dialogue about AIDS among young people. What better way than to create a dogtag-like fashion accessory that would keep on speaking?

Through thought-provoking statements such as "Most of the people infected with HIV don't know it" and "8,000 people die every day" and startling black-and-white images shot by worldrenowned fashion photographer Peter Lindbergh, we created billboards, magazine articles, taxi tops, bus shelters, and full buses decorated with the campaign. Through the leverage of ALDO's media buying, outdoor companies and publishers donated millions of dollars' worth of advertising space. Within three months of launching the campaign, we had sold over 225,000 tags, and they were even selling in countries where we did not have a campaign. The message was everywhere.

Just recently, I sat in a restaurant with members of the ALDO team. They had just received a footwear industry award before their peers and competitors for an advertising campaign that did not include a single pair of shoes yet sold an important message to millions, increased the company's visibility, and in the process not only accomplished good but also increased sales—the best of all worlds. By way of thanks, they marched me into one of their stores and let me pick out a pair of cowboy boots—my new favorites!

Shoes are a recurring theme in my story, and not just because they are an accessory I love. They actually sum up the essence of *Robin Hood Marketing* especially well: Do as the private sector does, and always act according to the perspective of the people you want to reach. Marketing well is all about walking a mile in someone else's shoes—those of our partners, our audiences, and anyone else we need to influence. What this book does so well is put us into that footwear and make that journey so we can advance farther and faster on the road to achieving our mission. You'll find that *Robin Hood Marketing* is an irreplaceable guide for your own trip. *Bon voyage* and good luck!

Washington, D.C.   Kate Roberts
February 2006   *Founder*
                                                YouthAIDS

                                                Vice President
                                                Population Services International

ACKNOWLEDGMENTS

The first person who should be acknowledged is you, one of the people out there promoting a good cause. People like you astonish me every day. I am fascinated by your stories and moved by your passion—so moved, in fact, that I set out to write a book because many of you made me feel compelled to help in some way. My hope is that the ideas in these pages will serve as a rocket booster to propel your important cause onward and upward. The more you succeed, the better off the world will be.

Writing a book is an act both vain and humbling. Vain, because to sit down and write you must believe yourself an expert. Humbling, because in writing you discover you do not know everything. Here, I would like to thank the people who helped me retain enough vanity to keep writing and enough humility to keep learning.

Among the most important are two pioneers of marketing for good causes, Sharyn Sutton and Bill Novelli. I've worked for both in my career, and their brilliant, unconventional, and challenging thinking deeply influenced my own. This book would not have been possible without that experience. Other contributors of great ideas and suggestions during the writing process were Ken Weber, Liz Heid Thompson, Tinker Reddy, Caron Gremont, Irina Negreyeva, Paul Malley, and Diane Meier.

Other people's thinking is made more visible in these pages in a series of interviews. Thanks to the following individuals for sharing their wisdom, reviewing the manuscript, and agreeing to be profiled in the book: Ken Weber, Bill Strathmann, Jack Fyock, James Browning, Leslie McCuaig, Mark Dessauer, Kristin Grimm, Kathy Ryan, Diane Bloom, David La Piana, Jan Pomerantz, Paul Bloom, Brian

Krieg, Dwayne Proctor, Jim Towey, Andy Goodman, and Raphael Bemporad.

While these people held me to high standards on content, others reminded me to keep my writing coherent and clear. Elisabeth Cohen Browning and Dorothy Hearst made invaluable and encouraging suggestions and edits. I also owe a great debt to my writing mentor, Nancy Tilly.

Two people taught me that selling a book is a lot like selling a good cause: Noreen Wald and my agent, Mollie Glick. I would not have been able to publish *Robin Hood Marketing* without them. At the same time, one person reminded me that selling a book doesn't matter as much as the act of writing. I don't know Anne Lamott, but the dog-eared state of my copy of *Bird by Bird* attests to how much her advice about writing and life has meant to me.

A small circle of people treated me as their own good cause while I was writing. I owe so much to my brother Matt Andresen, who contributed greatly to this book and to my life. I am grateful to my father, Jeffry Andresen, for reviewing the manuscript and for teaching me the importance of listening—in the most attentive way—to those around us. My mother, Julie McClintock, has fundamentally shaped my life not only in her role as mother but also in her work as an effective advocate for many good causes. I appreciate her always showing me that determined actions, not just intentions, are necessary to change the world. I also thank Teri Andresen, Amanda Andresen, John Morris, Margaret Kajeckas, Michele Moloney-Kitts, Katita Strathmann, Tom Walsh, Rebecca Baggett, Leslie McCuaig, and Lyudmyla Shulgina for their support and encouragement at critical times.

Last and most important, thank you to my daughters, Sophia and Kate, who often awoke to the sound of my tapping on the computer keyboard and patiently endured my many hours of work on the manuscript. I hope their future, so dear to my heart, will someday benefit from this effort.

—K.A.

Robin Hood Marketing

For Sophia and Kate

Lost in Sherwood Forest

Facing the Fact That Marketing Is a Must

The Robin Hood of modern folk-mythology is a creature built up, generation by generation, to meet the needs and desires of his audience. The earliest Robin Hood was a yeoman, not a wronged nobleman, who haunted Barnsdale Forest, not Sherwood; he didn't become a Saxon or mere Englishman fighting the Norman oppressor until Sir Walter Scott dressed him up for his walk-on in Ivanhoe. *The original outlaw behind Batman and Zorro and the Scarlet Pimpernel was a ragged ruffian who might have worn Lincoln green, whose shadow stretching across the centuries tells us much about our changing understanding of order and honor and justice.*[1]

PAULA KATHERINE MARMOR

We all have moments in life when we happen upon our calling, and mine was when I encountered a giant, smiling condom in Cambodia. A reporter at the time, I had been milling around a World AIDS Day event at a scruffy Phnom Penh city park and observing with boredom the usual collection of government signs and pamphlet-wielding health workers when I suddenly came upon a flurry of excited activity. Looking up, I saw the source of the commotion: a towering, condom-shaped balloon emblazoned with the words "Number One." People were flocking to the balloon, which had a friendly smile strategically sketched on its tip. At its base, a crowd was eagerly grabbing free samples of Number One condoms, as well as Number One paraphernalia like T-shirts, hats, and shorts.

The enthusiasm was refreshing. It was the mid-1990s, and I'd been covering the bleak story of Cambodia's HIV epidemic. I had spent many hours talking to frustrated health workers, as well as to cavalier and careless men who visited sex workers for less than the price of a beer and to many bewildered and fearful wives who'd contracted HIV from their own husbands. Very few people I met grasped the threat of the growing epidemic, and those who did either dismissed HIV/AIDS as irrelevant or greeted it with a stony sense of resignation. Either way, they weren't abstaining from risky sexual behavior or lining up to use condoms. There was not much good news to report.

Yet here was a rare smiling face to HIV prevention, bobbing in the hot afternoon breeze above the crowd. For once, I heard no doom-filled message of fear or shame. In its place was an appealing sense of pride and fun. The balloon, which touted the one English phrase everyone in Cambodia knew and loved, said it all. Who didn't want to be number one?

It turned out the giant condom belonged to Population Services International (PSI), one of the nonprofit organizations that is highly effective at marketing items that keep us healthy. PSI had just launched the Number One brand in Cambodia, and, as in all its work, it was taking a business-minded, results-oriented approach to its cause. It had a well-researched and branded product for combating the spread of HIV/AIDS and the infrastructure to sell it: a strong team of salespeople with corporate backgrounds, an aggressive promotion strategy, and a sophisticated distribution system.

I went to see that entire marketing machinery in action a few nights later, when I accompanied PSI salespeople through the underbelly of Phnom Penh. They were out selling in their target market's milieu: brothels in the ramshackle red-light district of Svay Pak. In Cambodia, many men visit sex workers, so PSI had targeted brothels as critical to halting the spread of AIDS. The PSI staff were selling deeply discounted but high-quality condoms in bulk for only about $1 per box of one hundred, and the salespeople had their positioning and sales pitch for this audience down pat.

The brothel owners told me they approved of the Number One brand because of the allure of its foreign name, and they liked the low price because they could sell the condoms to customers for several cents apiece and make a small profit. The men who frequented the brothels seemed to see the product—which was affordable but, importantly, not free—as a status symbol because of its name, and consequently they agreed to use condoms. And the young women working in the lean-to brothels got protection from exposure to HIV. In short, the product offered something for everyone, and that something was closely linked to the personal values of each of the audiences involved.

Number One condoms are now available in virtually every brothel in Cambodia, and, helped by a law that has since mandated condom use in sex establishments, HIV prevalence among sex workers and the general population has dropped dramatically. Now PSI is tackling a troubling problem of rising transmission among married and sweetheart couples in Cambodia.

It's worth noting (especially for those troubled by the culturally ingrained sex industry in Cambodia or the whole idea of condom use) that PSI also sells abstinence and fidelity, with the same results-oriented approach. That means working with the people, places, and events that matter most in a culture. PSI has done everything from creating soap operas to campaigning with religious leaders to convince people to change behaviors that hurt their health. In the process, they have accomplished far more than a finger-wagging message or government-sponsored abstinence campaign or condom giveaway ever could.

The common thread in all those efforts is approaching social good with a marketing mentality borrowed from the business world. The customer is always the focus. Great power inheres in that combination of good intentions and customer-centered marketing, as I was reminded in watching the smiling condom and the surrounding crowd. That day in the park presented both a personal and a professional epiphany. The personal epiphany was that after witnessing many sad events as a reporter, I was ready to return to doing something about them. I knew I would eventually leave journalism and go back to my previous work for good causes. The professional epiphany was that I wanted to work with causes that were interested in tapping and harnessing corporate savvy to accomplish their goals. I'd long been a believer in persuasion over preaching and selling over scolding, but I had encountered some resistance to that approach in the past. I'd ended up leaving the nonprofit field, but now I was ready to return and persevere.

I have since found stealing corporate know-how and applying it to good causes to be so successful that I decided to write this book so everyone from organizational leaders to volunteers unfamiliar with marketing principles can quickly master this approach and gain an advantage in the marketplace. It works. I have seen causes move toward their goals by leaps and bounds and double or triple their impact by embracing and applying basic marketing concepts.

The world would be a better place if all of us had that kind of success. Nearly eighty-four million Americans volunteer their time for good causes, and nearly nine in ten U.S. households contribute to good causes.[2] More than twelve million Americans work for non-profits.[3] *Robin Hood Marketing* aims to increase our effectiveness so we can unleash the potential for positive change that these numbers represent. Imagine what would happen if we all became twice as persuasive as we are now. How many millions more could we convince to join our organizations, volunteer their time, donate money, or change their lifestyles? Don't we owe it to our cause to try?

WHAT MARKETING MEANS

Marketing is how we get to those goals. It is how we motivate people to buy the product we are selling by demonstrating how it meets their needs and wants. As workers for good causes, we are all looking for ways to convince people to take an action (that's the selling part) that carries a price tag (the buying part). For example, the action may be buying a condom, volunteering, writing a check, quitting smoking, or voting for new legislation. The price may be time, money, discomfort, loss of a beloved or convenient vice, or political capital. Marketing gets people to pay our prices by convincing them they will get something of immediate, personal value in exchange.

Many of us may wish marketing were not necessary and that people would pay our prices without expecting anything in return. "Why should we have to do this when our cause is so worthy?" is a common refrain I hear from do-gooders. "If people would only listen, they'd see that (fill in the blank) is the right thing to do." These comments fly straight as Robin Hood's arrow to the heart of the myth this book will debunk: that right is might. It's not. Regrettably, simply being right is rarely enough to secure the victory of our cause. If it were, the world would be a perfect place.

Still, the do-gooders of this world—and I count myself as one—tend to stick to the same approaches. We continue to operate under the assumption, conscious or not, that if people just took the time to listen to us wax poetic about the urgent problems we are tackling—or if they just had more information—they would change their perspective, embrace our worldview, and take action. We end up lost in Sherwood Forest, marketing to an audience of one: ourselves. In our haste to pour our hearts into what we say, we forget to use our minds.

Commercial marketing requires us to think more dispassionately than we often do. It requires us to orient ourselves not according to our mission and our convictions, but according to the perspective of our audiences, the actions of our competitors, and the reality of our marketplace. We have to go from being inward-looking to being outward-minded, switching from the perspective of "what you should do for me because it's right" to "here is what I can do for you." Not even a legend escapes this rule. Consider the story of Robin Hood himself as quoted at the start of this book. Robin Hood is who we need him to be. Even our heroes are a reflection of ourselves, our culture, and our time. It's all about the audience.

ROBIN HOOD'S ORIGINS

Once upon a time, in the early 1950s, a clever professor named Gerhart Wiebe asked, "Can brotherhood be sold like soap?" In a now-famous *Public Opinion Quarterly* article, he argued the answer was yes.[4] He maintained that the more commercial the approach, the greater a social-change campaign's likelihood of success. The first in a long line of noble Robin Hood Marketers was born.

In the decades since, great marketing minds have developed and refined Wiebe's concept and created an entire professional field around it: *social marketing,* a term coined by marketing gurus Philip Kotler and Gerald Zaltman in 1971.[5] These trailblazers encountered some resistance. People weren't accustomed to using marketing principles in this way and feared that marketing was akin to propaganda or that it wouldn't work. These detractors have been proved wrong. Thousands of professionals have taken marketing principles and successfully applied them to good causes throughout the United States and the world. Social marketing is taught at universities, and a host of academics and practitioners develop and debate the topic in books, journals, and classrooms.

So the premise of *Robin Hood Marketing* is well-proven, and the principles in this book are based on a solid foundation of professional experience and academic study. Marketing good causes with a corporate mind-set delivers results. Yet many—if not most—causes do not apply marketing principles to the extent that they could. In my own work with dozens of good causes, I have found that many of us choose either to eschew marketing or to pursue it in a way that is not wholly effective.

Why? Perhaps because we think of marketing as glib and facile, something lighter than the serious work we're involved in. Or we may have mixed feelings toward corporations and their operating style and be reluctant to copy their approach. Our reluctance is also probably a reflection of the fact that the private-sector marketing approach has not reached a critical mass in the nonprofit area. As a result, most of us have limited experience in applying these principles.

In *Robin Hood Marketing* I seek to popularize the marketing approach of the first Robin Hood Marketers and the innovative volunteers and organizations that followed them by presenting memorable principles, practical examples, and good stories. It's social marketing for the rest of us.

THE ROBIN HOOD APPROACH

Robin Hood Marketing covers ten key marketing principles, mostly from the private sector, each of which is the topic of one chapter. Each of the principles, with the exception of the one focused on media relations, is illustrated at the beginning of the chapter by a famous corporate marketing effort. Many of the marketing examples I've chosen are advertisements, not because advertising is the same thing as marketing—it is only one aspect of it—but because advertisements are often the most visible, familiar, and understandable aspect of a marketing campaign.

Each chapter then covers how the marketing principle, the Robin Hood Rule, has been applied by a full range of advocates for good causes, from big U.S. nonprofits to neighborhood committees to shoestring organizations halfway across the world. Many of the examples are from my own wide-ranging, world-wandering background, which has included marketing work for dozens of good causes over the years, including CARE International in the United States and the Institute for Sustainable Communities in Ukraine; in addition, I draw on my work as a journalist, which included assignments for Reuters in Cambodia and for the Associated Press in Madagascar. Finally, each chapter ends with a section on how good causes can apply the Robin Hood Rules and interviews with people who have successfully advanced their own good causes by using the rule highlighted in that chapter. I interviewed people working for causes both big and small, as well as experts in aspects of marketing ranging from competitive positioning to storytelling.

As we cover each of the ten principles of Robin Hood Marketing, we will be creating a marketing arrowhead, which organizes the ideas I'll be introducing into a series of steps to follow in developing a marketing effort. By crafting a strong arrowhead, we will be able to hit our targets and inspire them to action. In the first chapter, we start with the assumption that our cause already has a mission and a set of programs it wants to advance through marketing, and we take that thinking a step further by setting a marketing goal, which is the action we want our audiences—the people we want to reach—to take. This action is the point or tip of our marketing arrowhead. Then, in Chapter Two we look closely at our audiences, so we can align our cause and desired action to their existing values. Next, Chapter Three analyzes the cluttered marketplace surrounding our audiences and describes how to recognize and react to forces that influence audiences. Chapter Four indicates how to tell the difference between friend and foe. Chapter Five shows how to take advantage of allies to effectively market our cause. Finally, in Chapters Six through Nine, we learn how to create and deliver a powerful message. This last part of the arrowhead can be crafted only after we fully understand our marketplace and the values of our audience. If our arrow is well honed through this insight, it will fly straight to our audiences' hearts and minds. Chapter Ten summarizes the ideas from all the chapters and explains how they fit together in a marketing campaign.

Working through all ten chapters will enable readers to put together a marketing plan, but for those who want to focus on specific aspects of marketing, I offer some advice. Each chapter begins with a section that covers the highlights of the chapter. If time is limited, read those sections and then focus on the chapters dealing with the individual marketing issues that are most pressing. For those working for good causes that want to improve their messages, the most important chapters are One, Two, and Six through Eight. Those focused on media relations should read Chapters Seven through Nine. Those wanting to improve their competitive positioning and pursue partnerships will find Chapters Three through Five enlightening. Chapters Seven through Nine provide useful background for establishing partnerships.

MORALITY AND MARKETING

Before we turn to those issues, I want to recognize that at times in this process some of us may find ourselves wondering where marketing ends and manipulation starts. This is a good question to contemplate because marketing requires us to strike a graceful balance between who we are, what we can offer, and what our audiences want. I encourage readers to consider that marketing, when practiced professionally and ethically, is about influencing, not manipulating, people. There is nothing intrinsically immoral about it. Isn't that what good causes are trying to do every day—to influence people to donate money, recycle their plastic, stop smoking, or feed the hungry?

I would argue, instead, that wasting precious resources by dealing with social issues ineffectively is immoral. There is no nobility in preaching to an audience of one. Those of us working for the public good have an ethical responsibility to be effective and efficient in reaching as many people as possible. If we can't make a compelling case that prompts people to act, then we have failed to make a difference and wasted valuable time, effort, and, often, donor and taxpayer dollars.

Still, we have to be true to ourselves. Marketing allows us to meet our audience where they are, physically and mentally, but it does not require us to lose our own way. We should stay true to our mission, represent ourselves honestly, and promise only what we can deliver. In that way, we gain a competitive advantage over all the other folks using marketing for more nefarious ends. We have credibility and sincerity on our side, and we should never lose sight of that.

Finding a way to strike the right balance between our goals and our audiences' wants can be an epiphany. I have heard many people call it an "aha!" moment. Aha! moments allow us to see the world in a new way and to grasp creative ways to increase our impact. By sharing the inspiring aha! experiences of dozens of good causes, I hope to generate new ones for the readers of this book. Here's to many epiphanies and much success.

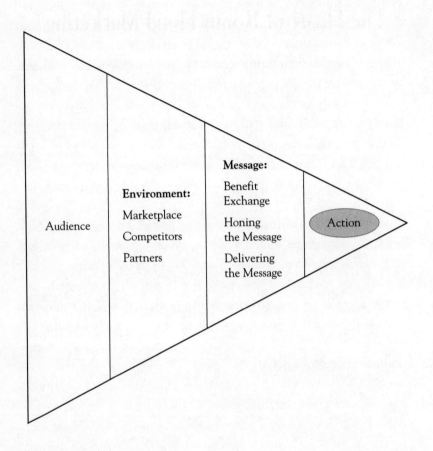

1

The Heart of Robin Hood Marketing

*Focus on Getting People
to Do Something Specific*

WHAT THIS CHAPTER SAYS

- The key to marketing is to focus on our audiences and not just on our mission and our organization.

- Marketers set goals according to what they want people to do and then work backward into how to make that action happen. They use a specific audience as their starting point.

- In reaching out to audiences, think of them as customers rather than potential converts. We don't need to strive for a shared worldview; we need to have people take a specific action that advances our mission. They don't have to know everything; they simply need the information that is immediately relevant to them.

- To apply the principles in this chapter: Determine what we are trying to accomplish, define an action for each audience that will help us meet our goals, and then test those actions to ensure they are sufficiently specific, feasible, and free of barriers.

JUST DO IT.

In three words, Nike marketed one of the best-known brands through one of the most oft-repeated slogans in marketing history. "Just do it" instantly fills our heads with images of the Nike swoosh, the grace of Michael Jordan, and the grit and glory of a can-do attitude to stretching our own limits. We feel inspired—perhaps not to go work up a serious sweat right this minute, but certainly to buy the shoes that imply we are the kind of person who could. The marketing campaign, launched in 1988, helped Nike sprint past competitor Reebok and establish itself as the market leader at a time when the jogging and fitness craze was taking off and athletic shoes were increasingly fashionable. The campaign has since earned a place in the Smithsonian Institution and is viewed as a gold standard of marketing.

So what makes those three words so powerful and the campaign so successful? "Just do it" focuses less on the product and more on us. Nike often quotes cofounder Bill Bowerman as saying, "If you have a body, you are an athlete."[1] And if you're an athlete, you are a potential Nike customer. The athlete-customer is the centerpiece of "just do it." Adman Dan Weiden, who created the campaign, explicitly and elegantly focused on us and what Nike wants us to do: to see ourselves as athletes, to desire a determined self-image, and to buy Nike shoes.[2]

> The key to marketing is to focus on our audiences and not ourselves. Nike succeeds by focusing on the people who buy the shoes, not just the shoes. We must focus on the people we need to take action, not just our mission and organization.

I'm not saying we should put our audiences before our mission. Every organization, including Nike, has a mission. It explains why we exist and guides our work. But to achieve that mission we need marketing. And to do marketing, we need more than just a mission statement; we need a clear idea of which people need to take which actions in order for us to achieve our mission.

Robin Hood Rule 1

Go beyond the big-picture mission and focus on getting people to take specific action.

For example, Nike's mission is to bring inspiration and innovation to every athlete in the world (which by Nike's definition is every person). The mission statement sounds nice, and it probably helps guide Nike's corporate sensibility, but it doesn't get to the marketing end point of selling Nike shoes. What action does Nike want people to take so they will feel inspired? Nike wants us to buy Nike shoes. We "just do it" because Nike's marketing strategy is to show us that buying its shoes makes us inspired, cool, athletic, and part of the world where Michael Jordan and Tiger Woods play. Nike is asking us to do something specific, and that specific thing is doable. Nike doesn't ask us to run ten miles. Nike tells us to buy the shoes that other people wear when they run ten miles, or to buy the shoes that may inspire us to run ten miles. Nike doesn't market with its mission. Its marketing is a means to get to its mission.

We need to make that same distinction by speaking in terms that resonate with our audience and asking for actions that are feasible. To apply the running metaphor to good causes, we should not assume everyone loves running (or our mission) as much as we do, and we should avoid asking people to go cover a quick ten miles right now because it's good for them. Although we need a mission, our audiences don't need to fully understand or embrace our mission in order for us to advance it. Rule 1 reminds us that we may get further by convincing people to take a walk around the block rather than to run ten miles.

GETTING STARTED BY
GOING IN REVERSE

→ Marketers set goals according to the action they want people
to take and then work backward to make that happen. This
process reverses the way most of us work. Traditionally, good
causes attack a social problem by starting with a mission and
planning forward, putting the focus on the organization. Marketing planning, by contrast, uses a specific audience as its
starting point.

In traditional planning, a nonprofit organization or volunteer
committee goes on retreat, wrestles to get consensus on a mission
statement, analyzes various options, and then devises a "strategic
plan" or "strategic vision" based on a staff-driven understanding of
the cause and its goals. Sound familiar? The exercise emphasizes collective reasoning, shared decision making, and group consensus.
The group wants everyone to agree on a direction, and so the direction is determined by the perspective of the group. The marketing plan is then an outgrowth of that process.

This process is important to an organization, but it's ultimately
an inwardly turned exercise. By contrast, marketing is outwardly
turned. Because marketing starts with an end result for a specific audience, it challenges us to dwell in the world of our audiences and
their marketplace. Audience actions, not our own ideas, are its
focus. To do marketing planning, we have to get beyond our far-off
mission (like helping people overcome poverty, increasing consumer
access to affordable health care, or strengthening schools) and zero
in on specific audience actions that are tangible, achievable, and
measurable. Then we plan backward from there. We ask, what
needs to happen so an audience will take an incremental step? How
will we convince them to act? That is the work of marketing, and
we'll tackle the answers in this book.

JUST DO WHAT?

In trying to convince our audience to act, we are typically tempted to do two things: convert people to our cause and impart vast amounts of information about it. By reversing our planning process, we begin to see these two approaches are unnecessary and, worse, are unlikely to work.

➤ Think in terms of customers, not converts. For our customers, a shared worldview is not a prerequisite to action.

To get people to take action—which is the whole point of marketing—we don't need an army of "mini-me's" or true believers. Although we may want to create fundraiser clones or health nuts or environmental crusaders with a profound understanding of our cause, doing so is unnecessary, as well as nearly impossible, for accomplishing good. We simply want to get people to take a specific action: give $50 online, eat five servings of fruits and vegetables a day, or tell their town-council members to vote against an environmentally damaging development. These people may not be experts on our issue, and that's fine. The reasons people take these actions may be entirely different from our own, and that's OK too. It's important only that they take action. They need only jog around the block and thus take a small step toward advancing our mission, whether they are fully aware of our mission or not.

We don't need to impart massive amounts of information, tempting though that may be. For example, when I buy a computer, I ask whether it has Intel inside. I have no idea how a Pentium processor works, and I don't want to know. There is not that much time in the day. I "just do it"—buy the Pentium—without ever becoming a computer expert or knowing Intel's mission statement. Similarly, we should not saddle people with the burden of becoming an expert on our topic before asking them to do something about it.

A little information goes a long way, and too much can be counterproductive and unconvincing. The brilliant social psychologist Elliot Aronson has written about the dilution effect, which describes how neutral or irrelevant information can weaken people's opinions or impressions. He cites an experiment by Henry Zukier in which two students were described to the research subjects as studying thirty-one hours per week outside of class. For the first student, that was the only information provided. For the second, additional, irrelevant information was added about the number of siblings the student had, how often the student visited his grandparents, and other facts. The study found that people believed the first student was smarter.[3] The additional information seemed to dilute the main point, which was the number of hours the student studied. If we have a good point to make, it can get lost if we provide too much information around it.

⇉→   People don't need to know everything; they simply want to know what is immediately relevant to them.

Here is a story from a good cause that vividly illustrates these concepts. Just a few weeks after the tragedy of September 11, 2001, and the anthrax attacks that followed, a group of public health professionals gathered to talk about their efforts to restore the crumbling U.S. public health system. The field had been trying to modernize its facilities and operations for many years, but it had struggled to get attention and investment. Before September 2001, no one had much cared. But now an unfathomable terror attack and anthrax-laced mail had changed everything. Suddenly, the ability of the United States to protect the health of its people was of paramount importance. You could not turn on the television or pick up a newspaper without learning terrifying facts about bioterrorism— or about the long-neglected and woefully weak line of defense available from the underfunded public health system. The country had started caring about public health. People were listening. They wanted to be safe, and they wanted to know what had to be done to restore the protective system that public health provides.

Despite my severe post-9/11 trepidation about flying, I boarded my flight out West for the public health conference with a sense of optimism. Like many Americans, I wanted to do something to help our country, and I was eager to spend time with the vitally important, committed people who worked day in and day out to protect my health. For too long, they'd been ignored, taken for granted, and targeted for budget cuts. But now was a chance to change that perception, and, as a consultant, I was there to help them do it.

At the opening night of the conference, a funder interested in helping the cause of public health gave a speech, then asked the attendees to reflect on how September 11 and the anthrax attacks had changed life for them as professionals. I pulled out pencil and paper in anticipation of the front-line information that could be taken back to spur action among other funders, policymakers, and the public. I'd heard stories of public health officials having to go home at night to send their work e-mails because they had no Internet access at the office. I knew the public health system lacked the equipment and staff necessary to quickly identify and report an outbreak of a dangerous disease.

A microphone was passed. The first person spoke. "This anthrax situation—it's terrible but it's such a distraction," she said. "Smoking is a far greater threat to public health than this, and yet all anyone wants to talk about is anthrax." Another person spoke up. "We have to get people focused on the broader work of public health. This isn't just about terrorism; it's about so much more." Vigorous applause followed. And so it went. One by one, these caring, devoted people talked about how the public's attention was misdirected. They asked, why couldn't the public understand public health in all its dimensions? Why weren't they paying attention to the many other aspects of the field? Why wasn't anyone talking about obesity or smoking?

The session ended on that note, and I grumpily returned to my hotel room. I opened the minibar and turned on the television—like everyone, I spent a great deal of time watching the news then. The first image on the screen was an advertisement. General Motors was telling viewers to buy a vehicle (at zero percent financing) to "keep America rolling." I stared at the television and its fitting commentary on the evening. Someone was seizing this moment of collective concern over the future of our country to urge action, but it was carmakers, not the public health professionals in the ballroom downstairs. Public concern was being harnessed to sell cars, not protect people's health. My goal was getting people to rally around the public health cause, but instead four-wheel-drive vehicles were speeding into the sunset in the name of patriotism.

If funders, policymakers, and the U.S. public finally wanted to invest in public health because terrorism had gotten their attention, why didn't the vital protectors in the ballroom downstairs see that as an opportunity? The answer was that they were focused more on what people thought of their field than on the actions people needed to take to strengthen the field's infrastructure. They didn't have an immediate, concrete "just do it" idea, such as having people demand additional government funding. They wanted people to see public health the way the profession saw it, to embrace a healthier lifestyle, and then, and only then, advocate for adequate funding for the field based on a full appreciation of the spectrum of services it provides. In essence, they wanted their audiences to become experts and change their worldview before taking action. Unfortunately, that is the equivalent of demanding of the U.S. public an instantaneous love of running and sending everyone out for a ten-mile sprint.

People are never going to see our cause exactly as we see it because they have their own view of the world. That leaves us two choices: either we can try in vain to get them to see the world the same way we do, or we can work from their perspective. Working from their perspective means asking them to do something realistic. I am not saying that "keep America rolling" is the right approach or that every good cause should wrap itself in the flag and capitalize on tragedy in the name of crass self-interest. Rather, instead of pleading with people to think like us, we should ask them to take concrete action based on the values that already matter to them. We don't ignore our mission, but we choose the most expeditious route to accomplishing that mission by appealing to our audience's perspective.

Let's step back into the hotel ballroom in the wake of 9/11. Public attention is focused like a laser beam on bioterrorism. Our cause (public health, in this case) addresses that concern. This is an opportunity to link our cause to our audiences' priorities, to win their support, and to ask them to take specific action. What do we want those people to do? If I'm a public health advocate in 2001, my immediate concern is my field's crumbling infrastructure. I need money to fix it. I want donors to give money for computers, communication systems, and training. I want my political representatives to earmark government funding for my cause. And I want the public to pressure lawmakers to do so. To get all that to happen, I don't need people to love the public health field or to understand its nuances. I don't need them to turn over a new leaf and quit smoking, eat better, and exercise more. Right now, I just need them to fund my project, pass my bill, or call a member of Congress and ask for money to protect the health of the country. If people give money, pass a bill, or make that call because they get a sense of safety from improved infrastructure, then that is success by my estimation. I get the investment that will help me to address their concerns as well as to fulfill the whole gamut of the public health system's responsibilities. People may not care about that larger good, and they don't need to. But they will get the benefit of it.

Fortunately, this story has a happy ending—or at least as happy as it gets in this day and age. Leaders in the public health field, including a few people in that ballroom, successfully showed their work's relevance to Americans in the post-9/11 world. They made these links. A survey at the time showed the result: a whopping 80 percent of Americans supported public health infrastructure investment—defined as funding for local and state health departments. The message got through. We may question whether the funding was sufficient or properly allocated in the end, but Americans and their political representatives "just did it" for public health.

➤ We must make complex issues understandable, or we can't market them.

Some people would say this is oversimplification. I would call it effective communication. People are bombarded with thousands of messages a day. They don't have time to become specialists in our cause, whether it is Social Security, public health infrastructure, stem-cell research, or local greenways. Social psychologists like Elliot Aronson and Robert Cialdini have documented this phenomenon of information overload extensively and describe how people seek to conserve their mental energy, screen out data, and rely on cognitive shortcuts.[4] For good causes, if we don't make an issue as clear as possible and the call to action as simple as we can, we will lose our audience.

Once people get one clear idea and take one small action, we can ask them to take another. It's a process. Momentum starts with one action and then takes time to build. Over time, some members of our audience may develop a greater understanding of our cause or a larger commitment to its aims. They may even want additional information or become converts. But we can't assume they will, and we can't start with that goal as a first step. That's the ten-mile run, and that's too far, even if we're wearing Nikes.

EXAMPLES OF CLEAR ACTIONS

Let's look at a couple of hypothetical examples of good causes and the specific actions they might seek. Suppose we're an antismoking group that wants to increase consumer access to and use of low-cost programs that help smokers quit. Who are our audiences? Obviously, smokers would be one. What are we asking them to do? We aren't asking them to quit smoking. That's not specific or feasible enough. What if we asked them to call a toll-free number to sign up for a program providing nicotine-replacement therapy and phone counseling to help them quit smoking? That's better. What might our action for our audience of donors be? We would want them to provide funds to run our campaign to enroll people in the program. How about other financial players, like insurers? We could ask them to pay for antismoking programs. Or we could be specific and ask them to provide a health benefit to all members that includes nicotine-replacement therapy and phone counseling.

We might want still more audiences to act. We might ask businesses to ask for quit-smoking benefits for their employees in their health-insurance package. We might ask policymakers to pass a law restricting smoking in public places, including offices. We might ask researchers to let us publicize evidence that nicotine-replacement therapy combined with phone counseling significantly increases success in quitting smoking and ask them agree to media interviews arranged by our cause. We might also have a specific action for sympathetic causes, such as including information on the program in their newsletters and other outreach vehicles. In all cases, the actions are tailored to the audience, specific, and feasible.

Now let's try another example. Suppose we organize a small neighborhood association to improve the quality of life and safety in the neighborhood. We want both to increase communication and cooperation between neighbors through meetings and a neighborhood-watch program and to lobby the town council on issues of importance to the neighborhood. If we are action-oriented, how do we communicate with our neighbors? Instead of simply telling them about the association, we might specifically ask them to join it, to come to neighborhood meetings, to speak in support of neighborhood initiatives at town-council meetings, and to participate in the neighborhood-watch program. The town council might be another audience. We might want its members to recognize the top problems of the neighborhood, approve speed bumps, and vote against a proposed zoning change that would allow higher density and commercial development. The police might be another audience; we might, for example, want them to respond to neighborhood-watch reports.

As these examples show, the actions chosen should reflect the many forces and players that contribute to a problem and solutions to that problem. My favorite example of this kind of thinking was a program to reduce the number of orphans in Crimea. Many newborn infants were being abandoned there, and, when placed in orphanages, they had little chance of being adopted. It was a tragic problem. The Crimean Charity Fund, a grantee of the Vermont-based Institute for Sustainable Communities, identified a web of problems contributing to the situation: village teenage girls were becoming pregnant at high rates, and many abandoned their children; some disadvantaged mothers were forced to leave their children at maternity wards if they could not pay hospital charges levied by corrupt administrators; and many families who wanted to adopt children did not try because the adoption process was perceived as complicated and expensive.

The organization decided it needed a range of audiences to take action in order to improve this situation. To tackle the problem of teen pregnancy, which had increased in many villages more than tenfold in the previous decade, the Fund targeted the most influential group for teen girls: boys. They were asked to attend a Fatherhood School, which prepared more than a thousand teenagers in several villages for the realities of family life and acted as a deterrent to risky sex. The result: in the project villages the following year, there were no new instances of HIV among teenagers and no unwanted pregnancies. When it discovered 15 percent of new mothers were forced to abandon their newborn babies until they could pay extortionate rates for hospital linens under a scheme devised by unscrupulous folk preying on the poor, the Fund successfully lobbied the mayor's office to stop the practice and provide public money to fund the service for low-income women. They got previous charges refunded to other disadvantaged women.

The Fund also launched a large-scale public-information campaign that successfully addressed the major barriers to adoption: it communicated to parents that adoption was not as legally difficult as they perceived and that the Fund could provide free legal counsel. The campaign was covered in more than one hundred local media, and local newspapers further supported the effort by publishing photos of orphans with disabilities. Posters in infertility clinics also generated interest. Thanks to these efforts, adoption rates increased sevenfold overall in Crimea and fourfold for disabled children. Calls to the adoption-consultation center increased tenfold. The Fund even got the regional administration to create a program promoting adoption, and that project works with a diverse group of lawyers, doctors, like-minded organizations, and local government officials to build on all the campaigns' successes by seeking to address adoption delays caused by problematic waiting-period legislation.

HOW TO USE ROBIN HOOD RULE 1

Here are six steps we can take to apply "just do it" thinking in our organizations.

1. Determine Marketing Goals

Here's a test I often use: I state what I think I want to accomplish with marketing, then repeatedly pose the follow-up question "To what end?" This exercise helps me hone in on the audiences and actions that are most important. For example, I once conducted training for a group of advocates for Social Security reform. They told me their marketing goal was to increase people's understanding of the Social Security program, its solvency, and its challenges. To me, that sounded more like a mission statement than a marketing goal or a rallying cry. I asked them, "To what end?" They said they wanted people to be fully informed so they would "make sound decisions" about their position on the issues. But the question remained: "To what end?" Why did people need to be experts on actuarial approaches to projecting surplus levels or progressive price indexing? What specifically did they want people to do? What kind of "sound decision" did people need to make? What policy did they want people to support, and how should people express that support?

A few people ultimately decided they wanted their audience to be against privatization and personal accounts and to express that opposition by actions such as e-mailing their congressional representatives. Others decided they wanted people to express support for other policy changes. But all pinpointed a specific idea and action. Those decisions changed their audience focus, the actions they were asking their audiences to take, and the amount and type of information they needed to impart. By the end of the training, the action was no longer "understand these complicated issues," but rather "protect Social Security by calling this number."

Many of us will find ourselves answering the "to what end" question with a statement such as "I want people to be more aware of my issue" or "I want people to understand what's good for them." If that's the case, go a step further. Why do our audiences need awareness or understanding? To what end? What action are we really after?

2. Identify All the Audiences That Need to Take Action

To achieve a mission, most good causes need numerous audiences to take action. As our earlier examples showed, social change requires action by people on many levels, from those directly affected by the problem to those in a position to address its root causes. Our audiences may include the people we are trying to help, as well as the people who influence or control access to them, like opinion leaders or gatekeepers. For many causes, donors and potential donors are important audiences, as are competitors and partners. We also may need certain actions from board members, media, businesses, policymakers, regulators, and the research or scientific communities to achieve our goals. Make an inclusive list of all types of audiences.

Each audience should be reasonably specific. "Everyone" or the "general public" are not audiences. Examples of clear audiences are eighteen- to twenty-four-year-old males, members of a neighborhood association, health reporters at large newspapers, or wives of men who need to get screened for prostate cancer. We want well-defined groups that likely share some characteristics and need to take similar actions. Each will require a different marketing approach. We'll be examining those audiences closely, refining them and grouping them—as well as defining the marketing approach for each—in the following chapters.

3. Define a Specific Action for Each Audience

Make the action as active as possible. Asking for concrete action is always better than telling people to think a certain way. For example, asking parents to read to their children for fifteen minutes every night is a better action than asking them to be supportive of reading readiness. Make sure the action stipulates who should do what, when, how much, and how often. Once we know our audience better, we may end up modifying the action, but we need a starting point.

The more specific the action the better for two reasons. First, in defining specific actions, we are forced to focus on the realistic and the explicit. Everyone working for our good cause will understand what marketing aims to do, and we will uncover any differences of opinion among our colleagues at the start of our efforts. We thus avoid misunderstanding, confusion, or stagnation down the road. The second reason concerns our audience: specific actions are easier to do and harder to decline than nonspecific requests. If I asked you to join the fight against cancer, how would you react? You'd probably say yes. But what would you do? Probably nothing. It's hard to know how you're supposed to "join the fight." You'd probably simply think, "Yes, cancer is terrible and I'm against it," and then go on with your day. Now imagine I asked you to go on-line and buy a Lance Armstrong Foundation Live Strong wristband to raise awareness of cancer and generate funds for the Foundation's work of providing cancer patients with information and tools. How would you react? You might buy the wristband because doing so is easy and hard to decline. It also gives you a nice benefit of taking action (that popular yellow wristband), a concept we explore further in later chapters.

A good test of whether our action is simple and specific enough is to ask if it would be possible to film the audience taking the action we desire. If we don't have a simple visual, our audience certainly won't. Even if they want to do what we request or buy what we are selling, they won't know how. Make it easy for them by being clear. If we are asking people to donate money, how will they do it? By calling a phone number? Going to a Web site? Writing a check? All of the above? If we are asking people to practice good hygiene, what are we really saying? Wash their hands? When, how often, and how long?

4. Test the Actions for Feasibility

Next, consider how easy the action we're asking of our audiences is. We may need to focus on a few simple steps an audience can take toward making a difference, rather than a grand goal. I feel overwhelmed by being asked to "reduce-reuse-recycle" or to "save the earth," but when my city gave me a new recycling bin with wheels and told me to throw in paper and boxes and newspapers and push it to the curb on Tuesdays, I did it. Tackling unemployment is not feasible for me; donating my business clothes to former welfare recipients looking for jobs is something I can do.

For most people, if the action doesn't seem doable, they won't do it. People want to do easy things, and they want to be able to test whether they like an action by taking small, reversible steps. They want to get out of a commitment if they don't like it, so a modest commitment is better than a large one. Most people like saving the earth and solving unemployment in theory, but those issues aren't going anywhere. Meanwhile, daily life calls. Our audience may need to drop their children at day care, walk to the bus stop, and get to work by 9:00 A.M., and they won't see how it's possible to fit enormous undertakings into their lives.

Asking for only small acts may seem like a cop-out, but in fact, small steps are more likely to add up to a big change than are ambitious calls to action. Cialdini cites ample research showing that if a person makes a trivial initial commitment, like signing a petition, that person is far more likely than those who didn't sign to make larger commitments later.[5] This is even more the case if the commitment was public in some way, like signing a petition or making a pledge. This "momentum of compliance" or "foot-in-the-door technique" works in part because people begin to change their self-image. Even a small act can start to convince them they are health-conscious people or active citizens. People seek to rationalize their actions and effort (especially if they perceive the effort as significant) and reassure themselves they made a wise decision. Once they perceive they were right to take action and experience some of the rewards associated with the action, they are more likely than those who don't act to take further actions reinforcing their initial commitment and self-image.

5. Identify and Remove Barriers to Taking Action

If someone has to travel, invest time, or search for services in order to take our action, then we need to remove those barriers. Line up transportation, reduce the amount of time required to take the action, or provide a list of places to get service to increase the chances the action will be taken. If we discover we have significant obstacles we cannot overcome, we need to change the call to action. It's worse for someone to try to take action and have a negative experience than for that person to have not taken action at all.

Think through each step from our audience's perspective. Say we ask our audiences to get their children vaccinated. Will they know where to go to do that? And when they try to get shots for the baby, will they get prompt attention? Are there enough places they can do it, sufficient supplies, and enough staff to administer the shots? Ask what will happen if we generate interest and demand for a service and then are unable to meet that need. For example, we might tell women to get mammograms. Yet waiting times for appointments have gotten long because demand exceeds capacity; it can take months to get an appointment in some areas. The government and several foundations and good causes are trying to address the problem, but meanwhile we may have worried women who have been directed to get a test that is hard to schedule. Maybe those bottlenecks are OK if our strategy is to create unmet public demand that creates pressure for change. In the case of mammograms, this problem has prompted the government and several foundations and good causes to devote funds and effort to increasing women's access to mammograms through initiatives such as mobile mammography vans.

6. Be Flexible and Willing to Change the Action over Time

In the coming chapters, we will learn how to gain insight into our audiences and marketplaces, and this information may change our thinking about the actions we seek and our marketing goals. We need to retain some flexibility so we can adjust our calls to action based on the valuable intelligence we gather. We also should be willing to set new goals when many people take action. Recognize when a goal has been met, declare success, and move on to the next step.

CONCLUSION

Marketing guru Philip Kotler summed up the essence of marketing well when he said it is less about pursuing a sale than about creating a customer.[6] Nike created customers by focusing on the people who buy the shoes, not on the shoes. When we have a clear call to action for each of our audiences, we have established a customer focus.

➤ We will succeed if we can transform ourselves from missionaries into marketers with a mission.

What do I mean by that statement? People with a cause are passionate, committed, and driven to make a difference. (We may even feel compelled to write an entire book to express our views.) As a result, we can be insufferably focused on our cause, despite the fact that most of the world does not care about the issue that burns in our hearts. Whether we are part of an organization or a single volunteer, we have much to gain by breaking free of this nonprofit narcissism and reaching out to our audiences from their perspective. Our customer focus will save money, time, and effort, and our audiences will be more inclined than before to pay attention, listen, and act. This result is important because most of us face great public scrutiny and pressure to spend our limited resources wisely.

We're going to retain our audience focus for the next nine chapters until we've reached the point of our arrow and our audiences are taking the desired actions. We'll reach that goal by getting to know our audiences, tapping into their values, cutting through the clutter of the marketplace, identifying competitors and collaborators, and creating and delivering a winning message. Each of these elements is a part of the arrowhead we must fashion for each audience, and together they create a marketing strategy that will motivate people to take the actions we want. The goal is to build a relationship with those audiences, so they will take additional actions over time.

Let's turn now to getting those audiences to "just do it."

Interview 1
Selling Soap and Good Causes

William Novelli's career has been the living, breathing answer to Gerhart Wiebe's question "Can brotherhood be sold like soap?" Novelli started his career at Unilever, where he marketed laundry-detergent products. After several years of selling soap, he went to work for the ad agency Wells, Rich, Green. There, he first was confronted with the question of how soap related to good causes. "I had come from Unilever and was working on the same kind of product—packaged goods. I was marketing laundry detergent, cat food, dog food, kids' cereals, whatever," he recalls. "Then they gave me another account, which was public broadcasting. This was the first time public broadcasting had hired an advertising agency to build its audience. The first thing I did was to go to a press conference run by the woman who had created Sesame Street, Joan Ganz Cooney. And she was applying what I thought of as marketing to Sesame Street, which is education. So I thought to myself, you can do more with this thing. You can apply it to education or perhaps other issues, other ideas, other sectors. And that got me going."

Novelli, an engaging, quietly intense man with a good sense of humor, had found his calling. He went on to direct marketing efforts for another good cause: the Peace Corps. He then founded his own public-relations firm with Jack Porter in Washington, D.C. He built Porter Novelli into one of the largest public-relations firms in the world, and in the process pioneered the application of private sector savvy to social causes. "In the early days, I liked to call us a bunch of soap salesmen who were trying to work on high blood pressure and cancer. Then I discovered the academic literature. I read the seminal paper on social marketing by Phil Kotler and Gerald Zaltman. I thought to myself, these guys are framing this very nicely. I'm using my lessons from laundry detergent, and they're framing it better. I need to marry the academic and the practical. That's how I started, bringing in theory, bringing in the academic perspective, and saying, boy this helps me to do my thing."

Novelli went on to apply that thinking as executive vice president of the international relief and development agency CARE, president of the Campaign for Tobacco-Free Kids, and in his current position as chief executive officer for the AARP (formerly known as the American Association for Retired People). In each role, he has paired his dedication to good causes with business sensibility and convinced the rest of us that yes, we can indeed sell brotherhood like soap.

Q: What is the goal in marketing good causes?

A: I think a lot of programs make the mistake of stopping at attitude change—in other words, getting people to believe as you believe. They think, well, what can I do about teen pregnancy? Well, I'll get these kids to understand X. There's a difference between understanding and doing. We need to understand we are in the persuasion business, not the information-dissemination business. When people tell me "It's not our job or our place to tell people what to think or do," I think we might as well be shoveling pamphlets out of airplanes. If you really want to get someone to do something, close the sale. If we want to communicate to people that the world's oceans are in trouble, ask what you want the consumer and the audience to do. Do you want them to drown themselves or write a letter to a congressional representative?

Q: Is brotherhood just like soap?

A: A company looks to potential market demand when developing a product. People say, "If you build a better mousetrap, the world will beat a path to your door," but that is not marketing. Marketers start with the consumer, not the mousetrap. Do the people with the mice in their homes want to get rid of the mice? How satisfied or dissatisfied are they with current mouse-removal systems? How much would they pay to remove mice? Nonprofits are by contrast product-driven, not market-driven. That makes it more challenging.

Q: So how do we know what will close the sale?

A: I really like the idea of positive deviance. Don't study the people who aren't doing it, study the people who are and see what motivated them. One of the tenets of marketing is that your best prospects are people like your customers. You want to sell laundry detergent, see who's buying it now. These people are predisposed. If we're thinking about smoking cessation, people who have tried to quit smoking twice are more likely to try a third time than people who've never tried at all. If we're thinking about physical activity, people who already own a pair of walking shoes are more disposed to get back into it than those who have never gotten off the couch. If we're thinking about social change, I think it's a mistake to focus only on individuals. People are swimming in a larger sea. They're influenced by the media, by normative behaviors. If you look at a neighborhood where all the kids smoke, that's what you see. It doesn't matter if your parents are telling you to quit. If we could make physical activity normative behavior, if everybody was doing it—movie stars, your neighbor, Oprah—it would help. If the media and policymakers are behind it, that is part of it too. Then there is private policy change, through corporations and organizations.

Q: How can good causes manage all these audiences?

A: Nonprofits have so many more stakeholders than a corporation has. We've got this many-layered onion. Maybe at the core is the board of directors, and we have to inform, educate, and persuade our board. The next layer is staff. They tend to be socially oriented, mission-driven. They need to be involved. Beyond that, you might have volunteers, members, and the general public. You have to work with all of them in sequence. If you have the board, you have a better chance of getting the outer layers.

Interview 2
Spurring Citizen Action

Leslie McCuaig is a businesswoman in foreign-assistance clothes. Those who know her say she uses the combination to great effect. She holds within her a highly productive creative tension that she has used to bring innovation and effectiveness to a variety of good causes. A hard worker who is both lively and composed, McCuaig got her start in international aid and development in Russia. There she applied both her background in Russian studies and her M.B.A. training to the design and funding of groundbreaking programs that fostered small and micro enterprises. She then tackled rule-of-law issues for a U.S. consortium working in the former Soviet Union before joining the Institute for Sustainable Communities to head the U.S. Agency for International Development's flagship civil-society project in Ukraine. That project, the Ukraine Citizen Action Network (UCAN), helps Ukrainian organizations and citizens become actively engaged in setting the country's economic, political, and social agenda. I worked with McCuaig to apply marketing to those efforts, and all the Ukrainian examples in this book come from grantees of the UCAN project.

McCuaig is now vice president of program development for the Institute for Sustainable Communities in Vermont. Here she talks about how she conceived the UCAN project by focusing on specific actions that would advance Ukraine's small but growing civil society.

Q: How do you tackle huge, amorphous issues like civil society?

A: I think you have to break it down. As mission-driven organizations, we tend to have global, idealistic notions. It's great if we want to stop hunger in the world, but you can't easily design an intervention to reach that goal, much less market to it. We need to get to a realistic level where we define what we can actually influence and what we can accomplish and then design an intervention according to that concrete perspective.

Q: How did you focus your approach in Ukraine?

A: With UCAN, we tried to avoid the more political definitions of civil society—which are those that stress democracy and human rights. Because building democracy is fairly abstract, people tend to fall back on tangible things like elections and building representative institutions, which assumes that these in and of themselves constitute democracy. Instead, we asked the question What does civil society mean to the average citizen? And the answer was that democracy is not just about voting once in four years, it is about playing an active role every day. It's not just about citizen participation in the political process but about people interacting with each other on a regular basis to address problems in their society. When we looked at civil society at that level, we realized that we needed to design interventions to remove the barriers to having people participate in that process. One of those barriers was that people didn't believe they were allowed to participate. They didn't realize how much laws had changed since Soviet times. They also thought their participation would not make a difference. Many people lacked the confidence to take action because they simply had never been involved before.

So the project introduced a focus on changing those mentalities. We wanted to overcome passivity, make people feel empowered, and help them see what could happen if they began organizing to address community problems. We worked to strengthen Ukrainian advocacy groups that already existed, especially to encourage them to reach out and involve more people. The project was designed to include as many people as possible in experiencing the rewards of civic participation firsthand. That influenced the way the people understood their role in society. And that, in my view, is the essence of democracy.

Q: What's an example of someone heeding that call to action?

A: In Ukraine, I was lucky to witness firsthand an incredible example. In 2004, presidential elections were held, and they were extremely corrupt. Right down the street from my office in Kiev, citizens from every walk of life took to the streets and stood in the snow and freezing temperature for days on end to protest the false vote count. They were participating in democracy very directly, and they were doing so because they felt their dignity as citizens had been disregarded—a sign of just how much mentalities had changed in Ukraine since the passive days of the Soviet Union. The "orange revolution" showed how change happens because of the acts of individuals. It's people, not institutions, that make a civil society.

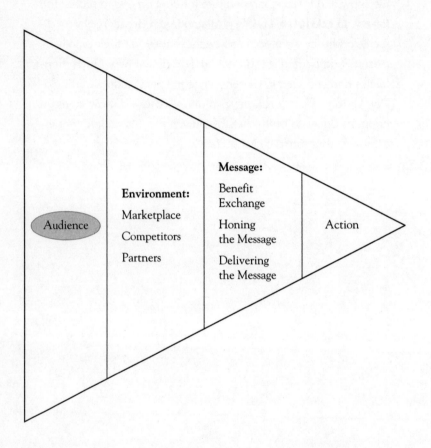

2

Robin Hood Reconnaissance

*Appeal to Your Audiences' Values,
Not Your Own*

WHAT THIS CHAPTER SAYS

- Everything we communicate will get twisted according to the minds it enters.

- As marketers, we have to accept people for who they are and work within their framework.

- The closer we align with our audiences' values, the higher our chances of motivating them to take action.

- We're not compromising our mission because we're not changing ourselves any more than we're changing our audience.

- To apply the principles in this chapter: Through research gather the information that will enable us to tap into our audiences' values and motivate them to take action. The goal is to uncover actions that are fun, easy, popular, and rewarding for our audiences.

- We're never done with our research. Uncovering the information we need is not a static, one-time effort. We must track attitudes and actions over time by monitoring how they evolve and forecasting what they will be in the future.

YOU'LL FEEL THE DIFFERENCE
THE MOMENT YOU LIE DOWN.

In the summer of 2000, the mattress maker Serta launched a new marketing campaign on air and in stores to distinguish itself from its alliteratively named competitors, Sealy and Simmons. The campaign featured endearing "counting sheep," who were out of a job because people were sleeping so well on Serta mattresses. The sheep, dejected because no one was awake to count them, wandered from bedroom to bedroom looking for work. In stores where confused customers struggled to distinguish Serta, Sealy, and Simmons, retailers displayed Serta-supplied plush toy sheep to prompt people to ask for the "counting sheep" brand.

Serta's reputation and popularity skyrocketed in response to these marketing efforts because the company did its homework and understood its audience's priorities. Serta knew that people do not think much about mattresses. Most of us can't even name the brands of mattresses we have. What we do think about is relief, rest, and comfort at the end of a long day. We want a good night's sleep. Serta did not wax ecstatic about its mattresses; it spun a story about sleep: "You'll feel the difference the moment you lie down." Then Serta gave us an easy and entertaining way of remembering which brand of mattress would put us to sleep.

In this chapter we steal Serta's simple appeal to people's wants and values.

Robin Hood Rule 2

The most important values are those of our audiences, not our own. The closer we align with our audiences' values, the higher our chances of motivating them to take action.

In Chapter One, we established the importance of focusing on our audience and the action we want them to take. This focus is the point and purpose of our marketing arrowhead. The Serta campaign shows us how to get there: by appealing to what our audiences—the base of our arrowhead—personally want and value. Serta may care about inner springs and foam encasements and the other nuances of its product, but the company knows that people value comfort and sleep.

We must be as smart, if not smarter, than Serta because Robin Hood Marketing is harder than commercial marketing. We aren't selling a comfortable mattress; we are often peddling the equivalent of sleeping on the floor without a pillow. Telling people that sleeping on the floor without a pillow is "right" is not going to get them to do it. Instead, we must show how our equivalent of sleeping on the floor is worth it from our sleepy, uncomfortable audiences' perspectives. We do that by appealing to their strongest wants and values.

GETTING TO KNOW YOU

To uncover our audiences' wants and values we must do some reconnaissance. Keep in mind that wants and values are distinct from needs. As people who work for good causes, we rightfully spend a lot of time thinking about how to meet certain needs—by providing life-saving help, training, exercise, literacy, vaccinations, and so forth. But we should not confuse what we know people need with what they want or value. The gap between the two is usually big. For example, my two-year-old daughter needs to brush her teeth in the morning so she won't get cavities. But she wants only the simple joy of using another product with Dora the Explorer on it. I need for her to have good oral hygiene, but I value her brushing her teeth without a pitched battle. That's why I willingly paid extra for the Dora toothbrush.

➤ We can't change who our audiences are, but we can change what they do. The trick is to show our audiences a new way to get what they already want.

Trying to change our audiences, or any individual person, is a recipe for failure. People of every age are highly resistant to change. In fact, social psychologists like Elliot Aronson and Robert Cialdini have shown that people continually reinforce their existing values by selectively processing new facts and experiences according to their mind-set.[1] Have you ever watched a presidential debate with opinionated friends on opposite ends of the political spectrum? Your friends on each side think their candidate won because they filter out any data that don't support their position or that challenge their identification with their candidate.

People want to preserve their mental framework and the sense of self and autonomy it provides, so they interpret information according to that framework. If information doesn't fit within it, they either ignore the information or assume the source of the information is crazy or can't be trusted. Or if the new information comes from someone the audience truly respects and trusts, they may adjust their beliefs and integrate them into their existing set of values. But those values don't suddenly change. For example, say I value a sense of safety. I decide I want to buy a security alarm for my house. But then my neighbor, who knows about recent break-ins and alarms that went unheeded, tells me I'd be better off with window locks. I decide to install window locks with my limited money rather than an alarm because I now believe they are a better option. My value, safety, has not changed, but I've changed my belief as to what will make me safe. If my neighbor had told me I was wrong to value safety, I would have ignored him or considered him crazy. I paid attention because he showed me a different way to be safe.

Anything we communicate will get twisted according to the mind it enters. Our ideology is simply not as powerful as our audience's own mental machinations. As marketers, we have to accept people for who they are and work within the framework they have.

I believe that accepting the perspective of our audiences shows respect. Telling people they need to change their values or that their values are wrong is not only ineffective, it is disrespectful. It's certainly no way to start a relationship, and that's ultimately what we want with our audiences. In our haste to be seen by them, we should not forget to see them. Humans have a basic need to be recognized and understood. By meeting our audiences where they are and communicating from their perspective, we are showing them respect and fulfilling that human need for connection. Meeting our audiences where they are has the added benefit of making our cause attractive to them because the more similar or familiar we seem to people, the more they tend to like us.[2] When we pay attention to our audiences, they pay attention to us. We get the actions we want by caring about what they want.

It's important to reiterate a key point from the previous chapter: we are not compromising our mission by telling people what they want to hear. We bring to the table a vision of our goal and a set of capabilities for reaching it. That will not change. But through marketing we recognize the person across the table from us—our audience. We don't market by saying, "Hello, let me tell you about myself." We market by listening to that person's thoughts and wants (which are often surprising) and proving our relevance to that perspective and those desires. We're not changing ourselves any more than we're changing our audience. We are uncovering the values we have in common.

CONNECTING CAUSES TO VALUES

Let's take some examples. One of the most famous is the American Legacy Foundation's antismoking campaign for youth. The Foundation set out to prevent smoking among young people because it knew that 80 percent of smokers begin using tobacco before they are eighteen years old. Its antismoking marketers decided to define their audience as twelve- to seventeen-year-olds, a savvy, jaded, and notoriously fickle audience.

The first step was to venture into the minds of teenagers. That meant starting with the value-based question "What do teenagers want?" rather than the needs-based question "How can we prevent them from smoking?" The campaign organizers thought about teenagers and their desires as they live through the transition that time of life presents. Young people are seeking to assert their independence and individuality, feel a sense of control, gain respect from their peers, and maybe even rebel. Many of them are attracted to smoking as a way to fulfill these fundamental adolescent desires.

So the Foundation began thinking about how it could allow teenagers to maintain control and to rebel in a new way. With the help of an alliance of prominent advertising agencies, the breakthrough "truth" campaign was conceived to provide a different way for teenagers to act on their values. The truth campaign urged teens to protest against a tobacco industry that it said was systematically seeking to manipulate them. The campaign set out to expose Big Tobacco's marketing practices and to highlight the toll tobacco takes in gross-out, extreme ads targeted to appeal to teenagers. By demonizing the tobacco industry, the truth campaign sought to provide teens with appealing new means for asserting themselves.

The campaign involved teens in all its planning and made them the public face of the effort. It organized a youth summit, a bus tour, a protest outside a tobacco company, and a slew of controversial advertisements. The theme was "Ask questions. Seek truth." One of the most memorable truth ads showed twelve hundred teenagers with numbered T-shirts pretending to drop dead in front of the headquarters of a tobacco company (symbolizing the number of people dying every day of smoking-related causes). Another showed teenagers raising an American flag to half-mast to honor those "loyal customers killed" by tobacco each day. A fake campaign for a product called Shards O'Glass freeze pops satirized tobacco-industry marketing. "At Shards O'Glass, our goal is to be the most responsible, effective and respected developer of glass shard consumer products intended for adults," says the faux mission statement on the shardsoglass.com Web site. It concedes, "We now agree with the overwhelming medical and scientific consensus that eating glass freeze pops can be dangerous." In the stilted language of cigarette warnings, it admits that its customers suffer a far greater incidence of "shards-related ailments" than nonusers do. As for addiction, it says that although it can be "very difficult" to break the habit, that fact "should not deter" those who want to try to quit.

This groundbreaking campaign, which has contributed to the lowest rate of high school smoking in nearly three decades, would not have been possible had the American Legacy Foundation focused solely on the need to curb smoking and failed to take into account the adolescent desire to act up. By giving teenagers something they wanted instead of taking something away, the campaign changed their behavior.

I experienced this same phenomenon halfway across the world in Ukraine. A small organization funded by the Institute for Sustainable Communities was working to motivate apathetic teenagers to care about politics, the future of the country, and voting. The group was frustrated because its message wasn't getting through to this tough audience. So it attended a marketing training. At the session, I asked them what they were telling teenagers. "We're telling them about our organization and how they should care about the future of the country," the twenty-seven-year-old director of the organization said. "If they vote, they can have a brighter future."

He was only twenty-seven, but he was already too old to instinctually think like a teenager. Eastern European teenagers aren't that different from American teenagers: they don't focus on the distant future, and they tend to be cynical. Promising a better country or brighter future isn't exciting to them. The organization's director and I talked about what teenagers did value, based on his informal research and work with them. What interested them? What got under their skin? He said his staff and volunteers always talked about Ukrainian teenagers as cynical and somewhat rebellious. Teenagers were especially tired of lecturing from their babushkas (grandmothers). What did the country's babushkas want? "They want things to be the way they used to be in Soviet times, with a good pension system. And they don't like the way young people dress and act. Teenagers don't agree, of course."

He was on to something. During a year and a half of living in Ukraine, I had found that babushkas on the street relished verbally assaulting unsuspecting pedestrians with unsolicited advice. One had lectured me for long minutes on a temperate spring day because she thought my children weren't bundled up in enough layers of clothing. I'm not a teenager, but I knew the feeling of being on the receiving end of a wagging finger. It didn't spur me to action—it made me resentful and rebellious. Just like the truth-campaign masterminds, this organization's director was putting his finger on fundamental adolescent frustrations.

We talked about how to change his marketing approach according to these insights. He ended up making a slight change in his message that made an enormous difference in its meaning. The new approach (in rough translation): "You decide your future, or your babushka will do it for you. Vote on October 31." Because of the work of hundreds of such organizations and an increasingly involved and engaged citizenry, some 80 percent of Ukrainians went to the polls during that historic 2004 election. Plenty of babushkas were at the polls, but so were many young people.

Let's take one more example from the same training in Ukraine. A community foundation named Dobrata was trying to encourage businesspeople to give money to charitable causes. This was not an easy task in a country emerging from decades of Soviet rule and with no history of corporate philanthropy, and when Dobrata staff came to the training, they expressed some disappointment over their efforts to motivate entrepreneurs.

They showed everyone at the training their latest advertisement, which they had aired on local television. It was animated, in black and white, with mournful music playing in the background. A stooped babushka (there is that powerful cultural icon again) enters a pharmacy. She looks up at the shelves and then down at a few stray coins in her pocket. Tears slowly course down her cheeks. She is unable to buy the medicine she needs. A voice-over and accompanying text urge people to help by calling Dobrata. What happened when the ad ran? Dobrata was flooded with calls from babushkas asking for money to buy medicines. Virtually no one called to donate money. The main problems: lack of a clear audience and an appeal to that audience's values. Businesspeople didn't see the ad as meant for them. It was depressing—everyone in Ukraine knows the collapse of the Soviet Union hit pensioners hardest—but not personally motivating. No one believed a call to Dobrata could resolve this enormous social problem.

After two days of thinking about their audiences and reflecting on their values, Dobrata went back to the drawing board. The next time I saw their staff, they handed me a disk with their new ad. It was a colorful, animated spot to be shown in movie theaters. This was a far better venue than television for reaching their audience because only those who are relatively well-off, like businesspeople, can afford to go to the movies in Ukraine. In the spot, a businessman is shown slumped over his desk, signing paper after paper handed to him by a secretary. He goes on autopilot, numbly working his way through massive stacks. The picture zooms into his brain, which has the cogs and wheels of a robot. Life has become mechanical and without feeling. Then an alarm clock goes off on his desk and suddenly the scene brightens. The secretary places before him a donation request from Dobrata, and he signs, breaks out of his rut, and regains his human self. A friendly voice-over and call to action (wake up and give to Dobrata) end the spot. The ad was funny, motivating, and memorable. It clearly spoke to businesspeople by whimsically highlighting the drudgery that comes with any job, especially in a country with lots of red tape. It positioned its "product"—charitable giving—as a way to fulfill a desire to break out of the grind and feel good. Dobrata hit its mark. With this kind of thinking, we can do the same.

HOW TO USE ROBIN HOOD RULE 2

To apply Robin Hood Rule 2, we need a clear sense of our audience's wants and values. We get that information through research. Here's how.

1. Identify the Information Needed

It's tempting to start researching our audiences by compiling a list of questions to ask them. But first think about the answers we are trying to obtain. We need information that will enable us to tap into our audiences' values and motivate them to take action. The right questions will lead us to that information. There are a lot of theories about human behavior, but most can be boiled down to this: people take actions they perceive as fun, easy, popular, and rewarding.[3] By fun, we mean the audience wants to like what they are being asked to do. By easy, we're referring to the need for the audience to perceive the action as feasible. By popular, we're saying people want to fit in with others and enhance their own self-image. By rewarding, we mean people want to receive a personal benefit that exceeds the costs of taking action—a topic we explore fully in Chapter Six.

> Through research we want to uncover actions that are fun, easy, popular, and rewarding for our audiences by understanding them as groups and as individual people.

Imagine our research as a zooming satellite telescope. Through the lens, we would first see a country, then a state, city, and neighborhood. Then, our zoom lens would focus on a home, a person, and, finally, the inside of that person's head. We want to know the groups the people in our audience belong to (the telescope view from far away, showing nationality, geographical location, race, religion, cultural values, social class); whom they associate with (their families, friends, acquaintances, groups they join); what they do (their job, finances, lifestyle, stage of life); and how they think and feel (their psychology). This composite picture helps us begin to understand what makes a group of people tick.

Make a telescoping list of the information we need about each of our audiences. Here are some suggestions:

- What demographic and geographical groups do they belong to?

- What do they most care about? What are the most important problems/issues in their lives? What are their values and wants? What concerns keep them awake at night?

- Have they ever taken the action we're seeking? What happened? If they have not taken that action, what do they do instead? We want to talk to people who are taking our action and those who are not.

- What or who constitutes our competition? What messages have they heard regarding the actions they now take or regarding our issue? How do they talk about our issue? How did they react to what they've heard, seen, or read? Research often goes astray in focusing on one good cause's agenda as if people react to that cause in a vacuum. We won't be the only one speaking to our audience, so we need to understand where we stand in relation to competing ideas, causes, organizations, and actions. We can then use this information to determine how to deal with competitors, the topic of Chapter Four.

- What appeals to them about our action, and what do they see as easy or hard about it? What is their decision process? How much do they seem to know about taking

action? How close are they to taking action? Does
the action seem relevant? Feasible? What would make
it easier? What do they see as the relative costs and
consequences of taking action versus not taking action?

- Who approves or disapproves of their taking action?
Who influences them? Do other people around them
take our action? What do they think of those people?
Where do they get their information? How do they
interact with the people/sources that influence or
inform them?

In thinking about our audiences and how they might answer
these questions, we should not limit ourselves to the people we are
trying to change. We can also ask people who have already adopted
the change why they did so. In developing countries, researchers
have used a research approach called "positive deviance," a tantalizingly interesting term. Jerry Sternin developed the concept, based
on the idea that the solutions to change already exist in many communities.[4] For example, in an impoverished country with low birth
weights for babies, why in one village do babies weigh healthy
amounts? In your community, why do certain students from groups
with poor graduation rates manage to finish high school? Are they
unique, or can their reasons for taking certain actions inform your
efforts? Say we have a marketing goal of increasing the number of
older people who exercise in our community by 15 percent. After
comparing walkers and nonwalkers, we discover the nonwalkers are
different in one of three ways from the walkers: they are sick and
can't go out for a stroll; they don't have a nice area to walk in near
their house; or they feel unsafe or uncomfortable walking by themselves. Those contrasts are helpful. We might decide the solution to
turning nondoers into doers is to provide biweekly buses to neighborhood parks for "walk and talk" programs that provide the safety
and sociability that the nondoers seem to value and currently lack.

2. Choose a Research Method

Now we want to determine what kind of research will get us the answers to our questions. The two basic kinds of research—quantitative and qualitative—are best used in combination. Quantitative research seeks to quantify, or count, people by categorizing their thinking, feelings, or behavior. It provides the broad view of our entire audience. Qualitative research probes the minds of individuals through questioning and observation to understand how they think, feel, or behave. It's the zoom-lens view of our audience. Qualitative research gives us words; quantitative research gives us numbers. Together they provide a vivid picture of our audiences.

Here are some qualitative methods to choose from:

- *In-depth interviews* allow us to explore an audience member's thinking in great detail, one-on-one. Audience members are contacted individually, and the interviewer can ask questions, follow up, and fully explore what people say about their attitudes or behaviors.

- *Focus groups* attempt to get at the same information by questioning a group of similar people gathered together. A researcher serving as facilitator asks exploratory questions and guides discussion for a group of four to twelve people who are representative of an audience. In this case, the insights gained tell us more about how people think as a group and how they influence each other than about how they think individually.

- *Observation* involves immersing ourselves in the milieu of our audience and studying what they say and do. This technique is useful because people often can't identify or articulate all the information we seek.

Quantitative methods include the following:

- *Phone, mail, or Internet-based surveys* collect information about who people are (demographics, regional backgrounds), how they act (their behaviors), and what they feel (their psychology) by asking quantified questions. This method is useful for two reasons: it gives us an idea of how pervasive the attitudes and behaviors we measure through qualitative research are, and it gives us a baseline of the current situation that we can use to measure progress.

- In *intercept, or arranged, interviews* surveyors go to malls or busy streets and ask people who walk by whether they will answer some questions. The researchers typically ask screening questions to see whether a person is a target audience member; if the person is, the researcher conducts a brief survey.

- *Purchased databases* are expensive but useful for some larger organizations. Companies sell information about various audience segments, which they describe in great detail. For example, PRIZM, a segmentation system from Claritas Inc., divides U.S. consumers into fifteen groups and sixty-two segments.

In deciding among these methods, we need to take into consideration how much time and money we have. If we have a big budget, we can bring in a professional researcher to choose the methodology and conduct the research. If we don't, we need to assess the kind and amount of research we can realistically do ourselves. The fourth step below describes how we can manage to do some research even if we can't conduct a focus group or survey ourselves.

3. Check Assumptions at the Door

Before conducting research we must remember that our audience is not like us. Most members of our audience do not wake up thinking about our issue, and they don't go to sleep reflecting on it either. They look at life differently, hold different values, and have different needs and wants. They take action for reasons other than ours. We need to seek and accept research that shows all those differences, as strange and surprising as they may seem to us. Our assumptions may very well be proved wrong in the course of research, and that's good. An acute sense of the contrast between our audiences and ourselves is a huge advantage because it can help us look at our issue in a fresh way and forge audience connections we never imagined.

I once conducted research for a client who was addressing at-risk drinking, defined as regularly consuming more than one to two drinks per day. We held focus groups with people who were consuming more than recommended levels, and we asked them in an open, nonjudgmental way to talk about their lives and the kinds of alcohol they preferred. We even had them cut out pictures from magazines that showed how they felt about their favorite drinks. Interestingly, they did not perceive themselves as at risk; they saw themselves as social, responsible drinkers. They noted they did not drink and drive. They described at-risk drinkers as people who were different from them—people who were nearly alcoholics, drank alone, and got behind the wheel after drinking too much. In other words, their idea of "at-risk" was very different from that of the client. "At-risk" to them was more about behavior than quantity.

This difference was useful to uncover. If the client had launched a campaign about at-risk drinking, the entire target audience would have ignored it because they would not have seen it as personally relevant. Telling those people they were wrong about what at-risk drinking meant wasn't likely to work either. But redefining the amount of alcohol consumption that constituted "responsible, social drinking" was promising because that redefinition created a link between the image of themselves the people in the audience wanted and the action the client wanted that audience to take.

4. Conduct the Research

We can now delve into our quantitative and qualitative research. Ideally, we bring in experienced researchers to do this work. They can do it better than we can for ourselves because they are not immersed in our issue and are less likely to be biased by certain attitudes and assumptions. We are so close to our issue we can be overly swayed by evidence that supports our assumptions and can ignore evidence that does not. We may become too focused on details, or we may interpret a few people's opinions as fact. In addition, our audience may be more inclined to tell us what we want to hear if they're communicating with us rather than with a neutral third party. But let's be realistic. Hiring professional researchers may be impossible. If there is no research budget, we can first find out whether existing research can provide insights into our most important audiences. Perhaps our cause has relevant past research, records, databases, or staff insights, or we can look at governmental statistics, journal articles, partners' research, or go to universities for help. If we need to do our own research, interns or university students may be willing to assist us for little or no cost. If we conduct interviews, focus groups, or surveys ourselves, how-to guides like *Hands-On Social Marketing* can be useful references,[5] and Web sites like surveymonkey.com make it easy and inexpensive to e-mail survey questions.

We can also conduct informal research. What trends have staff or volunteers noticed among our members, clientele, or donors? We and our colleagues can use all interactions with our audiences to gain insights. If we run a homeless shelter or a legal-aid organization or a health clinic, we should listen carefully to how our clients answer questions such as "How have you been doing?" or "What do you need?" If we are fundraisers meeting a major prospect, small talk can tell us a lot about what's inside that person's head: "How are things at your foundation?" "What are people focused on these days?" If we are knocking on doors as a canvasser or answering a toll-free line, we should listen as much as we talk. Find out how people feel about their lives, our issue, and current events. We can also gain important insights by simply observing our audiences. I worked on a project where policymakers were a key audience; I wangled an invitation to a health-policy forum and heard them discuss their priorities firsthand. The forum provided a gold mine of information. Go wherever the audience congregates. If we work at a museum, we can observe the people coming in the door. Who are they? Greet them and ask them how they are. Try to figure out why they came or how they learned about our exhibit. If our audience members are online, go to their chat rooms, blogs, and Web sites and read what they are saying. Watch the television shows they watch and read their magazines.

Our research questions should not probe directly for the information we want, which is why people think and act the way they do and what we can do to change their thoughts and actions. Unfortunately, our audiences cannot easily explain their thoughts and behavior nor predict the messages that will cause them to change. Human behavior is complicated, and most people are unaware of why they are the way they are. They can often provide a logical explanation for why they behave and think as they do, but unfortunately, that self-justification has more to do with what they believe the "right" explanation to be than with their true motivations. Asking "why" will not tell us "why." People are emotional, busy, and preoccupied with paying the mortgage, losing weight, helping their children with homework, and being loved—often all in the same moment in the middle of the night when they can't sleep. All those thoughts are influenced by a host of factors, such as the events of the previous day, their social and economic status, or their sense of self-esteem. We can find out what's going through their head in the middle of the night and what they've been up to lately, but we can't expect them to make sense of this information for us. As marketers, that's our job.

We can understand "why" by listening to their stories and getting at their feelings. The psychiatrist does not ask patients, "Why are you depressed?" but instead talks to them about how they decided to come for an appointment and elicits from them stories about their life that contribute to a picture of who they are. In hearing a story, an attentive listener comes to see the truth. The person who tells the story, in turn, benefits from that attentiveness and may see life in a new way through speaking about it; in this way talking about experiences can be therapeutic.[6]

Good research gets at the truth in a similar way, for different purposes. To return to the example of at-risk drinking, we did not ask people to explain why they had four drinks on Saturday night. Instead, the participants cut out pictures that described how they felt about drinking. They chose pictures of a child laughing on a swing, a woman relaxing on a beach, a hockey game, and a man clowning around, surrounded by attractive women. Each picture told a story about why they liked to drink and about the kinds of pleasures they might feel they were giving up if they drank less. These insights provided the keys to how "responsible" drinking at lower levels could be favorably positioned. Rather than saying to our audience they were drinking too much, we said that by drinking at lower levels regularly, they would get not only the current benefits of relaxation and socializing—so clear in the pictures—but also increased energy, weight loss, and the health benefits of moderate drinking.

Just as people aren't reliable sources about the reasons for their behavior, they are also poor predictors of how they will behave in the future. They may readily express intentions to take action if they believe taking action is "right," but we cannot be sure they will follow through. Most of us would say, yes, we will try to exercise more this year. But will we? Good research recognizes that gap between promise and action. For example, imagine a car company has gathered a group of people in a room and asks them, "Would you buy a military vehicle with a combined weight of 4.3 tons and drive it on errands around town? If not, what would convince you to change your mind?" The people sitting in this focus group would probably look at each other, then the moderator, and declare this a crazy concept. They might say they would never buy such a "car." But if we gather a focus group of wealthy men and learn in the course of a conversation about their daily lives that they care about power and appearing bigger and better than the next guy, we will know how to persuade some of them to buy a Hummer. It turns out plenty of people think driving a 4.3-ton truck is fun, easy, popular, and rewarding.

When framing questions, ask people about their daily lives, their priorities, their experiences, and their stories. Then ask how they perceive our issue in this context. This changes the type of information we get. For example, if we had started our at-risk-drinking focus groups by asking about at-risk drinking, we likely would never have learned why people valued the experience of having their cocktails. Instead, people revealed that information by showing pictures and telling stories about the last time they had a few drinks. Similarly, if we had surveyed people about what they thought about the Hummer or the iPod or a $4 cup of coffee at Starbucks when these products were first conceived, we would not have necessarily discovered whether those products would sell. But by learning that people seek relaxation, power, convenience, or social contact, we could have known these products had the potential to meet unmet wants.

5. Identify Groups of People Who Share the Same Values

As we review the results of our research, we should be able to start identifying some common values and desires. Here is a list of wants we might encounter: rest/sleep, convenience, comfort, health and well-being, time, safety, security, predictability, control, pleasure, fun, excitement/thrills, sexual fulfillment, love, friendship, emotional support, participation, self-improvement, beauty/physical appeal, pride of ownership, independence, privacy, conformity, achievement, style, social status, admiration, approval, attention, profit, savings, power, hope, happiness. These are the values to look for in listening to our audiences.

As we do our research, we may find that certain groups within our audiences, which we'll call segments, share certain values. We want to profile those segments so we can market to them specifically. Think about the examples earlier in the chapter and how they show the effectiveness of segmentation. The antismoking truth campaign picked rebellious twelve- to seventeen-year-olds. The Ukrainian groups targeted young voters and businesspeople, respectively. When segmenting the audience, choose groups that are small enough to share core values or to desire similar benefits but large enough to have an impact on our mission if they take action. Divide or combine them by aspects of who they are (for example, gender, marital status, parental status, age, income level, type of job, health status, religion, race). Or segment them by their attitudes toward our issue or their behaviors. A segment worth targeting is one that is likely to act, one that we have the resources to reach, and one that promises a level of impact worth the money needed to reach it.

We talked about the Hummer as a vehicle that appeals to people who crave power. Think how other automakers have differentiated themselves according to audience segments and their values and wants. If I care about safety, I think Volvo. If I am thrifty, I think Hyundai. Predictability and reliability? Toyota or Honda. I desire prestige? BMW. I want to communicate class? Mercedes. How do good causes do the same? We appeal directly to the audience segments with the same types of values. Rather than trying to explain to our audience why we're right or arguing the finer points of our position, we head straight to the rich, emotional territory of their desires. Serta doesn't lecture us on mattress coils; it entices us with sleep. We entice with some of the other values on our list, and how we can do that is the topic of the rest of this book.

6. Write Down the Results

Whether we are just one volunteer or a marketing director at a big nonprofit organization, we should make a record of what we learn and share it with as many people who work with us as possible. This task sounds obvious, but often valuable intelligence and institutional memory get lost. People transition in and out of jobs, committees turn over, and volunteers come and go. I have worked on countless efforts—from a major fundraising mailing to an elementary school benefit—and found insufficient records of past research and marketing results. We do our cause a big service when we capture the insights that derive from our research. Put them in a place where people will find them the next time they undertake a marketing effort, and track marketing efforts over time so the chances of success are increased and mistakes are not repeated.

Also be sure to share research with leaders, and get high-level staff members involved in research so they will see its value, be attentive to the results, and budget for more research next time. Also keep leaders and staff posted on the impact of a research-based marketing effort on bottom-line results.

CONCLUSION

It is tempting to assume we know our audiences' values and skip doing research. Research can be time-consuming and costly. But the results nearly always surprise us, test our assumptions, and lead us to some highly productive creative thinking about how to reach our audiences. If big research projects are not possible, consider some of the relatively easy, informal ways of doing research that are outlined in this chapter.

The good news is research can make us far more effective than we would otherwise be as marketers. The bad news is we're never done with research. It is not a static, one-time effort. We must track attitudes and actions over time, monitor how they evolve, and forecast what they will be in the future. We need to go back to each of our audience segments time and time again to ensure we still understand how to motivate them. In that process, we may refine our segments, identify new target audiences, or alter the actions we're seeking. Research is an iterative process and a learning experience, and we should expect to make adjustments as we go along.

Marketing is not a scientific system as much as a messy, living, breathing process. With neglect, it shrivels and fades. But with consistent care and attention, it grows and thrives.

Interview 1
Fishing for the Right Audience

Kristen Grimm has worked on stopping land mines, saving swordfish, and selling ecofriendly coffee. The causes are disparate, but her approach is consistent. "Know your audience and how they experience life. Then ask them to do something small. Social change starts with small steps," she says. Grimm, who is president of her own firm, Spitfire Strategies, has made social change the work of her entire career. "I was an Irish history major headed for law school, but then I was drawn to my early work by good causes," she says. She got her start as an intern at Fenton Communications and went on to become president. Grimm has also worked as a fellow at the Vietnam Veterans of America Foundation and is a frequent speaker and trainer on communications and advocacy for good causes. Here she reflects on how to fish for the right audience segments, as she did in the award-winning Give a Swordfish a Break campaign.

Q: How do you choose the right audiences to target?

A: The first thing to remember is the general public is not an audience. You have to feel comfortable knowing you may have to knock off certain markets at different times. Be able to say, right now, I'm going to go after single, eighteen- to twenty-four-year-old, college-educated women. They are likely very different from males thirty-five to fifty-five. You may feel that you need to be marketing to both these audiences at the same time, but vague efforts don't take into account how differently people experience life. Start by looking at the so-called low-hanging fruit. That can get you some early wins, excite your organization and its funders, and give you a sense that you can succeed. For example, if I'm promoting fair-trade coffee, I'm going to first look at women who are already buying coffee and really focus on their values. If you look at the ads of TransFair USA, it's interesting to see they always start out by talking about the great taste of the coffee. Then they go on to talk about helping coffee farmers. If you're going to the woman spending $3.52 on a latte, you must immediately tell her that your coffee tastes great. Start with that because you know such a woman cares about that. Then, when that's taken care of, you can add that she can feel good about drinking your coffee because it's fair-trade certified. It's less about where people live than about how they live. Find the clumps of people who live in a way that makes them a good target for you. In general, in the nonprofit sector, people think of their targets too widely. A small group of people who are really committed can be very powerful in achieving change. Mothers Against Drunk Driving was a small but activated and successful group.

Q: How can good causes research their audiences?

A: Watch television and read because that's what your audience is doing. You will learn a lot from the advertisers in those media because they are devoting a lot of time worrying about how to reach your audiences. They are fairly transparent in their strategy, and you can grasp it quickly and use it for your own ends. For example, we tear out advertisements from consumer magazines and look at the trends there. You see companies marketing time because people don't have it. You see Nike ads with young women running, and you can see implications for causes like choice and fair-trade coffee. If one of those ads has been running for a long time, pay attention. That means the company has hit a sweet spot. Ask yourself, what emotions are they playing on?

Get your hands on research that other organizations have done. How many times have nonprofits gone out in the field and done research very similar to the research someone else has done? Look at what else is out there because it's not so dramatically different and you can learn from it. If you're an environmental group addressing land issues, and there is research on how people feel about water issues, use it.

Be skeptical about what you hear. People say things in polls and focus groups all the time that they don't then act on. They say they will buy organic coffee, but then they don't do it after they leave the focus-group facility and go back to their lives. You have to get into the heads of consumers, go where they go, and see what they see. Get out in the marketplace and observe. One research company did focus-group research with young people on Sony boom boxes, and they all said a yellow boom box was a great idea. At the exit, they were offered a free boom box in black or in yellow. Everyone took the black. You have to pay attention to what people actually do at the end of the day.

Q: What's your favorite example of a campaign that reflected a good understanding of audience?

A: In Boston, we're working to attract young members to NARAL Pro-Choice America. Young women experience reproductive rights very differently than our mothers did, so we wanted an approach that would reflect that. Although these young women support choice, they don't have a militant image. They are not out of the mainstream; they like to be fashionable. As consumers, they value choice in all aspects of life. So our campaign is Choice Is Always in Style. We're doing it in partnership with spas, clothing boutiques, and cafés because young women trust those places as shoppers and are influenced by the styles and attitudes these places reflect.

The Give a Swordfish a Break Campaign was a great one because if we'd approached it in a traditional way, we would have issued a report saying oceans were overfished. Industry would have shot it down. It would have been one day of news in the *New York Times*. But SeaWeb and the Natural Resources Defense Council thought about who makes decisions about eating swordfish, and it was chefs. They recruited all the leading, trendy chefs in New York City restaurants and had them say they wouldn't serve swordfish. It was a food story, not an environmental story, and people who eat at those restaurants listened because they wanted to be "in the know." Eventually, a thousand chefs, cruise lines, and magazines were involved. You still see the effects of the campaign today. People ask in restaurants, "Is this a fish I can eat or not?"

Interview 2
The Surprising Side of Research

Jack Fyock is a social psychologist who loves to divulge the surprises that lurk in the hearts and minds of target audiences. As a researcher who has examined everything from retirees' understanding of Medicare to teenage girls' love of television, he has seen his share of the unexpected. "What I like most about my work is showing the extreme disconnect between what a cause is trying to accomplish and what's going on in the target audience's head. It's a different world," he says. "The great findings in psychology are the ones that are counterintuitive."

Fyock, who loves to tell a good, counterintuitive story, has explored that terrain as a social science researcher at the Centers for Medicare and Medicaid Services, as a senior manager at BearingPoint, and at Market Strategies. He also does adjunct teaching at American University, where he helps students grasp the finer points of strategic communication. He received his Ph.D. from the University of Maryland at College Park, where he specialized in strategic self-presentation. But perhaps this social psychologist's work as a bartender years ago was the best training ground in the wild and unpredictable territory of the human mind. "When people are sitting on that barstool, they tell you a lot about what's in the deepest recesses of their brains, whether you want to hear it or not," he says.

Here, he offers his thoughts on finding out one of the hardest things to know: what people really think.

Q: One of the tricky things about research is we want to find out our audiences' values but they can't be relied on to articulate them. What do you do?

A: When I teach my social psychology class, I spend the first three weeks telling students that they have no idea why other people do what they do. I tell them not to rely on their own experiences to draw conclusions about the motivations of others. Because you can't trust self-reports from people, you do stories. For example, one technique we use in focus groups is to draw a picture of a person. Then we draw a dialogue box in front and a thought bubble behind. And we ask, for example, a group of people with diabetes to respond to the following questions: "If a casual friend asks you what it's like living with diabetes, what do you tell them?" And then, "What do you think?" We say, "Fill in the dialogue box with what you tell them and the thinking box with what you 'really' think." Surprisingly, the simple act of writing in a thought bubble gets people to open up. In many cases, it gives people permission to appear vulnerable and weak. It appears that because they feel they are one degree removed from their thoughts and speaking from an "objective" perspective ("it's not me, it's what is written in here"), they are more honest. It's amazing what they will say.

We recently did a focus group of caregivers of people who have chronic illness. The thought bubble responses were very honest: they revealed exhaustion, depression, and "giving up one's life" to take care of someone. In the study, we were testing various names for a chronic-care improvement program. One of the names referred to "health support," and "support" matched completely with the caregivers' bubbles. For them, it was exactly what they needed. One of the challenges of human research is that you have a hindsight bias. At the end of this project, people said, "Of course! Of course 'support' makes sense!" But going into it, nobody liked any of the names that used the word "support." When I present research findings, I sometimes ask people to predict the findings before I state them. In general, nobody has any idea, or they have wrong ideas. And then when I present the findings, everyone says, "Of course!" Good research sometimes seems like common sense, but it's frequently not so obvious before the research is conducted.

Q: Whom do you choose to research?

A: I like to focus on both doers and nondoers. Look at people who are opposite, and that's where you clearly see differences. For example, when you research people who are trying to manage their diabetes and those who are not, you might find that what sets the groups apart is that the doers had been nondoers until they ended up in the hospital, and dealing with their disease then became highly personal. Similarly, I was involved in research that looked at the use of blood thinners. The doers checked their blood regularly, took their medicine as required, used many of the medical terms associated with their condition (for example, "My INR score was 3.2, so they had to reduce my dose"), and could articulate why they were on a blood thinner. By contrast, the nondoers were less compliant with blood checkups, indicated that they missed doses, and used less sophisticated terms when discussing their condition ("They told me my blood is too thin"). The nondoers said that they had "never" been told why they were on a blood thinner and were likely to remind everyone that blood thinners are "really rat poison." Doers talked about blood thinners as providing them with "peace of mind." What drove these differences? It didn't appear to be education, or any other demographic predictor. Instead, doers tended to mention traumatic health events as the impetus for taking blood thinners. Nondoers frequently mentioned that they didn't know why they were taking blood thinners. By looking at these two groups side by side, we were able to see clearly the challenges of motivating people who had not experienced a significant life-threatening event to take their blood thinners.

Q: What are some pitfalls to avoid?

A: Human behavior is complex, and we should recognize that it is hard to research and understand. Some common mistakes in focus groups include asking questions without understanding their impact on the rest of the group. For example, we feel like we have to talk about our issue right away in a research setting, which impacts everything else in the group. People like to feel smart, and if they figure out what we're looking for, they tend to say things that support "good" behavior instead of talking about the stuff they really do. Focus groups are very much affected by the power of social norms. I watched a group discussing long-term-care insurance. Adult children of parents who might obtain that insurance were asked if they were concerned about having an inheritance. Of course everyone denied that they wanted money. But it's hard to know whether these comments represented their true beliefs or their need to appear "good" among strangers. In cases like that, in-depth, individual interviews are better.

Q: What is one of the surprises you've encountered in your research?

A: A few years ago, we did focus groups with volunteers who work with an organization that helps Medicare beneficiaries with their health-insurance decisions or problems. We asked them what they liked about their jobs. Theoretically, you'd think they would like the fact that they help get seniors enrolled in programs that could save them thousands of dollars or that they help seniors obtain discount prescription cards to save money.

Yet, when we asked, "At the end of the day, when you're driving home from your volunteering and say, 'This was a great day,' what made it a great day?" overwhelmingly, people said, "I spent time with a very lonely woman who was so happy to have someone to talk to for an hour or two." These volunteers liked the idea of the difference they were making for someone who needed a friend. In other words, making helpful human contact was a more important motivator to get them to volunteer than was helping people save money or obtain drug discounts.

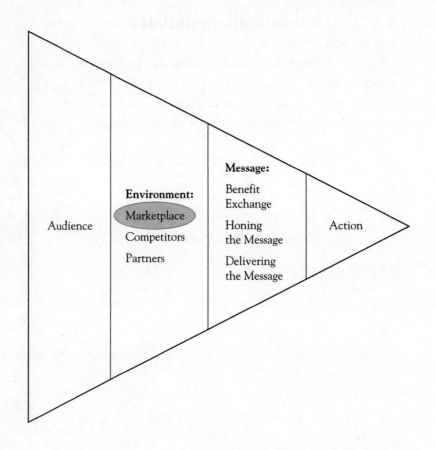

3

The Village Square

*React to the Forces at Work
in the Marketplace*

WHAT THIS CHAPTER SAYS

- We must recognize the marketplace forces that influence our audiences and their actions and harness those that work in our favor.

- Our audiences' actions are affected by demographic, lifestyle, social, cultural, health, natural, economic, infrastructural, legal, scientific, technological, political, media, business, and competitive factors.

- To apply the principles in this chapter: Take a walk in our audiences' shoes and consider which of these forces affect their likelihood of taking action. Then identify those we can use to our advantage, those in our way, those that require partners to leverage, and those that we cannot control.

THINK DIFFERENT.

What do Albert Einstein, Samuel Beckett, Martha Graham, Bob Dylan, Martin Luther King Jr., and Maria Callas have in common? According to Apple Computer, they "think different." Apple placed arresting images of these unconventional achievers in the media beginning in 1998 in a bold bid to rev up their brand and revive slumping sales. The famous faces, which spoke volumes about the nature of creativity, appeared with minimal adornment: only Apple's logo and the two words "Think Different." The award-winning campaign's execution was simple and stark, but the ideas behind it were big and ambitious. The Think Different campaign celebrated people who had succeeded by walking to the beat of a different drummer. An Apple logo next to their likenesses suggested that those people were somehow the essence of Apple. Apple made an innovative product that would make us innovative. Buying a Mac meant becoming a free thinker.

The campaign, which was aimed at increasing sales, worked especially well for two reasons that should be familiar to us because they were the topics of our first two chapters. Apple and its ad agency, TBWA\Chiat\Day, had a clear focus on action and a specific audience in mind. They knew that current and likely Apple customers considered themselves smart, creative, and discriminating, and the company embraced and projected those qualities through the appropriation of cultural icons like Einstein, Dylan, and King. Like Nike, Apple focused on its audience's sense of possibility. It sold its products by focusing not on the computer itself and its features but rather on the idea of inspiration and what its audience might do with the computer.

A third factor also played a part in Apple's success: the campaign positioned Apple relative to marketplace forces. Apple knew it was fighting a tough battle in a market gravitating toward other personal computers, but it also saw some possibility in the strong position it held with artsy, independent-minded consumers. It took a hard look at those trends and decided to acknowledge and amplify its unique position by accentuating the characteristics that made it different. Apple created a rallying cry for both consumers and itself.

Apple understood the forces that were working in its favor and those that were not, and it acted accordingly. This marketplace savvy is the third private-sector principle we will steal.

Robin Hood Rule 3

Recognize and react to the forces at work in the marketplace. We must identify the forces influencing our audiences' actions and harness those that work in our favor.

The marketplace is in the middle of our arrowhead. It's the environment where our audiences live and where our efforts will take place, so it's vital that we understand it. It's also where our competitors lurk and our potential partners reside. We'll be dealing with those factors in the next two chapters.

THE MARKETPLACE

None of us works in a vacuum where we can command the full attention of our various audiences. Instead, we work within a messy context of people, ideas, events, and environmental factors that all affect our ability to be heard. This context is our marketplace. Companies like Apple seek to understand the forces at work in this marketplace to sell their products; we need to understand them in order to succeed in our mission. Marketplace forces can undermine or advance our mission, affect our relevance to our audiences, increase or decrease our advocacy power and visibility, and make or break our fundraising efforts. The better we understand them, the greater our chances of harnessing them to work in our favor.

Let's take an everyday example of the forces that are at work around us. Say I'm driving down the interstate in Ohio. What determines how fast I'm going? One factor is my personal circumstances and values, which we covered in the previous chapter. If my children are in the car, I'm not behaving as if I'm on the Autobahn. I drive carefully because I know that obeying the speed limit saves lives. But if my children are not in the car and I'm late for an important job interview, I may brush those thoughts from my mind and drive faster. If my mother is in the car telling me to slow down, that might have the reverse effect, depending on our relationship.

Other forces are also at work. The speed limit affects my driving. That law and its enforcement—such as the cop car parked in the median with a radar gun or the traffic camera snapping pictures of speeders—slow me down. A factor that may speed me up is the rate of speed of other vehicles. If all the cars around me start flying past, I may press harder on the accelerator. If a sudden rainstorm descends on the area, and I can't see well, I may slow down so I don't get in an accident. If I stray onto the shoulder, textured pavement alerts me to danger, and I may ease off the accelerator. If a red light appears on my dashboard and I notice I'm low on gas, I may decide to drive slower to get slightly better gas mileage and make it to the next filling station. I may decide that's a good idea anyway because the price of gas is high these days.

Each of these factors represents a marketplace force. Let's look at each more closely, imagining that we are a good cause focused on getting people to obey the speed limit on the interstate. We should think about each of the following categories:

- Demographic: Who are speeders, and what demographic trends do we see among these groups? For example, if we know speeders are increasingly male commuters, we will have a different audience and marketing approach

than we would for teenaged drivers or truckers with
lead feet.

- Lifestyle: Is our audience short on time, focused on
family, young and reckless, or retired and relaxed? The
type of life they lead certainly affects their values as
well as their driving habits.

- Social and cultural: What social and cultural expectations and trends affect our speeders? My mother's plea
to slow down may affect me. The speed of other drivers
on the highway is also influential. For example, I don't
see myself as part of the group that drives one hundred
miles per hour in the left lane. I adjust my speed to that
of the majority of cars around me. What are our speeders' peer groups doing? Could we influence them?

- Health: One reason people drive reasonably carefully is
they don't want to die or be injured in a car accident. It
may not always be the main thought in our heads when
we get behind the wheel, but it is a factor.

- Natural: Mother Nature has an effect on any business
or cause through the supply of natural resources, the
state of the environment, or natural disasters. If it's
pouring rain or the roads are icing over, drivers are
likely to go slower.

- Economic: People care about their wallets. For example, the cost of gas can affect driving habits.

- Infrastructural: Potholes make drivers slow down, but
they can also make drivers swerve. Textured pavement
may make drivers slow down at off ramps.

- Rules and laws: The speed limit and the presence of police greatly affect the average speed on a road. Everyone

needs carrots to take action, but we often also need the stick of enforcement.

- Scientific: Studies showing that speeding increases fatalities or has no effect on safety can influence my speed. We want to stay connected with the research community relevant to our cause and anticipate the impact of new findings.

- Technological: We may want to encourage the police to install more traffic-enforcement cameras because they slow people down.

- Political: Who are in office and what is their agenda? What reelection issues are they worried about? During the gas crisis of the 1970s, speed limits were lowered to fifty-five miles per hour. During the decades that followed, politicians increased limits because they weren't popular.

- Media: Keep tabs on topics of interest to the media. If the media are focused on the price of gas or the safety of SUVs, we can use that attention to put a spotlight on our issue.

- Business: Successful good causes look at the private sector as a force to co-opt, not fight. We may want to partner with Volvo or Michelin to deliver safe-driving messages to our audience.

- Competition: Who else is talking about driving and speeding and how may they influence our audiences? If auto clubs are lobbying for increased speed limits, we need to counter that message; if they are promoting safety, we can align with that cause.

AN EXAMPLE: EAT YOUR FRUITS AND VEGETABLES

Let's take an example of how a good cause—getting people to eat their fruits and vegetables—handled some of these forces. In the late 1980s, the California Department of Health Services got a National Cancer Institute grant to change nutritional habits in order to prevent cancer. It set a tangible audience action as its goal: eat five servings of fruits and vegetables per day. Clearly, the action being sought was good for people's health, and plenty of scientific evidence backed it up. But the payoff—avoiding cancer—lacked immediacy for many people. In fact, people were eating about three servings instead of five because of demographic, economic, and lifestyle forces at work around them. In many homes, both parents worked with less time than ever for shopping and food preparation. People were simply too busy to wash, peel, or prepare fruit or make a salad. Fast food was quick and convenient. People knew fruits and vegetables were healthier than burgers, but burgers were cheap and easy. Social forces were at play as well. Most people didn't see their peers eating five servings. It seemed like a lot. Surely only health nuts ate like that.

The Five a Day for Better Health campaign worked with, not against, this audience environment. It acknowledged people's lifestyles and the other factors that made them demand convenience and speed, and it showed how people could still eat their fruits and veggies within that context. The campaign focused on showing people how to add two servings "the easy way." The program slogan became "Fruits and Vegetables: The Original Fast Food."

The campaign also recognized that the private sector played a role in the marketplace. McDonald's wasn't helping matters, but the campaign organizers realized other corporate entities might be allies. For example, the produce industry benefited directly when people increased their consumption of fruits and vegetables. The California Department of Health Services ended up becoming a partner of that industry to strengthen the campaign's position in the marketplace. The relationship was so successful that the National Cancer Institute created a national campaign with the produce industry, forming the Produce for Better Health Foundation. That alliance has since grown into the nation's largest public-private partnership for nutrition. (In Chapter Five, we meet the man who helped broker the original partnership and learn how he did it.) The private-sector campaign partners brought the "easy," "fast" message to grocery stores, cafeterias, and kitchens, spelling out how to add two servings a day easily with convenient packaging, microwaveable meals, simple recipe changes, and easy recommendations like drinking a glass of orange juice.

The National Cancer Institute began evaluating the campaign in 2000 and found it raised the daily serving of fruits and vegetables from 3.9 to 4.4 nationally and nearly quadrupled the number of consumers who knew the correct number of servings for good health. Children's consumption went from 3.1 to 3.4 servings per day. That is a lot of carrot sticks and applesauce.

HOW TO USE ROBIN HOOD RULE 3

1. Go for a Walk in the Audiences' Shoes

Imagine waking up one morning in our audiences' shoes and seeing the world as they do. In the course of the day, our audiences encounter many marketplace forces that affect the likelihood of their taking action. Some of these forces will have surfaced in our audience research. Others may not have because our audiences may not be aware of all the factors in their environment that influence them. Speak to front-line staff and leading thinkers on the issue at hand to fill in the picture. Call or visit the organizations and companies that the audience comes into contact with, imagining the experience they have and the message they hear. Read, watch, and listen to what our audiences read, watch, and listen to.

2. Make a List of Marketplace Forces

Draw up a list of marketplace forces influencing each audience we have. Consider the following types of forces:

- Demographic: Which demographic trends affect the size of our audiences or our ability to reach and influence them with the resources we have?

- Lifestyle: With an understanding of our audiences' lifestyles, we can determine which actions are reasonable to request and feasible for our audience.

- Social and cultural: How might we influence our audience's peer group as a whole?

- Health: The more our audiences see our issue as immediately important to their health and welfare the greater the likelihood of their taking action.

- Natural: What natural or environmental trends might bring attention to our issue, undermine it, or otherwise affect our efforts? For example, if we're promoting water conservation, a drought would make it a lot easier and a rainy season might make it a lot harder to get people to take action.

- Economic: Always think about whether audiences can afford to take action and emphasize any cost savings to them.

- Infrastructural: Is the infrastructure in place to encourage action, or might it stand in our way?

- Rules and laws: Are laws or regulations in place or proposed that might affect our audiences' actions or willingness to take action? Which laws might help us succeed?

- Scientific: Many good causes successfully piggyback their issue onto research that has the attention of the media and is in the public eye. They are also ready to react if research flies in the face of their claims or the actions they promote.

- Technological: Which technological advancements can bolster or hinder our efforts?

- Political: Which ways are the political winds blowing?

- Media: What are the media saying about the public's current mood, its priorities and concerns, and possible openings for our cause?

- Business: Which private-sector organizations benefit if we succeed? Could we co-opt them?

- Competitive: Who else is talking about our issue, and how might they influence our audiences?

3. Divide the List According to Ability to Influence the Marketplace

Narrow our list to the forces that have the greatest effect on our audiences. For example, if the natural environment and health are not especially relevant to our audiences' behavior or our issue, we should remove them from our list. We want to hone in on a handful of highly influential forces.

Next, ascertain the forces in this smaller list that we can use to our advantage, those in our way, and those that may require partners to leverage. That's what the Five a Day campaign did. Imagine if that campaign had ignored lifestyles, economics, and private-sector forces: "Eat your fruits and vegetables because they are good for you!" Fortunately, Five a Day thought about how to use the marketplace context that made convenience and time so important to consumers, and they took advantage of the complementary agenda of the produce industry. In other words, the campaign figured out how all the marketplace forces aligned with the action it was seeking. It also had an idea of how those forces, like busier lifestyles, were evolving. We need a clear idea not only of the current status of our marketplace but also of where it is headed.

In the next three chapters we focus on how to use a similar approach to dealing with competition, building partnerships, and creating messages for our worthy cause.

CONCLUSION

Our marketplace is as competitive as Times Square. In this environment, we never command the full attention of our audiences. Each major marketplace force is like a giant electric billboard. If we ignore those forces, we're one person standing on Broadway, holding a small, handwritten sign. Meanwhile the world is flowing around us, people are gazing upward, and we go unnoticed. Aligning with the right forces is like getting our message flashed on one of those Times Square billboards. We gain attention, and we greatly increase our odds of getting results. May the forces be with you.

Interview 1
Tapping Marketplace Forces for Belarus

In rising through the ranks of America Online (AOL), Kathy Ryan covered every aspect of creating and selling product. "I did product development, public relations, product positioning and marketing, and, in the process, I learned what makes a really good product. It needs to target an audience and meet their needs," she says. Ryan sold AOL products for over a decade until she left to care for two children she adopted from a Russian orphanage. When she was ready to go back to work, she realized she wanted to promote a new kind of product. "I started wondering how I could put my background to use for nonprofits. So I began consulting and volunteering for causes I really cared about."

Ryan now applies her marketing expertise to Chernobyl Children's Project International Inc., where she donates her time as executive director of the U.S. office. In this way she gives back to a part of the world not far from where her children were born. The project helps young victims of the aftereffects of the Chernobyl nuclear accident in Ukraine; during a test in 1986 the complex spewed one hundred times more radiation than the atomic bombs dropped in Japan. The Project provides humanitarian and medical assistance to children in Belarus, just north of Chernobyl, where the wind blew 70 percent of the radioactive material released in the accident. It addresses the domino effect of poverty, poor health, and social and psychological problems that the disaster created. The organization's board reflects expertise in this field, as well as corporate know-how. "Our board includes experts on our issue, but also people from the worlds of business, finance, and law. Donors, who tend to be from the corporate world, like that we know how to get the job done, but they also like the fact that we have private-sector members who treat donations as an investment."

Q: What is the marketplace like for your donors?

A: One of challenges of communicating about Chernobyl is that it doesn't have the disaster-of-the moment factor that an earthquake or tsunami or extreme poverty has. People don't think about an event that happened more than twenty years ago in a foreign country. They don't realize the disaster is not over because we are all accustomed to disasters with beginnings and ends. With breast cancer, you have a Race for a Cure. The cure is your end point. We don't have that end point. The antinuclear lobby has an interest, but their focus in really on using the disaster to advance their goals. People in favor of nuclear power have an interest in underplaying the consequences of Chernobyl. Radiation scares people, and it becomes the focus. That's OK, but we also address the broad picture and want to inform people in a credible way about that situation. This is a health problem. It's an economic problem because Belarus was the breadbasket of the region. It's a political issue because it was wrapped up in the fall of the Soviet Union and later political changes in the region.

Q: So how do you handle those challenges?

A: We are strictly a volunteer organization with no paid staff, and we don't want to spend a lot so we find economical ways to get attention. We have experimented with Google advertising. I bought the keyword Chernobyl, with the idea that only a defined number of people are typing that keyword into the system, and they are likely a good audience. We'd like them to come to our Web site (http://www.chernobyl-international.org). We can target messages and track response rates faster and far more cheaply through Google than by direct mail, which is very expensive. We could test different headlines and found that "Chernobyl: the facts" worked best. We can capture people's interest. Then we treat them as part of our community by contacting them with information. We took a filmmaker with us on a mission, and she made the documentary *Chernobyl Heart*, which won a 2004 Academy Award and appeared on HBO. That made a huge difference.

Q: How have you harnessed marketplace forces?

A: The twentieth anniversary of the Chernobyl disaster was in April 2006, which attracted attention. We marketed around that idea. Then there are all the political developments in the region. The fact that Ukraine and Belarus are emerging news stories puts a spotlight on that part of the world, and we can take advantage of that attention to bring the event up to date. In showing its relevance, there is also the issue of nuclear-power plants as targets for terrorism. People don't pay as much attention if they don't believe it could happen to them. Martin Cruz Smith has a book called *Wolves Eat Dogs*.[1] It takes place in the Chernobyl exclusion zone. Then there is a new video game called Stalker: In the Shadow of Chernobyl. I wrote the manufacturer of the game and suggested adding information about our cause for people who want more information about Chernobyl. Because I come from a consumer-marketing background, I am not afraid to grab onto these opportunities in the popular culture.

Interview 2
Swallowing the Cause

Sharyn Sutton likes to tell nonprofit organizations to "swallow your cause." She says that, as with pride, if we are consumed by our cause, we are likely not to see, hear, or understand those people we most want to reach. If we want to make a change, we must stifle a desire to preach and instead learn about our audiences and our marketplace. "I was asked to talk about marketing at a very high-profile conference on improving care for the dying. I'd given a lot of thought to how I could shock people into understanding that their passion for a cause does not lead to good messaging. So I walked into my session and announced I'd like to start by asking, 'What are you doing to make sure our kids are better educated? The schools need help, and there is nothing more important than our children and their education.' The audience looked at me as though I was nuts. They were thinking I was at the wrong conference," she says. "Too often we think people are just as impassioned about our issue as we are. Because it is heartfelt for us, it must be heartfelt for everyone. No. There is something called reality, but that reality is different for everyone. Creating effective messages means leaving our reality and understanding the reality of others." Sutton, never far from her Blackberry and always working on a cause, is a high-energy woman who likes to reveal people's alternative realities through pragmatic but probing audience research. "Good research should feed directly into our campaigns and ensure they will penetrate the unique and mysterious world of others," she says.

She is best known for her work on the Consumer-Based Health Communications model and has led some of the best-known national social-marketing campaigns. The Five a Day nutrition campaign (in partnership with the produce industry), the Once a Year for a Lifetime mammography campaign (with Revlon and Avon), and the U.S. Department of Agriculture's (USDA's) Team Nutrition campaign (with Disney and Scholastic) reflect her vision. Each of those campaigns bears her hallmarks: taking advantage of marketplace forces and forging unique public-private partnerships.

Sutton is managing director of communications and social marketing at the American Institutes for Research, which acquired her own firm, Sutton Group, in 2005. A former executive vice president at Porter Novelli, she also directed public-outreach programs at the National Cancer Institute and the USDA. Here, she shares her insights into how good causes can survive and successfully navigate the cold, hard reality of a competitive marketplace.

Q: Just how competitive is it out there?

A: You can market a good cause the way you market Coca-Cola, but it is a whole lot harder. We have far fewer resources, and yet we are trying to make huge changes. Coke has legions while we may not even have marketing staff. We have no infrastructure for creating social change like the infrastructure in the private sector. Businesses have distribution systems, sales forces, ad agencies, and some of the best audience research you can find. But that does not mean we must create a social-change infrastructure from scratch. If nonprofits were competing in a car race, they would want to start by building a car. Why not co-opt the cars in the race and emblazon every one with our cause? It would be a lot easier than starting from scratch. We need to connect with the vehicles in our marketplace and get behind the wheel. This is what public-private partnerships are all about.

Q: How have marketplace forces made a difference in campaigns you've worked on?

A: When I was at the National Cancer Institute, we launched the Once a Year for a Lifetime campaign to encourage women to have mammograms annually. We got that message out with great partners. We worked with Revlon to create nationally broadcast television dramas in English and Spanish; with Avon to run a cause-marketing venture that raised over $6 million in two months for local breast-cancer education; and with grass-roots organizations to sponsor screening and education. At the same time, we took advantage of positive marketplace forces. Insurance companies were beginning to cover mammograms; the White House held a breast-cancer summit; and the courts were finding in favor of women who were not screened by their physicians. This campaign helped double mammography screening rates among all women—white, black, and Hispanic.

Q: What's your favorite example of "swallowing your cause?"

A: When I was at the USDA, we wanted kids to make healthier food choices than they usually did. But we couldn't just tell them to do it. Here's where we had to "swallow our nutrition cause."

We had to approach children around their own reality, not educate them about nutrition. What is healthy doesn't matter to kids, but they know that junk food is bad, grease is the stuff on their fingers, and fat is the white part of meat that wiggles. They don't want to eat healthy. They want to grow big, get muscles, go faster, have energy, and think better. So we asked them to "devour for power." And we knew it shouldn't be the USDA telling them. We partnered with Disney, which offered us the *Lion King* characters Pumbaa and Timon because they knew how to deliver a message. We also partnered with Scholastic, the largest in-school children's publisher, to distribute materials. The campaign was wildly popular, and research showed that the greater the exposure, the more likely kids were to make healthy food choices. This success can be credited to our partners; they had the ability to appeal to and reach the kids. If we can't reach people, we should look to the people who can. That's often the private sector.

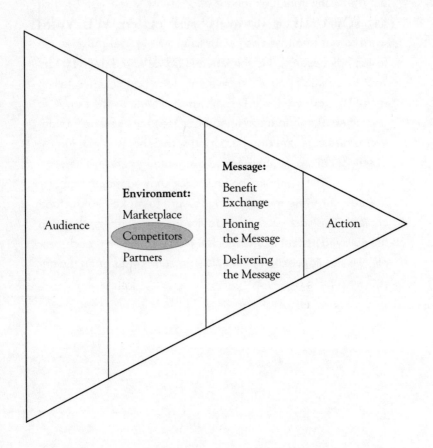

4

All for One and One for All—We Wish

Stake a Strong Competitive Position

WHAT THIS CHAPTER SAYS

- We need to understand our competition and then innovate, differentiate ourselves, or collaborate with a partner to achieve a strong and unique position in our audiences' minds.

- By finding the right niche in our marketplace, we will spend less time and energy fighting for dollars and duplicating effort.

- Our competition for money and attention includes good causes doing similar work (brand competition), as well as different causes competing for the same money, members, or clients (industry competition). It also includes form and generic competition—all the good causes and companies seeking to fulfill the same audiences' needs and wants that we are.

- To apply the principles in this chapter: Devise a competitive strategy that focuses on the audience while taking into account the competition, not the other way around. A strong competitive position is based on our strengths, is unique to us, is simple to understand, and is important to the audience.

ENLIGHTEN YOUR FEET.

Open your sock drawer and look inside. I am willing to bet that if you're a man, you'll own at least one pair of Gold Toes. Those are the dress socks with the distinctive gold thread at the toe. If you're a woman, you may have a pair of white work-out socks with that gold color on the toes. The odds are in my favor because more than half of all men's socks sold at U.S. department stores are the Gold Toe brand, and the company weaves more than 140 million pairs for men, women, and children every year.[1]

Why does Gold Toe hold such a strong position in the market? Because it has a clear competitive advantage. In the consumer's mind, Gold Toe stands for quality and durability. Gold Toe socks don't get little holes at the toe after you wear them a few times, nor do they lose their elasticity and start sagging around the ankles after a few washes.

The company gained its toehold in the sock market during the Depression, when it began weaving strong Irish linen into the tips of its socks so they would last longer during hard times. In the 1930s, a department-store buyer told one of the company's founders that the durable toes were great, but customers couldn't tell which brand had them. In a stroke of genius, the company decided to wrap gold acetate thread around the linen so its strong toe—now a Gold Toe—would be immediately visible to consumers. The company made its competitive advantage recognizable and unmistakable. That decision has made Gold Toe Brands Inc. the third largest sock manufacturer in the United States. Go to a leading department store today, and you can see why. In a sea of black and blue men's dress socks, Gold Toe practically leaps off the display shelves.

Gold Toe tells us to "enlighten your feet." We're going to enlighten our minds with Gold Toe's winning approach.

Robin Hood Rule 4

Stake a strong competitive position in the minds of the audience. We want to make our competitive advantage as clear to our audiences as if we'd adorned it in gold thread.

In the preceding chapter, we got to know our marketplace and the forces that can help us. Here, we are going to explore the groups and ideas that stand in our way within that marketplace: our competition. We then circumvent the challenges they present by identifying our gold toe: the one characteristic that makes us more special than everyone else.

THE WAR FOR WHAT?

Marketers love war analogies, from the marketplace as the "battlefield" to outreach efforts as military "campaigns." Jack Trout and Al Ries, authors of the classic *Marketing Warfare*, went so far as to base the principles of competitive marketing on the writings of the nineteenth-century Prussian general and superstar of military theory Karl von Clausewitz.[2] Another bestseller, *Guerrilla Marketing*, urges the small entrepreneur to outmaneuver larger but less nimble opponents just as a guerrilla army takes on the big guns.[3]

This dog-eat-dog, kill-or-be-killed, fight-to-the-death rhetoric sometimes extends to good causes too: think of the war on drugs, the war on poverty, the fight against cancer, the battle against Big Tobacco. Although we do-gooders may speak the corporate language of crusaders or generals, we typically stop short of using battlefield thinking in our work in the trenches. Many people who are passionate about their cause can't believe that anyone is competing against them to do social good. After all, who could be against someone trying to improve his or her neighborhood school or advocating a cure for cancer? Doesn't everyone want such efforts to succeed? Unfortunately, the marketplace for doing good is not a harmonious Garden of Eden. Forces good and bad work at cross-purposes on any issue. And sometimes our most acute competition is from do-gooders with similar agendas. They share our worldview, but they are competing for donor dollars, attention from audiences, and credit for success.

Corporations understand their competition in order to be profitable. Good causes need to understand their competition to succeed in their missions.

> The goal is not to obliterate other good causes or get into hand-to-hand combat with private-sector competitors. The goal is to understand our competition and then innovate, differentiate, or find a partner to achieve a strong and unique position in our audiences' minds. By finding the right niche, we spend less time and energy fighting for dollars and duplicating effort.

Think of our own theater of war as having two fronts. The first is money. In the late 1940s there were a few thousand nonprofits; today there are nearly a million and a half. Since the mid-1990s, the number of nonprofit organizations has been growing about 5 percent per year, more than twice the growth rate of the private sector, with health services and education organizations leading the pack.[4] Competition is therefore stiff for donor dollars, and we have to work twice as hard to distinguish ourselves in a world where donors receive a mind-numbing number of appeals and proposals. We may not be as special as we think we are. The nonprofit strategist David La Piana calls this the "belief paradox." If there is one belief that all good causes share, it's that they are all unique. Too bad funders also share one belief: that all good causes are the same.[5]

The second front is the war for our audiences' hearts and minds. We must compete with every organization that seeks to convince our audience to take actions that are the opposite of or that are opposed to the ones we desire. We need to position our cause favorably with respect to this competition or our audience will turn to our competitors when they want to take action.

In fighting on both these fronts, we have limited resources. We don't have the big guns, so we need the big brains. We should find the ground that is above the fray and relatively easy to defend, rather than fight over someone else's small square of turf. We require more than the courage of our convictions; we need a dose of von Clausewitz too.[6]

SIZING UP THE COMPETITION

So who is our competition on our two battlefronts of money and minds? The short answer is, anyone who stands to lose if we gain. Competitors generally fall into one of four categories. First, direct competitors for money, members, or clients are good causes that do similar work in the same field. This is the narrowest way to look at competition. In the private sector, such direct competition is called "brand competition"—the competition among companies offering similar products at similar prices.[7] Coke and Pepsi are in brand competition, as are Honda and Toyota. Yugo and Mercedes are not. This type of competition is most familiar to us. It's easy to grasp that Catholic Relief Services and World Vision are brand competitors in international-aid work, as are the American Cancer Society and the National Coalition for Cancer Survivorship in the world of advocacy groups for people with cancer. Another example would be two nearby elementary schools holding auctions to benefit the PTA or two causes fundraising to combat global poverty.

Second, indirect competition occurs when different causes compete for the same money, members, or clients. Most organizations are competing not only with similar groups but on the larger bat-tlefield of an "industry." In the private sector, industry competition is among all the companies making the same category of product. Hyundai and Mercedes are industry competitors because they are both car companies. Catholic Relief Services and the American Cancer Society are industry competitors in a sense because they are both nonprofits seeking donations for a good cause. The activist canvassing in our neighborhood for signatures and money to reduce mercury poisoning can be seen as an industry competitor if we're canvassing the same neighborhood for a different cause. People may not want to answer the door again and give twice in one day. These indirect competitors may also be competing for staff members, board members, or media attention in our community.

Third, a still broader kind of competition occurs when causes and companies offer competing actions to fulfill the same audience needs and wants. "Form competition" is competition among all the organizations that provide products that meet the same need we do. In form competition, a car company competes against other forms of personal transportation, such as motorcycles, bicycles, and trucks.[8] After 9/11, auto manufacturers offered a way for Americans to feel they were supporting the country in the wake of terrorism—by buy-ing a car. They were form competition for the many other causes, in-cluding that of public health, that were trying to encourage audiences to meet the same need with a different action—by, for ex-ample, increasing funding for public health infrastructure. Another example is a symphony orchestra competing with a compact disc recording; both offer a way to listen to classical music. If we're try-ing to get people to lose weight through exercise, we are competing with all the other ways an audience may attempt to look thinner—by eating less, eating healthier, getting a gym membership, buying Slim-Fast, taking diet pills, wearing all black, using a girdle, getting a gastric bypass or tummy tuck, or sucking in their stomachs.

Fourth, "generic competition" occurs between us and all others seeking our audiences' money, time, and attention; it is a step back from form competition. For example, a car company may see its competition as all other companies offering big-ticket items.[9] The American Cancer Society fundraising department is competing against all other ways consumers can spend their money. A museum may be competing with a movie theater and a football game because those are other ways someone might spend a Saturday afternoon. This competition can be thought of as latent competition; people in the private sector say these latent competitors from unexpected places often pose the greatest threat. For example, travel agents in the early 1990s may have viewed their competitors within the universe of other travel agencies; with the subsequent dominance of the Internet and rise in self-booked travel through sites like Expedia and Travelocity a powerful and latent competitor profoundly changed an entire industry. Just a year after Expedia was off the ground, it was already one of the biggest travel agencies in the world.

HOW TO COMPETE

Once we have an idea of our competition, we can think about how to deal with it.

> Competitive strategy should focus on the audience while taking into account the competition, not the other way around. We do not win solely by reacting to our competitors but rather by outperforming them in meeting our audience's needs and wants. An audience's mind, not the marketplace, is the real site of battle.

Think of all the also-ran ideas that were knee-jerk reactions to competition: Burger King's Magical Burger King as rival to Ronald McDonald or Mr. Pibb as an afterthought to Dr Pepper.[10] These ideas come from the "they did it, we'd better too" school of thought. This thinking can extend to nonprofits, especially with regard to marketing tactics. We don't necessarily need a silent auction or imprinted coffee cups or wristbands or a logo with clasped hands just because the other guy has them. We are better off finding a better, newer way to meet our audiences' wants.

→ So how do we outperform our competition in reaching our audiences? We establish a competitive position that has four attributes: it is based on our strengths, it is unique, it is simple to understand, and it is important to the audience.

The first attribute is our natural strength. We want to take an honest look at what we do well. Gold Toe knew it had the most durable toe in the sock market. To use a nonprofit example, let's think about the relative strengths of Greenpeace and the Natural Resources Defense Council. Greenpeace has a good infrastructure for what it calls "bearing witness" to enemies of the environment and grabbing headlines. The National Resources Defense Council has a band of relentless lawyers and scientists who are great at lobbying and litigation.

Second, define the characteristics that make our cause unique. If we think about our environmental example, one factor that differentiates Greenpeace and the Natural Resources Defense Council in the marketplace of environmental groups and the minds of consumers is how they use their relative strengths. Greenpeace goes after governments and corporations with confrontational tactics that expose environmental problems. This in-your-face style defines them in most people's minds. The Natural Resources Defense Council is good at tightening up environmental-protection policies by working within the system to effect change. It works at the policy level.

The third attribute is to stick to a simple, understandable idea when we market our cause. We want to stand for one idea, consistently. Greenpeace owns the mental real estate of extreme environmental activism. The National Resources Defense Council sticks to the idea that it is "the earth's best defense."

Finally, the competitive position must be important to the audience. If we stake competitive ground that's not relevant to our audiences, we will never get their attention. Our strengths, unique qualities, and single idea must be attractive to the market we want to capture. Greenpeace appeals to a certain kind of person, while the National Resources Defense Council attracts a different crowd. They each have an audience that likes what they do.

AN EXAMPLE: DIFFERENTIATING DIAPERS

Let's walk through a private-sector example of a company's using these principles to create a competitive advantage. Suppose we are brand managers for Kimberly-Clark in the 1970s, and we are competing with Pampers. Pampers is the long-time market leader in disposable diapers, a category it invented. Like most first products, Pampers is number one worldwide. In Russian, all disposable diapers are called "pahm-payrs." Pampers is to diaper as Kleenex is to tissue. It owns the idea of "disposable diaper" in our minds. Its advantage is that it is an established, big brand that is everywhere.

At Kimberly-Clark, imagine that we do a little research and find out that some mothers don't like the fact that Pampers leak around the leg holes. We see an opportunity and create Huggies, the first disposable diapers with elastic leg bands. Our new product builds on our strength as a product innovator. It has a unique and simple advantage in that it's leak-proof. That's a good advantage to have because it's important to the mothers who buy our product. (In case you think I'm discounting all the diaper-changing dads out there, I'm not; bless every last one of you. Women are the ones who usually buy the diapers, though you will be pleased to know a man invented Pampers.) Huggies used this approach to successfully distinguish itself as a new brand, and it has continued to innovate its design over the years. Pampers innovates too in a back-and-forth war to be the best-designed diaper. Pampers continues its role as the worldwide market leader, but Huggies today says it is number one in the U.S. market.

Now let's switch gears and imagine we work for Luvs. What is our competitive advantage? It doesn't make sense to go after Pampers or Huggies based on their relative strengths. What could make us unique? How about price? Those market leaders aren't cheap, so we could sell our brand as a quality diaper that costs less. Luvs did just that. The brand stands for "cottony and soft," but more important, it is less expensive. It goes after a segment of the diaper market that wants that advantage: the cost-conscious, practical mom.

Luvs had an effective ad in which a woman reflects on her first months as a new mom. She was terrified to let anyone else hold the baby or to use anything other than the priciest diaper on the market. The ad flashes back to her anxiously clutching her child, then shows her today, relaxed, laughing, and talking about how she now knows better. Who needs fancy, expensive brands when the experienced mom knows Luvs work just as well, if not better, she says. Live and learn, and then get Luvs. A Web site testimonial says: "Luvs seem softer than cashmere—without the pretense." Here we see the hallmarks of a good competitive position. Luvs has the unique, simple, and relevant advantage of quality for less.

Now let's look at a diaper that carved out another niche of the diaper-buying market: environmentally conscious moms. Seventh Generation diapers are positioned as a quality product that doesn't contribute to dioxin pollution. Seventh Generation diapers are for the extreme green mom who wants diapers that are free of chlorine, dyes, fragrance, latex, and tributyl tin. This is a small, niche market that works for Seventh Generation. It's unique, simple, and relevant to eco-moms. In addition, it's a big enough market for the company to be viable, but it's also small enough that Pampers, Huggies, and Luvs are likely to leave it alone.

Huggies, Luvs, and Seventh Generation all dealt with market leader Pampers through differentiation. They found a niche where they could be good—they would argue, the best—and used that position to their competitive advantage. They knew that the closer you are to your competition, the stiffer the competition. It's better to be opposite than identical.

DIFFERENTIATING A CAUSE

Differentiation is even more important with good causes than it is in the private sector. Good causes are more likely to get lumped together in people's minds than diaper brands. Let's take an example of how we can use these principles. Consider the good cause of helping sick children. Many causes help these children through a variety of approaches: medical aid, family-support programs, advocacy, and research. The Make-a-Wish Foundation has carved out its niche in this market as the largest "wish-making organization." Nearly half of all children with a life-threatening illness in the United States make a wish through the Foundation. The organization's position is unique, simple, and relevant to many people: it fulfills the wishes of very sick children, whether through helping them meet a famous person, letting them pretend to be a superhero for a day, or creatively helping other sick children. This approach works because the Foundation has the organizational strengths to back it up, including a huge volunteer structure, seventy-five chapters in the United States, and corporate partners like Disney.

A Harvard Business School Africa Business Conference profiled how Rwanda is using these same competitive principles to promote its tourism industry. It could have jumped on the African safari bandwagon, but it realized Kenya, Tanzania, and Uganda had better natural resources and an established market for safaris. It looked to its natural advantage—mountain gorillas—and is seeking to market a primate-discovery tour that combines visits to the gorillas with visits to other primates. Market research showed that a segment of ecotourists is wild about primates, and the government is working on developing this tourism product to meet that market demand.[11]

These are compelling examples, but how can this thinking work on a small scale? I'll give you an example. When my daughter was in kindergarten at a public school in Washington, D.C., our PTA raised money by getting donations from businesses for a silent auction each year. The problem was, so did every other school in northwest

Washington. A good idea would have been to innovate with a new product other than an auction, but that didn't go over well with the PTA committee. "We always do this, it's a tradition, it works" was the refrain, and it is a familiar one to those of us who are boat-rockers. It's not easy to innovate on a volunteer committee.

The auction was destined to happen, and, as the one-person PTA Marketing Committee, I was asked to write talking points for volunteers to use in asking area businesses for donations. The goal was to get them to give away products or services for the auction in return for a thank-you in the auction program and the knowledge they'd helped an area school. Knowing that each business would be approached by other schools, it was clear that "Sorry, I already gave to another school" was likely to be our biggest barrier.

We had to find a unique competitive position for our school auction. I looked at the natural strengths that made our school different: it was the most diverse, drawing students from all corners of the district and of all races. Parents from poorer school districts petitioned to get their children into our small school, so it functioned as a de facto magnet school. The strength of the other schools—that they represented the neighborhood—was a weakness because they had students from one small part of Washington composed of mostly well-off families. Their size—also a drawback for us as fundraisers—was a weakness if it meant that donors' money didn't go as far.

In soliciting donations, I asked volunteers to emphasize that our auction benefited the broadest array of children, and because the school was small, the businesses could have a big impact on that diverse group. The response to "Sorry, I already gave to another school" was "But not this school or these kids—they are different." We didn't hurt the other schools, which were bigger, better organized, and started soliciting donations earlier, but we also got businesses to give. Many gave to two auctions because they saw two different reasons to give—one for the neighborhood children and one for a wider need. We had successfully established a small square of competitive territory in our audience's mind.

HOW TO USE ROBIN HOOD RULE 4

1. List the Top Competitors

For each of our audiences think about the direct, indirect, form, and generic competition we face for money, audience attention, or whatever outcome we seek. Two sources of information—our research and our competition—will help. We identified much of our competition in conducting our audience research and in analyzing marketplace forces. Review this research once again and note the competition it uncovered. Search the Internet for information on our issue, and examine the competitors involved in our professional coalitions and conferences. Patronize competitors to understand their messages, products, and strengths or weaknesses. Make donations to competitors or use their products and services. Get on their mailing lists, use their Web sites, and call their toll-free numbers.

2. Prioritize the List

Just as we did with our analysis of marketplace forces, we want to select the competitors to challenge. For each competitor, we should ask ourselves how big a threat it is to our message and whether we have the ability to counter that threat with competitive positioning. For each audience focus on the two to three competitors we could challenge in order to significantly improve our chances of achieving our mission.

3. Stake the Competitive Position

As discussed previously in this chapter, a competitive position has four attributes: it reflects our strengths, it is unique, it is simple, and it is important to our audience. In thinking about each competitor, we want to establish an advantage in each of these four areas.

- Strength: What is our strong suit, or what strength can we create? What characteristics will make our audience choose us over the competition? Are we especially good at building relationships with our constituents? Do we have good services or an innovative approach to tackling our issue?

- Difference: What makes us unique? Do we have the most stellar reputation in our field? Are we the biggest or the first to offer a service? Are our services more accessible than those of our competitors or are our customers more satisfied? Is our overhead lower than that of other groups?

- Simplicity: Is our strength or difference a simple, easily grasped concept? At best, we can stand for just one attribute in each audience's mind, so we want that quality to be clear and memorable.

- Value to audience: Last, check ourselves. Is the quality we've chosen something that our audiences care about? The competitive advantage we believe we have is not an advantage if it's irrelevant or uninteresting to the people we want to reach.

Create a document or chart that reflects the competitive advantage we are establishing for each key audience. We will be reflecting that "gold toe" positioning in all our messages—a topic we turn to in the coming chapters.

CONCLUSION

The process of assessing and challenging the competition may be painful, but it is ultimately beneficial, not detrimental, to good causes and the common good. Competition spurs us to do better, to work more effectively, and to use our limited resources more wisely. It avoids duplication of effort and allows donors to focus resources on the best groups to fulfill their goals. Competitive thinking makes us more successful in our missions, and that improvement in turn makes the world a better place.

At the same time, we should not get carried away with the concept of competition. We need to stand for a unique idea, but we do not always want to stand alone. We want to reach beyond our niche when it helps advance our issue or spur action. If we share a common interest with another cause or corporation, we should fight together rather than fight each other. Good partnering can help increase our overall market; we can make a bigger pie rather than struggle for a piece of the existing pie. In Chapter Five we learn how to find those partnerships and make them flourish.

Interview
Competitive Thinking in Business

Matt Andresen is president of Citadel Execution Services, an affiliate of a $12 billion hedge fund headquartered in Chicago. It's a big job, but he got there by being the little guy. He is an example of a shrewd latent competitor who climbed to the top. Andresen made a name for himself in the late 1990s by transforming Island ECN from a three-employee firm to the largest electronic stock market in the United States. An electronic stock market is a computerized stock-trading system that matches buyers and sellers directly, rather than routing orders through dealers or trading floors. Island handled six hundred million shares a day and surpassed the size of Nasdaq by the time Andresen brokered its eventual merger with competitor Instinet.

In the process, Andresen gained the reputation of being an iconoclast with a love of rattling big competitors with bold moves and bombastic rhetoric. He liked to tell market makers that if they profited from the kinds of market inefficiencies that Island eliminated, they'd better prepare their résumés. "Someday, you'll be out of business," he warned. Perhaps Andresen likes to put his competitors on guard because of his early passion for fencing (he was an alternate on the U.S. Olympic team). Or maybe he got his competitive start at birth through acute sibling rivalry. He is, after all, my brother.

Here he shares some of his favorite insights on competition.

Q: How would you summarize the essence of competition in the private sector?

A: In business, you have two choices: innovate constantly or milk what you have until it runs dry. The first works; the second doesn't. No opportunity lasts. You desperately need to have something new and of value to customers at all times or you're dead. Out of the original twelve companies listed on the first Dow Jones Industrial Average, only one is still in the index—General Electric. The rest died, dissolved, got bought, reinvented themselves beyond recognition, or—in the case of Laclede Gas—are still around but were removed from the Dow Jones long ago. Today's giant could be tomorrow's U.S. Leather Preferred.

Q: How is this relevant to businesses of any size—or, for that matter, to the nonprofit sector?

A: Every day, I wake up worrying how to convince my customers that I have something they want and get them to stay with me, all while staying half a step ahead of the people who are as hungry for those customers as I am. It's not pleasant, but it brings out your best, it brings out the best in your competitors, and the winner is the customer.

I believe the same holds true for good causes. Island succeeded because it did a better job than its competitors in meeting the needs of its customers: traders. We offered them faster trades at a lower price. We proved we cared about them more than our competitors did by offering them a product and then promoting it aggressively. We didn't have the marketing dollars of the major stock exchanges, but we were creative. We put up ads with photos of real traders and the slogan "You, the trader" on every bus and subway in the vicinity of Wall Street. We went into several Starbucks in the financial district one day and paid for everyone's morning coffee. We made sure our audience knew we were most concerned about them, and that is key to any enterprise that needs to reach people, whether it is a for-profit or not-for-profit. We made ourselves look unique and different. Being unremarkable looks safe only on paper; in real life, it gets you run over. People just don't see you.

Q: What is the most important thing for a CEO to think about?

A: Most successful companies got where they are for two reasons. First, they had some luck—they blundered into a good thing. Second, they maximized that opportunity by being self-aware and self-critical. They continually asked, Does my way of business still work? Is my message still resonating out there? Is what I am building still solving my customer's problems? Do I understand my customers today? Microsoft didn't sit back and relax after MS-DOS. They watched what Apple did, they anticipated changes in the marketplace, and they create new products all the time. You have to be like the nervous suitor, always wondering whether you are liked and always looking to meet your customers' needs in new ways. That doesn't mean you listen to everything your customer says. Customers have a hard time identifying or articulating their problems. They typically cannot describe the new software product they want. But they can say what is bothering them, and the smart company figures out what product fixes that.

Q: What you are essentially saying is that business succeeds by innovating to meet customer needs. If you were running a good cause, how would you do that?

A: The first thing I would ask is, are we prepared to run this organization like a business? We need to focus on our customers because they are always king. Do we have the right people to accomplish our goals, and do we understand our competition? Then I'd go out and really connect with the people I wanted to donate. Everyone underestimates the importance of being a nice guy who operates on the same level as another person. There is such power in making that connection. It shows a respect for the other person and who they are, and it gives you credibility. If I were going into a low-income neighborhood, I would dress one way; if I were fundraising from super-wealthy people I'd dress that part. Wherever I was, I'd remember what my customer wants. The wealthy donors are looking for immortality. I'd find a way to give them that—for instance, by putting their name on a park bench or a paving stone.

Q: How can the little guy prevail in the marketplace?

A: When you and I were growing up, Katya, we played P-I-G at the bottom of our long, steep driveway. For those who haven't played, you take turns making basketball shots. Each time a player sinks a basket, the opponent has to make the exact same shot from the exact same spot or they get a letter. Whoever gets P-I-G loses. I was the bigger, more skilled player at P-I-G. I could sink lay-ups, jump shots, and free throws. You could maybe half the time.

But you knew my weakness: lack of patience. You invented the "beekeeper shot." This shot involved placing a basket upside-down on your head in a rough estimate of a beekeeper's head-gear and holding a net in the left hand and the ball in the right. The beekeeper had to start beyond the top of the driveway, in the cul-de-sac, and run one lap around the cul-de-sac, sprint down the driveway, climb onto an old bench under the basket (symbolizing the hive), and make a one-handed shot just under the basket. Who knows what the neighbors thought, but I know the effect: I would be so fed up by the end I would miss. In the language of marketing, I was a classic market leader. You could have spent hours trying to master a jump shot, but you chose the more expeditious position of the guerilla, flanking me with the wacky beekeeper shot. I conceded the shot.

The small players in this world have to do things in a very original way. Don't lament over your shortcomings or your opponent's strengths. Think about how you can be refreshingly different. Find your beekeeper shot. You may not win the whole marketplace, but you will score the points you need to get and keep a niche.

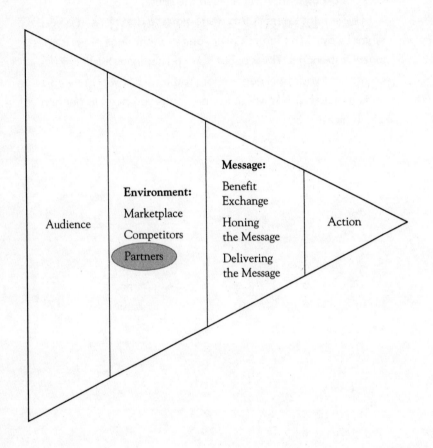

5

Building a Merry Band
Partner Around Mutual Benefits

WHAT THIS CHAPTER SAYS

- Partnerships should yield clear wins for each partner, and the partners should share a customer base or have complementary bases.

- In thinking about partners, instead of asking who is like us, ask who wins when we win. Look for partners with a compatible agenda with respect to our audience.

- No partnership is perfect. The bottom line is to go into the partnership with open eyes, more positives than negatives in regard to fit and benefits, and a plan for compensating for weaknesses within the alliance.

- Inevitably, the benefits that partners receive will change, and one partner may perceive diminishing value. Create new benefits if commitment is flagging on one side.

- To apply the principles in this chapter: First consider all partners aligned with our agenda and weigh the relative pros and cons of working with them. Choose those with the best fit, and make a plan for staying on track toward mutually compatible goals.

HOT DOUGHNUTS NOW.

Fall 2003 was a heady time for Krispy Kreme Doughnuts Inc., which was then churning out three billion doughnuts annually.[1] The chain was growing like gangbusters, the stock was on the rise, and the media loved to describe the cult status of those super-sweet glazed doughnuts. Everyone from characters on *Sex in the City* to then-President Bill Clinton were devotees.

Krispy Kreme decided the time was ripe to aim still higher: Why not put its bakeries in the number one food retailer in all the land? Krispy Kreme decided to "hole up" at Wal-Mart.[2] It opened five outlets in Wal-Mart stores to sell "hot doughnuts now" in a test program. A bevy of breathless retail analysts praised the concept, which was succeeding at other companies. Barnes & Noble customers were happily ordering venti skinny lattes from in-store Starbucks as they shopped. It seemed logical that doughnuts at Wal-Mart might have similar allure.

But was the customer fit for Wal-Mart and Krispy Kreme similarly strong? In the minds of consumers, Wal-Mart stood for abundance and value, from the size of the stores and parking lots to the display and pricing of products. When Wal-Mart shoppers thought about doughnuts, they likely pictured them in a big box at a bargain-basement price. Krispy Kreme stood for relative scarcity and mystique. Getting the sugary doughnut required a pilgrimage to a store, where customers might have to stand in long lines to buy the indulgent luxury. If they were lucky, they would arrive just when a new batch was ready and the "Hot Doughnuts Now" sign was alight. This effort was part of the Krispy Kreme experience: the quest, the timing, and the satisfaction of scoring the elusive treat.

So what happened when these two experiences came together? Unfortunately, not the same synergy we find in simultaneously lingering over a cup of coffee and a good book. An in-and-out trip to Wal-Mart is not the same thing as a pilgrimage to Krispy Kreme. When Krispy Kreme is juxtaposed with "Always Low Prices!" signs, vacuum-cleaner bags, and patio furniture, it just doesn't feel quite so tantalizingly elusive or appealingly hip. And from the Wal-Mart side of the equation, a high-priced hot doughnut does not look like a good deal to a customer who has just been cruising aisle after aisle of everyday low prices.

At the time its Wal-Mart pilot was launched, a Krispy Kreme spokesperson told *USA Today*, "We're just checking it out, exposing ourselves in the marketplace to more people."[3] If that rhetoric conjures up images of Krispy Kreme caught with its pants down, it should. Marketing partnerships are not about exposing ourselves like a trench-coated flasher. They should be about understanding and meeting the needs of the consumer in a way that benefits everyone involved.

The doughnut shops in Wal-Mart stores not surprisingly faltered, generating only about a third of the average sales of Krispy Kreme's stand-alone shops.[4] Those shops were not doing so well either, as the Krispy Kreme fad cooled, concerns rose over obesity, and low carb became the popular mantra. In Spring 2005, the doughnut maker pulled the plug on the Wal-Mart outlets. The experiment was not yielding the benefits Krispy Kreme had anticipated. This cautionary tale provides us with some food for thought about the nature of partnerships.

Robin Hood Rule 5

Build partnerships around mutual benefits or you won't be partnering at all. Partnerships should yield clear wins for each partner and, most important, the partners should share a customer base or have complementary bases.

The moral of the Krispy Kreme story is that a partnership without benefits for the customer and common goals and shared benefits for the partners is like a bunch of people holding hands in a circle. It's nice and it feels good, but there's nothing in the middle. We don't want this kind of hollow, doughnut-shaped and half-baked partnership, which may often amount to no more than regular meetings and logo exchanges. We want to build a different kind of partnership with two key ingredients: fit and filling. The fit is compatible goals for a common audience. The filling is the benefits that should accrue to each partner when we win our audiences' hearts and minds.

FINDING PARTNERS THAT FIT

We need partnerships because it's hard to make a difference by working solo. Harvard Business School professor James Austin has called the twenty-first century the "age of alliances," a time when collaboration is an increasing necessity for good causes.[5] Why? In the corporate sector, businesses have an extensive infrastructure for developing and selling their products. For example, they have research-and-development units, distribution networks, accountants, marketing managers, sales forces, public-relations departments, and ad agencies. A good cause may have none of that infrastructure, but by effectively partnering with other causes, the private sector, or the government, we can beg and borrow much of that infrastructure. Partners can help us reach our audience and advance our cause through their communication channels, distribution systems, political connections, money, and other resources.

Because the goal of a marketing partnership is to more effectively connect with our audiences than we have been, our audiences should be the starting point for all our thinking about partnerships. Starbucks and Barnes & Noble make sense together because they share a customer base and common goals with respect to that customer base. Both retailers want people to congregate in their stores and linger there, rather than brew coffee at home and order from Amazon.com.

Let's apply this thinking to a good cause. What good causes might match up nicely with Starbucks? One long-time partner of Starbucks has been the international relief and development agency CARE.[6] Starbucks and CARE share an audience that is likely not only to want good coffee but also to be concerned about responsible corporate practices. The organizations also share the goal of promoting the well-being of people in coffee-growing countries. Their partnership is a nice strategic fit.

In another example, Procter & Gamble's Pampers division was an excellent fit for the U.S. National Institutes of Health and Health Canada's fight against sudden-infant-death syndrome (SIDS). Pampers put messages on its smaller-sized diapers to encourage parents to put babies to sleep on their backs and thus reduce SIDS-related deaths. The Back to Sleep campaign and Pampers had a shared audience of parents and the common goal of reducing infant deaths.

On a far smaller scale, when my daughter's international school in Ukraine raised money, it had to keep in mind the notion of fit when accepting contributions from corporations where parents worked. For example, the school did not solicit corporate support from parents who worked for the Altria Group (which includes Kraft and Philip Morris) because neither the school nor Altria wanted to appear to be marketing tobacco products to an audience of kids.

FILLING THE DOUGHNUT

The filling is the benefit to each partner that should come from working together to reach an audience. It's the win-win proposition that brings each party to the table and keeps them there long enough to achieve success. The benefits for each party may be entirely different, and that's to be expected. Each partner has its eye on the unique opportunities and barriers within its own marketplace. Strong partnerships don't require a shared worldview. They just need some of the following types of filling:

- Philanthropic fulfillment: a sense of connection to a cause and the ability to make a difference in a way important to each partner

- Financial: money, an increase in revenue, or shared costs for one or both partners

- Image: a positive image, increased credibility, or heightened visibility

- Expertise: capability or capacity in an area (business acumen, philanthropic impact, marketing expertise) that one partner may be lacking

- New markets: access to additional or different customers/audiences, ability to broaden or deepen a constituency

- Marketing resources: the capacity for increased outreach, including new communication vehicles and distribution networks

- Efficiency: the elimination of duplicative efforts and the sharing of administrative tasks

- Products and services: the ability to add products, services, or related benefits for customers or audiences

- Competitive advantage: a characteristic that sets partners apart from competitors, builds customer loyalty, increases market share, or helps ward off competitive threats

- Employee morale: a boost to the recruiting and morale of employees, especially for corporate partners

In the Back to Sleep campaign, the National Institutes of Health and Health Canada got huge financial and marketing resources behind their message, Pampers expertise in marketing to parents, access to a huge constituency of diaper buyers, and the satisfaction of greatly increasing the number of parents who put their babies on their back to sleep. Pampers gained the benefits of philanthropic fulfillment, a positive image for its product, added expertise in a relevant area (preventing SIDS), access to new markets (for example, by the distribution of SIDS pamphlets to new mothers through hospitals), and quite possibly increased employee morale. Pampers also got a competitive advantage because, in today's increasingly competitive marketplace, philanthropic affiliations can be an important way for companies to differentiate themselves in the eyes of consumers.

Having philanthropic affiliations is worth emphasizing; it's a benefit increasingly recognized by companies and can be a strong selling point for good causes courting corporate partners. Paul Bloom, professor of marketing at the Kenan-Flagler Business School at the University of North Carolina, says it is harder and harder for companies to differentiate their brands through service, product features, or benefits. "What's happening now is they are being forced to compete on the basis of price or on heartstrings and affiliations. Those emotional affiliations might be with celebrities or sports teams or, increasingly likely, with a good cause. The style of marketing has become just as important as the product in securing a competitive advantage."[7]

To shift from diapers to coffee once again, Harvard's Austin notes that together Starbucks and CARE were able to communicate their support of people in coffee-growing communities more effectively than they would have alone. Starbucks added to the aura of its coffee-drinking experience by demonstrating that it treats its coffee suppliers and coffee-growing communities around the world with the same respect it shows toward Starbucks customers. CARE had the knowledge of the countries where Starbucks bought coffee and the experience in international development that could help Starbucks increase its ability to support its suppliers. In turn, CARE was able to get its cause in front of far more people than it could have otherwise because Starbucks had marketing savvy, and its stores featured brochures, banners, mugs, and other materials with the CARE message. CARE's relationship with Starbucks also helped CARE interest other corporate supporters in its work. The result was value for both partners and a greater, social good.

So far, we've focused on public-private partnerships. How does mutual benefit work with partnerships between good causes? Let's look at the example of the National Organization for Rare Disorders (NORD), which illustrates both fit and filling. NORD is a federation of nonprofit health groups that helps people with rare, "orphan," diseases and the organizations that serve them. An orphan disease is defined as one that affects fewer than two hundred thousand people in the United States. Each disease has a relatively small constituency on its own, but taken together, more than six thousand rare disorders affect about twenty-five million Americans. NORD was established in 1983 by patients and families who saw the potential of working together and increasing their political clout to get the Orphan Drug Act passed; the Act provides financial incentives for the development of new treatments for rare diseases. In the decade before the Orphan Drug Act, fewer than ten drugs for orphan disorders came to market. Since the passage of the Act, about two hundred have been approved.

The success of NORD shows how like-minded groups can combine over the long term for their mutual benefit. NORD members represent different diseases, but instead of seeing themselves as competitors fighting for attention, they came together around a goal held by all their audiences: increasing the attention and funding devoted to each of their diseases. They didn't fight over pieces of the metaphorical pie; they increased the size of the pie. In return, all the partners received greater funding, more capacity for outreach, increased visibility, greater political power, and advancement of their respective missions.

> This example also shows the importance of an X factor in a partnership: a catalyzing event. Catalyzing events can create a sense of immediacy that brings together partners expeditiously and improves their ability to work together.

The efforts to advance legislation supporting orphan drugs were a catalyzing force. For Pampers and Health Canada, the release of research linking sleeping position to reduction in infant deaths was a catalyzing event. We greatly enhance our chances of attracting partners by capitalizing on important developments such as these.

COURTING UNLIKELY BEDFELLOWS

Keep an open mind about the kinds of partners that can help us. The most effective partnerships are often with the most unlikely bedfellows.

> Instead of asking who is like us, ask who wins when we win. Don't rule out groups that have different motivations for wanting the same success. We don't need to share a mission to have a suitable fit.

We should, for example, be open to working with business. Although companies are passionate about making a profit and doing so may be a large reason for their support of good causes, that does not mean they don't care about making the world a better place (many do) or don't deserve to be a partner. We're missing out on huge opportunities to advance our mission if we rule out private-sector partnerships (which are becoming increasingly necessary to the survival of many causes) or if we refuse to work with groups that see the world differently than we do. Be open to partners beyond the usual cadre of like-minded groups because diverse partnerships can get much attention and significant results.

My current favorite example of this phenomenon is the Theodore Roosevelt Conservation Partnership, which brings together Environmental Defense, the National Rifle Association, the Safari Club, the World Wildlife Fund, ESPN Outdoors, and the Bass Angler Sportsman Society. This motley group of hunters, fishers, and green groups got foundation start-up funding and corporate sponsors to support causes such as preserving wetlands. By working together, they were able to achieve financial and political clout. They met with President George W. Bush and persuaded him not to remove large tracts of isolated wetlands from federal protection. Although the groups don't seem to have much in common and their reasons for wanting to preserve wetlands are different, their shared end goal provided enough filling to achieve an important victory.

Hooking up with unlikely partners can achieve unprecedented results, but these partnerships come with internal challenges. Trying to convince those within a cause that corporate "enemies" or "unrelated" causes are potentially valuable partners is not easy. The idea of right against might is romantic and makes many of us feel good, pure, and even self-righteous. If you are courting unusual partners, be prepared for raised eyebrows and occasional looks of horror from your colleagues, and try to persevere. Bloom, at the Kenan-Flagler Business School, says this reaction is common. He found it hard to get his running club to accept corporate sponsors because some members saw such partnerships as "unethical." Bloom eventually got his running buddies, who were having trouble paying the club's bills, to agree to corporate sponsorship of a couple of races. The partnership put the club back in the black and ended much of the criticism.[8] Get recalcitrant people on board by pointing out the successes of other unusual alliances, and, in the process, seek to redefine how colleagues think about partnerships. Partners don't need to be our clones or converts in order to help us accomplish good. The usual suspects mostly likely won't yield dazzling results, but the strangers who think differently just might.

HOW TO USE ROBIN HOOD RULE 5

We need to answer five strategic questions when identifying, as-sessing, and creating partnerships to ensure that we form partner-ships that effectively advance our cause.

1. Who Is Also Trying to Reach Our Audience?

At the start, we want to think as expansively as possible about the organizations, both nonprofit and private, that are reaching our au-diences or that want to reach our audiences. All of them could be potential partners. Include organizations that seem to be competi-tors at first glance, as well as groups working on different issues with our same audience.

2. Who Wins When We Win?

Now we want to ask, if we succeeded in motivating our audiences to take action, who on this list would benefit? Would organizations we haven't thought of benefit? The list we develop is our hit list of potential partners. Next, look for partners with a compatible agenda with respect to our audience and the potential for both parties to gain philanthropic fulfillment, financial benefits, enhanced image or expertise, access to new markets or marketing resources, increased efficiency, new products or services, competitive advantage, or in-creased employee morale. Note the relative gain for us and for the other organization.

3. What Are the Pros and Cons?

Now we need to weigh the relative assets and liabilities of working with another group. We should honestly assess the possibility for ex-ploitation, dependence, and blurring of mission, as well as cultural dif-ferences, level of commitment, and capacity limitations on each side.

Each type of partner has pluses and minuses. Good causes should think about how private-sector partners might affect their credibility or image (their most valuable assets), and be wary of appearing to endorse a company's products unless that is the intention. Recognize that the politics, profit motives, and the fast pace of business mean we will be dealing with a different culture. Partnering with government entities can bring regulatory muscle to an issue, but the relationship requires operating under bureaucratic, political, and legal constraints and dealing with the slower pace that required layers of approval will entail. Partnering with other good causes is a more flexible arrangement than the previous two, but funding is less predictable and a tendency toward competition between organizational leaders can cause tensions. Working with volunteer organizations can be challenging given their often loose structure, high turnover, and inexperience with partnerships.

We want to then create a balance sheet for ourselves and our potential partner. On one side, list all the potential benefits; on the other, the drawbacks and areas where the partnership might break down. Does it look like the pluses outweigh the minuses for us and for our partner? We want to ensure mutual benefit. If the partnership is working for only one side, it will be short-lived.

→ No partnership is perfect. The bottom line is to go into the partnership with open eyes, more positives than negatives in regard to fit and filling, and a plan for compensating for weaknesses within the alliance. Shared, realistic expectations and a common vision for the degree of collaboration can go a long way to establishing and preserving a successful partnership.

4. How Do We Form the Partnership?

Start the partnership at the top of the organizational chart. The higher the level of the person involved in each organization, the better the chances of strong results. It's best to have someone in charge on each side who has executive backing, commitment to the cause, and significant power within the organization. Those people should then assign effective staff members to carry out the work of the partnership. Good partnerships also start with realistic expectations and clearly defined roles. Each party should know and be capable of taking on the tasks asked of it. The more tangible and specific the request, the better. Time, resources, responsibilities, budgets, and deadlines should be clearly delineated. Agree up front about the consequences if an effort is far less or more successful than anticipated. Ask partners to commit to adding resources to deal with problems or to take advantage of big gains or opportunities.

5. How Do We Stay on Track?

Over time, the stronger the relationships between partners at all staff levels and the deeper their degree of commitment the better. Then, staff turnover, shifting individual roles and priorities, or isolated personality clashes will not undermine the partnership. We want to form numerous personal connections and be flexible with regard to the changing dynamics of relationships and organizational politics. We don't want to take our champions for granted, and we have to be willing to patiently cultivate new people internally when there is turnover.

➤ Partnerships based on long-term relationships and closely intertwined missions are likely to withstand competition from other players who offer better terms or greater financial incentives.

Communication is essential as the work of the partnership unfolds. Update partners regularly through a formalized process, ask for their input, and show appreciation for their efforts. Partners need to be continually reminded of the benefits that the partnership is yielding for each side. Regardless of the type of partner we have—

another cause, a business, or a government agency—we need to create and show value over and over. If the partner is a business, adding value is especially important. Build into a program traceable means such as coupons or codes to measure increased business from the partnership. Communicate the value to the cause internally and to outside stakeholders, so these audiences remain consistently supportive of the alliance.

For example, Mark Dessauer, communications officer for Active Living by Design, a national program of the Robert Wood Johnson Foundation, is working with twenty-five community partnerships across the country to increase physical activity through community design. The partnerships consist of unlikely allies such as public health officials, park rangers, transportation engineers, architects, and neighborhood associations, and so good communication is paramount. Dessauer says, "Our strategy for change includes promotions, policy, programs, and physical projects with the partnership at the center. These partnerships are funded at a very low level so they run on the passion of their partners. Planning for and then celebrating small successes is critical for keeping the partners involved and improving the efficacy of the partnership. If you cannot pay the partners, then media attention or public recognition is worth its weight in gold—assuming that the media attention is good."[9]

If problems arise in communicating or working together, those disagreements need to be confronted quickly and openly. Make midcourse corrections together. Strong partners with a long-term relationship have enough trust and mutual respect to work through challenges rather than abandoning an effort altogether. Address poor performance together and clarify responsibilities. Keep reminding everyone of the shared goal that unified the partners in the first place and mark progress toward it. Call attention to every small success, and give partners credit for helping to achieve it. Recognition is hugely important to partners, especially corporate ones. Each little victory can be rallied around, and sharing the glory greatly strengthens the relationship between partners.

➤   Inevitably, the filling of the partnership will change over time, and one partner may perceive diminishing value. Effective partnerships require a constant balance of the benefits each party derives from the relationship. Over time, it may be necessary to create new benefits if commitment is flagging on one side.

When overall victory is achieved, the partnership has fulfilled its purpose. Knowing when to stop a partnership is just as important as knowing when to start it. Declare success and move on when a goal has been achieved, or set a new, finite goal together. Better a clean finish than death by disintegration.

CONCLUSION

A partnership does not need to be for life.

➤   A short-term shared audience or one-time goal may provide a sufficient convergence of interests to form a limited partnership. We lose out when we focus solely on the elusive long-term love-match of a fully shared vision or organizational goals.

We may simply need a partnership that is short term or that is designed to accomplish a single, immediate goal. In fact, many long-term partnerships started with a limited collaboration, such as a one-time gift of money or single event, then grew into more transactions over time, and, ultimately, became highly integrated and cooperative ongoing collaborations.

If this process of constantly cultivating existing partnerships and seeking new ones sounds like a lot of effort, it should. Successful partnerships require effort, and for this reason we should be careful, creative, and highly selective in forming them. Familiarity is not necessarily best, and more is not necessarily better. Instead of signing on many friendly but insubstantial partners in an attempt to look good, focus on cultivating a few strong and complementary partnerships to accomplish good. Dollars to doughnuts, that refreshingly results-focused approach will bring success.

Interview 1
In Search of Unlikely Bedfellows

Brian Krieg loves unique partnerships that push beyond the usual nonprofit parameters. In his role as president of FocusPoint Communications in Portland, Oregon, and over the years as a veteran marketer and lobbyist, he has paired the most unlikely of players to accomplish good.

Krieg has held senior management and marketing positions at national and multistate trade associations, the U.S. Department of Agriculture, and the California Public Health Foundation. He served as vice president for one of Oregon's largest public-relations firms, overseeing promotional campaigns, lobbying accounts, and administrative services. He was a founder and original manager of the Five a Day for Better Health campaign, one of the largest public-private health promotions in history. Krieg also has masterminded many lobbying successes at the state and federal levels.

In his no-nonsense, high-energy, rapid-fire style, he urges good causes to view building partnerships as the art of finding convergent—not necessarily common—interests. "Understand the unexpected ways in which you overlap with others," he says. Here he offers his top tips on his favorite topic: cultivating unlikely bedfellows and unusual alliances.

Q: How can good causes find and cultivate unconventional partnerships?

A: Believing you are unique and different can really get in the way of creative thinking. Be willing to break that barrier and think of partners that may share interests with you. Don't always go after the same suspects. Many smaller organizations and companies are looking to give a little back. You miss out if you go after the same big guys all the time. Then focus. It's better to have one strong partner than twenty so-called sponsors. Find a leader who is willing to break the mold and even make some enemies because getting something done is bound to irritate someone.

Understand that this is a working relationship. Don't expect your partners to have the same passion or beliefs that you do. They most likely have a different set of reasons for getting involved than we do. They may simply want to sell more product or get visibility. Unless those aims are antithetical to our own, that is OK. This is not a jihad. We should live in the moment, focus on what we're trying to accomplish together, and deal with the fact that our partners may not share all our opinions. Maybe they will become true believers over time, but we need to live with the fact that they may not.

Remember that because their commitment may not be as passionate as ours, we need to be respectful of their time. They are making sacrifices to do this. Run meetings on schedule, have an agenda, have a recap, and assign responsibilities. Show progress at each meeting so they feel you're doing things. Partner representatives will need to be able to show a return on their investment of time and resources.

Step back and be willing to give your partners visibility. Put them in the limelight. For example, the maritime museum in Portland, Oregon, wanted to light a ship they have on the water. The International Brotherhood of Electrical Workers union did it with contractors from the National Electrical Contractors Association, and the museum was happy to let them get credit for that in promotion and press materials because the museum was happy for the donation. By contrast, when the electrical contractors did major wiring for a local housing group, the organization didn't let them have full visibility and instead promoted Nike's sending over a hundred people to swing hammers and frame walls.

Q: How did partnerships make the Five a Day campaign such a success?

A: We did not go it alone. I once heard a man in charge of produce at Kroger stores in Houston tell a gathering of an organization fighting diabetes that he worked in produce for Kroger for twenty years and never thought of reaching out to the nutrition community for promotion. He also told those folks, "At the same time, you never thought of reaching out to me."

I was hired because I could bridge the industry and public health worlds. I was a translator between those communities, and I knew people at the food and agriculture trade associations. In getting Five a Day together for the California Department of Health Services, we first sat down with the U.S. Department of Agriculture to gain an understanding of the economic hurdles we were dealing with and the barriers we were facing. We realized the dairy industry and the meat industries did not share our agenda; at that time those industries were rewarded for fat content because of policies dating back to World War II. By contrast, we knew the produce commodity boards were looking to promote fruit and vegetables, as were grocery stores, which saw them as underconsumed products that offered a high profit. We approached those boards and showed we had some marketing dollars behind us. We were serious. We talked to the vice presidents of produce for smaller, more accessible, and innovative grocery chains and got their input. They were interested in doing it, and the larger chains followed.

You can't underestimate the value of partners in spreading the word. For example, in Florida, Try Foods made recipe racks for stores to promote more unusual items like fennel. We worked with them on converting the higher fat recipes to low fat and including the Five a Day message and logo on the recipes and rack. This company's sales force got feedback that helped shape the program. When we went national, that sales force was key because they knew the business, had a system for promoting and distributing the message, and helped us sign up grocery chains. Their competitors were attracted and also got licenses to promote Five a Day. We thought of all the potential partners, like the folks who made produce bags. That may not be the primary message delivery point, but every bit adds to the mix and the way consumers absorb the campaign. That's why Coca-Cola puts its name inside the bottle cap. Maybe that cap ends up on a sidewalk and someone sees it. It triggers a response and reinforces a message. We were ensuring that people subliminally saw our message throughout the stores. And it cost us nothing.

Q: What's a favorite example of your work in forging unusual partnerships?

A: The Union of Operating Engineers wanted to improve minority recruitment for jobs in the field and to raise the profile of the union and its members in our community. They saw Head Start parents as a good match, and they wanted to reach out to that community. So we chose Head Start programs at schools near major construction sites, where people notice all the activity. We planned a special event and brought a front-end loader and construction toys to the school for the day. We talked with the kids about careers in construction. The school had different complementary activities like reading about construction and making construction safety vests. Then we sent home information about construction-industry jobs to the parents. It was such a success it's now an annual event. It is eye candy for television. Every year, we get perhaps four out of five local stations attending, and three out of five typically air the piece. It's a win-win-win. The union gets great PR, the school gets some useful teaching materials, the needy children get toys, and the parents get information about good jobs. Who knew we could build so much excitement over operating engineers? It really works.

Interview 2
Avoiding Partnership Pitfalls

David La Piana grew up the child of immigrants from Sicily in a poor and working-class California community, and that experience shaped his decision to devote his career to good causes. "I was the first person in my family to graduate from high school, let alone go to college," he says. "After graduate school, I realized that my heart was leading me back to where I had come from." La Piana became a VISTA volunteer and then worked in a variety of roles in the nonprofit sector, including staff member, executive director, trainer, consultant, and board member. He worked with the YMCA, the International Institute, and the East Bay Agency for Children, a human service agency that grew tenfold under his leadership. La Piana also taught at the University of San Francisco's Institute for Nonprofit Organization Management and at the Haas School of Business at the University of California, Berkeley.

Although an idealist at heart, La Piana's mind is strictly business as he helps nonprofits and foundations operate, build partnerships, and compete effectively. That is the work of the firm he founded, La Piana Associates, as well as the topic of his book, *Play to Win: The Nonprofit Guide to Competitive Strategy*.[10]

Q: What do you see as the most common problems in partnerships?

A: So many partnerships are not set up with goals. Goals, set early on and well, obviate some of the power struggles and relationship issues that can arise later. If people go in together to respond to a request for proposals and the only reason they are doing that is for the money, that's like getting married for the wedding presents. They will probably end up fighting over those presents. A more authentic relationship develops organically, from the work itself, and that can make it more successful.

One of the questions I ask is whether there's a motivation other than money for forming the partnership. Also, I ask whether there's a preexisting relationship. Often, I get a call from someone interested in forming a partnership who goes on and on about the possible synergies the partnership will create. I always ask, "How long have you been working with this other organization?" And they say, "Oh, we've never worked with them." I say, "You've been in the same community for thirty years and you've never worked together?" Well, it turns out a grant opportunity just came along. In such cases, I'm suspicious of whether this is a natural collaboration. I don't think foundations should give grants to collaborations that haven't existed for at least three years. That would weed out partners who don't have a natural affinity for each other or a shared purpose.

When they work well, partnerships provide great financial and logistical payoffs. But we have to be aware of several key potential downfalls. Number one, the parties may not be getting into the partnership because they want to but because someone is saying they have to. Maybe a grant maker wants to see a collaborative effort or a board member thinks the organization is too small. Number two, people may hugely overestimate the potential benefits of a partnership while hugely underestimating the amount of work it's going to take. They may have a rosy view: "We're all in this together, and so we'll all get along well." They may fool themselves into believing the synergies they posited in the grant proposal. Then people see they're spending large amounts of time working out simple problems like payroll or hiring joint staffers. Number three, some organizations are weak and unable to do much on their own, and, by partnering with other weak organizations, they compound the negative.

Q: What are some partnerships that work?

A: In Berkeley, near where I live, there are theological seminaries of every stripe. They established a union for courses they have in common, and then they built a library together. Jewish seminarians, Franciscans, and Unitarians all are coming together. They'll never merge, for obvious reasons, so it's clear what's separate and what's joint. They have been at it for decades; it's well institutionalized. I've also seen relationships where a group that serves younger kids, for example in mental health care, doesn't want to get into serving adolescents but needs a place to refer them, so it partners with a group that serves the older kids.

The most successful nonprofit-corporate partnerships I've seen result when the organizations share a businesslike culture. When nonprofits are more interested in relationship aspects and underlying values and the businesspeople are more interested in finances, it's like they're speaking a different language.

Q: What is the most important lesson you've taken away from your work in partnerships?

A: There's always one group that's stronger, more sophisticated, or richer, and they're going to be in the driver's seat. I tell them to treat the other group with respect, as if they were an equal partner, even if they're not. I tell the smaller or weaker group to recognize that they have a weaker hand but to advocate for themselves and expect to be treated with respect. It helps to understand the reality of one's position going in.

Interview 3
Finding the Filling

Network for Good is an e-philanthropy Web portal. It provides a central place where people can donate their time and money to nonprofits and where nonprofits can receive donations as well as access tools for online outreach. If eBay is a virtual marketplace for selling goods, Network for Good can be considered a virtual marketplace for doing good. Network for Good began in November 2001 as a partnership between technology giants AOL, Yahoo! and Cisco Systems; these businesses wanted to turn the Internet into a force for social good. Network for Good has since grown into one of the Internet's leading charitable resources, and it continues to partner successfully with all three of the companies that founded the organization.

Network for Good provides interesting insights into how an organization that bridges the cultures of corporations and good causes can successfully develop. Bill Strathmann, CEO of Network for Good, and Ken Weber, its president, have both private-sector and nonprofit backgrounds, a combination they say helps them understand how to build the relationships the organization has with both its corporate and its nonprofit partners. "If we focus on the differences between nonprofits and businesses, we exaggerate divisions and lose sight of what matters. We're focused on achieving social good through the Internet, and both nonprofits and corporations play important roles in accomplishing that good," says Weber.

Q: How does the partnership benefit both the cause and the corporation?

A (Strathmann): Network for Good has been rewarded by its corporate partners with funding, in-kind gifts, and the business expertise of the corporations, which at times have also lent staff to the organization. The corporate partners in turn get at least three important benefits. First, they receive philanthropic fulfillment. The three partners, although competitive in the technology marketplace, have long shared an altruistic vision of their marketplace's role in philanthropy. They see the Internet as a "rocket booster" to fuel individual giving to charities and expand people's involvement in good causes. Before joining forces, each company had separate initiatives in that area, but ultimately they felt they could accomplish more by pooling their resources and customer reach. They believe that in providing Internet-based resources to nonprofits, they can help to close the digital divide. Through Network for Good, even small charities without their own Web sites can reach donors, raise funds, and improve their sustainability.

Second, for each partner, Network for Good is a venture that matches their corporate aims. AOL and Yahoo! share a strategy of providing content that enables their customers to do every-thing online. Making online charitable giving accessible, efficient, and effective is a natural extension of that strategy. For example, after the December 2004 tsunami and Hurricanes Katrina and Rita in 2005, AOL and Yahoo! links to Network for Good's Web site drove millions of dollars in donations in just a few weeks. For Cisco, which makes networking products like routers, it is a nat-ural fit to help build the online infrastructure that Network for Good makes available to nonprofit groups.

Third, the partners gain competitive advantages. All have a strong desire to show their customers they are socially responsi-ble companies that care about a greater good. In today's ex-ceptionally competitive marketplace, a positive philanthropic image can set one company apart from another.

Q: How does Network for Good show it is providing value to its partners in all these areas?

A (Strathmann): We regularly share with our board, which in-cludes our partners, a custom-made "dashboard" that measures progress in areas such as generating funds and volunteers for the nonprofit organizations connected to us. It's also key to ded-icate staff to managing these relationships. We make it part of the job description. We are always on call to respond to any re-quests from our partners, and we give them plenty of visibility on our Web site. That visibility also benefits Network for Good by adding to its credibility with donors.

Q: What communication tips do you have for nonprofits that are in partnerships with businesses?

A (Weber): The ability to relate and translate what Network for Good does as a nonprofit in terms that businesspeople can un-derstand and talk about in their own cultures and within the pa-rameters of their own business agendas is critical. In fact, we try to see ourselves as a hybrid organization: a business that does good and a nonprofit with business DNA and a prevailing business sense. You can't really expect to win and grow partnerships with businesses if you aren't oriented that way, at least some of the time. There is a danger in going too far; you can't talk about what you do as a nonprofit in pure business terms (and it should be a red flag to you if you find yourself trying to do it). But you absolutely need to be able to talk about your work and your results in business terms. A lack of understanding and appreciation of the way businesses see themselves and look for value in partnerships is a recipe for false starts and failed partnerships. For better or worse, business is the dominant frame in our society. I think that's a net positive. Understanding business practices (goal setting, measuring, reporting) is extremely helpful in pitching and cultivating corporate alliances, and following such practices also can be transformative for a good cause and its effectiveness.

At the end of the day, perhaps with notable exceptions, businesspeople are people. They are good and soulful, particularly when it comes to applying company resources, making their jobs more interesting, and feeling better about themselves in what they do. Chances are, if you are in a partnership discussion with them, they are philanthropically minded or at least sensitive. There is more common ground than you might think, and making the most of it is largely a challenge of language and seeing things from their perspective and, ultimately, a shared perspective.

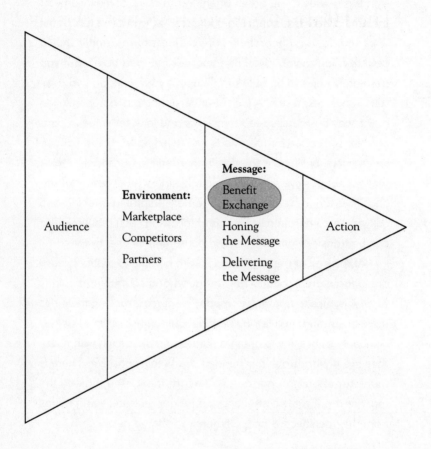

6

The Heart of the Good Archer's Arrow

Put the Case First and the Cause Second

WHAT THIS CHAPTER SAYS

- It is the reward, and not our own mission, that most effectively makes the case to our audience to take action.

- We create a compelling benefit exchange by offering a reward that has five important attributes: it should be immediate, personal, reflective of audience values, better than competing rewards, and credible.

- Positive rewards work better than scare tactics. Threatening dire consequences of not taking action is motivating only if the audience has an immediate, personal sense of danger and we make a specific and feasible recommendation for taking evasive action. So go negative only with the utmost care.

- To apply the principles in this chapter: We must return to the research we've done and review audience values and desires. Next we should shape a reward that taps into these values. We then have our benefit exchange.

I'M GOING TO DISNEY WORLD!

In 1987, the Super Bowl's most valuable player, Phil Simms, hollered into the television camera, "I'm going to Disney World!" So was one of Disney's most successful marketing campaigns launched and a new phrase in the modern lexicon was born. Since then, John Elway, Michael Jordan, Mark McGwire, and Miss America have all claimed in ads aired shortly after their victories that their next stop was one of the Disney theme parks.

The success of "I'm going to Disney World!" reflects the essence of marketing—the benefit exchange, which is a reward offered in return for taking an action. Every marketing effort in the private sector tells us what we get in exchange for our money. A benefit exchange answers the key question, "What's in it for me?" Disney cleverly positions its theme parks as the ultimate reward in two implied benefit exchanges. For the famous people celebrating victory, going to Disneyland or Disney World is the reward for their accomplishments. For us, we are promised the one reward that supposedly tops a Super Bowl victory or Miss America coronation in return for the price of visiting the parks.

Because Disney World is featured as the mother of all rewards, we will steal it for our next rule.

Robin Hood Rule 6

Case first, cause second. The reward, and not our own mission, most effectively makes the case to our audience to take action.

WHY REWARDS WORK

Good causes need to offer rewards for action because most people are not motivated by morality. They may know an action is right but make the wrong choice because doing so is easier or more compelling than making the right choice. Or their idea of what's right may be different from ours. Or they may be too busy to notice yet another cause telling them what they should and should not be doing. "Do the right thing" works only in the movies (in fact, it was the title of one); in real life, we need the benefit, the reward, the big carrot. That's why the most essential part of Robin Hood's arrowhead is the benefit exchange at its core. By offering our audiences a reward, we seize their attention in a crowded marketplace and stimulate them to take action. Without a benefit exchange, our marketing arrow won't strike anyone's heart or mind. It will sail off in an errant direction and land unnoticed in a sad, forgotten little spot of Sherwood Forest.

⇒ We create a compelling benefit exchange by offering a reward that has five important attributes: it should be immediate, personal, reflective of audience values, better than competing rewards, and credible.

Let's take those five qualities one at a time.

Rewards Are Immediate

⇒ The reward should be available to our audience right away. Few of us take action based on a reward that we expect to receive in the far future. It is human nature to seek instant satisfaction over distant gratification.

The private sector knows the importance of instant gratification well: nearly every product that companies offer claims to give the consumer an immediate benefit. Eating a hamburger satisfies our hunger, drinking beer makes the ball game more fun, and wearing cologne makes us sexier right now. Or at least that's what we believe. But it is harder to identify immediate rewards for good causes than for consumer products. We cannot simply tell people they are at risk and expect that avoiding that risk is a compelling reward. If our reward is not having a problem years down the road—for example, avoiding AIDS by using a condom—we have to address the lack of urgency in that idea. People may believe they are personally at risk—and that the consequences of no action are severe—but unless they see an immediate reward for action, they may not act. That's why people may live in an unhealthy way for years and change their habits only after a heart attack. For the first time, they realize they might die imminently if they don't act.

When I was a journalist in Cambodia in the mid-1990s, I interviewed young people for a story on HIV and AIDS. Teen boys and young men in that Southeast Asian country rarely used condoms despite the fact that Cambodia had one of the fastest growing epidemics of HIV and AIDS in the region. When I asked them why, young men told me they knew which girlfriends or prostitutes had HIV by the temperature of their skin. The prostitutes I met in shedlike brothels said they felt powerless to insist on condoms, and, anyway, many believed douching with toothpaste would kill HIV. These misconceptions were clearly a challenge for organizations battling HIV and AIDS, but the real problem became clear when I spoke to a teen boy in Phnom Penh. He was wearing a red-checked sarong and sucking on a hand-rolled cigarette when I approached him, and he regarded me with withering skepticism when I asked him about AIDS. "Why would I care about something that might kill me in ten years?" he asked. "I will die from something else before then." In a country plagued with land mines, poor water, infectious diseases, and (at the time) a guerrilla army, he may have been right. A cultural and religious sense of fatalism only reinforced his view. Where was the sense of immediacy?

Across town, in a pagoda surrounded by banana trees, people sick with AIDS had a different sense of immediacy. A monk clad in saffron robes was mixing a medicinal drink made of bark chips and served in old Sprite bottles. The monk said the elixir cured AIDS, and ill people from throughout the country traveled to Phnom Penh for the drink and his blessing. I spent an afternoon watching him receive visitors on a straw mat in the temple, and some of them spoke with me. In our conversations, it became clear that they were there because they needed hope, and the monk had that reward ready for them in a green plastic bottle.

Because a sense of immediacy is essential for a reward to be a good one, we have to create it if we don't have it. It doesn't work to tell a fatalistic young man in Cambodia that using a condom will prevent a disease far down the road. The example that opened this book illustrates the better option. Population Services International brought a sense of immediacy to condom use in Cambodia by putting a desirable brand—the alluringly English-named Number One condom—in the hands of people right at the moment they might use the product. The audience wasn't told to think of a deadly disease while seeking physical gratification, but rather to use an appealing product that provided an instant, positive boost to the ego.

Some good causes deal with the immediacy challenge by providing a reward like a T-shirt, hat, or wristband. These offerings give the person who donated money or took some action with an instant benefit—for example, recognition. Or the cause might offer rewards before the audience takes action. Have you ever received address labels in the mail from a good cause? They create a sense of obligation in the recipient, and so you probably felt some pressure to send money.

Gifts are a small incentive that may motivate people to take an initial action, but we can't expect them to be a way of keeping our audiences engaged over time. Once people take action, we need to remind them of greater immediate rewards than the gift. We can communicate with them about the people they helped so they get the more substantive reward of feeling good about themselves because they made a difference. When I order from drugstore.com, I often get free hand lotion or shampoo. I initially use it because it's free. Sometimes, I eventually buy the product if I get the benefit of smooth hands or shiny hair. Similarly, I may support a cause if it sends me address labels and seems like a worthy organization, but these rewards will never keep me giving over time. I donate to organizations that show me the immediate impact of my giving, again and again. I want to feel good today because I made a difference.

Rewards Are Personal

The second component of a good reward is that it is personal. Our audience members need to believe that the reward will make life better for them as individuals. The private sector understands the importance of making rewards personal. They don't sell you a car by explaining the way the engine is built; they tell you the car is reliable, safe, or fast, depending on who you are and your personal priorities. They take the attributes of their product and translate them into personally desirable benefits.

That translation is easy to make for most products. It's harder for good causes. We often promote changes that contribute to a collective, societal benefit. To ensure personal relevance, we need to figure out a way to translate that greater good into a specific, tangible reward that our audience members want. For example, I worked with several projects promoting citizen involvement in emerging democracies. When citizens voice their concerns and work with their representatives to address them, society benefits. People learn their role and responsibilities as citizens. The government becomes increasingly responsive to and representative of its citizens' interests. Policymaking is improved. Democracy is strengthened.

Are your eyes glazing over yet? The problem with these benefits is that although they are real and important, they are not the rewards that motivate a citizen to raise a concern or a government official to listen, especially in countries with no democratic traditions. These collective rewards need to be chopped into small pieces so they are relevant to individual people. For a citizen, learning about roles and responsibility in a democracy is not as personally satisfying as getting a local council member to listen to a problem and to take steps to correct it. For a local government official, being responsive is less personally relevant than getting complaining citizens off her back or winning reelection. For a businessperson, the merits of a strengthened democracy are a more stable environment for investment and greater economic growth. Each audience sees democratic society through its own lens and unique perspective, and each audience member looks for a reward that matters to her. We need to appeal to that subjective reality.

Good causes get themselves into trouble by agonizing over whether it's fair to make bold promises based on their audiences' subjective reality. We might wonder, can we really tell a citizen that the mayor will solve his problem? What if she doesn't? Can we be sure a more responsive government official is guaranteed reelection? Will economic growth be assured? Such questions miss the point. The idea is to make a reasonable promise that is personally relevant to our audience. It is reasonable to expect the benefits of civil society that I outlined for each audience; in fact, case studies show these results in many places around the world. But irrefutable proof is not as important as what our audience members believe is possible. We want them to see an opportunity. I buy antiwrinkle cream not because I am sure it works, but because I hope it will make me look better. If I am the mayor of a town and my constituents are happy because I solved a problem for them, I believe I may get reelected.

➤ Wild claims don't work, but bold ones do. We shouldn't shy away from making them.

The other way to make big ideas personal is to make them tangible. While I was living in Ukraine, the government tax authority launched a campaign to motivate taxpayers to stay honest and continue paying their taxes. The tax authority developed several ads. One was a cartoon illustration of a bee in front of a hive with a slogan celebrating the fruits of a collective contribution to the government. Another was a photograph of a new well and water pump;

city residents could fill containers with fresh water from the well. An accompanying slogan thanked taxpayers for making the well and other city improvements possible. In one of my trainings, I placed the ads side by side and asked a roomful of Ukrainians which was more effective given the tax authority's marketing goals. Not surprisingly, they were unanimous in their judgment that access to fresh water was far more personally relevant, and therefore motivating, than a role in building a metaphorical hive.

This example seems obvious, yet in our communication we often focus more on hives than on wells. We talk about saving the earth, ending poverty, or creating a great society. Every day, we have to remind ourselves that the hive is what we're building; the well is what our audience needs to see. When my young daughter asked me what this book was about, I said that it was about helping people make the world a better place. She asked me if I was writing about cotton candy. I was reminded again of the well and the hive. I was talking about the hive. I'd forgotten my own advice.

⟫⟶ At the end of the day, the personal connection, not the grand concept, grabs our attention.

Rewards Are Grounded in Audience Values

In Chapter Two, we learned about our audience's values. The reward we offer should be directly connected to these values.

⟫⟶ We can't easily change what our audiences believe, but by plugging into their existing mind-set we unleash great power behind our message.

The values of our audience may have nothing to do with our cause, but we can still use them. Consider the messages we see every day and the values they represent. Ads for women's running shoes are all about strength and empowerment. They practically scream,

"I am woman!" Pharmaceutical ads during the nightly news show how certain drugs help seniors attain what they want: a happy and independent life. During a televised basketball game, an ad for men's deodorant shows a woman ripping a man's clothes off in an elevator. No need for interpretation there. Each of these ads reflects a value the target users of the products care about, think about, and deeply desire. And each is fairly far removed from the product in question. Is self-actualization related to running shoes? Does arthritis medication buy happiness? Are deodorants the first thing that comes to mind when you think about sexual desire? Probably not, but the associations work because the values in question are close to each audience's heart.

A famous, frequently cited example of the value-based principle at work in social advertising is the successful Don't Mess with Texas campaign. The phrase has become so famous that many people outside Texas don't even realize that this is not a state slogan but rather a long-running marketing effort to get people to stop littering. The young Texan men who were the target of the campaign didn't care about littering, but they did care about their macho image, and no one doubted the fierce pride they had for their home state. By tapping into these powerful feelings with the Don't Mess with Texas concept, which didn't have a thing to do with trash, the ad agency that created the campaign (GSD&M) drastically reduced roadside litter.

Fundraising, like any other aspect of doing good, must be connected to personal values in order to work well. Think about the many reasons people give money to a cause and how those reasons are connected to their values. We need to understand these values, whether they are held by individuals or foundations, to determine how we should ask for donations.

We assume that people give to our cause because they value our mission. They probably do approve of our mission, but that's not why they write a check. When we dig a little deeper into the reasons behind the decision, we find that they are more likely rooted in that person's fundamental, personal values than in pure ideology. Giving is an action intertwined with self-identity. Here are some values-based reasons that I might give to a cause:

- I don't want to feel powerless in the face of a major disaster, like a famine, tsunami, or earthquake; I want to feel I am helping.

- I want to memorialize someone, as when I give to a breast-cancer fund after a friend dies from the disease.

- I feel a sense of closeness to a community or group, and so I want to generously support my alma mater or Lion's Club.

- I want to fit in and supporting this charity seems to be in style.

- It's a good way of meeting or connecting with people; it makes me feel a part of a group and builds my social network.

- I want to have a good image for myself and my business in my community, so I want my name on a brick in the new playground.

- I want to feel I'm changing someone's life, and I get a letter from the child I sponsor each month that shows I'm making a difference.

- I was raised to give to charity; it's a family tradition and value.

- I want to leave a legacy that perpetuates me, my ideals, or my cause.

- I feel fortunate (or guilty) and want to give something back to others.

- I give for religious reasons; God gave me affluence and wants me to share.

- I want to be a leader and create something important and good.

- Someone I know or trust asked me to give, and I gave because of that relationship.

I may give to a cause for any one of these perceived rewards or a combination of them, but all these rewards benefit me and fulfill my individual ideals. In most cases, they give me a sense of connection and the beginnings of a relationship that holds meaning. The importance of these benefits should be recognized whenever we talk about our cause to anyone, from a small donor to major philanthropists.[1]

I'll tell you a story that sums up the importance of appealing to people's values. I once worked in the marketing department at a large relief and development agency. We raised money, promoted our programs, and courted the media. On the other side of the agency was the program department. It oversaw all the relief and development work that was performed throughout the world. The departments were separated by a narrow hallway, but it might as well have been a yawning chasm. The people in the program department thought the marketing department hyped the agency's achievements, spent too much money to raise money, and oversimplified their complex mission of helping people help themselves. The marketing department thought the program department was out of touch with the average American and the realities of fundraising. The conflict got heated at times. The program department was weary of seeing appeal after appeal emphasizing emergencies around the world. Someone nicknamed the fundraising appeals "development pornography" because they emphasized the plight, not the personal strengths, of the people the organization helped. The marketing department replied that complex explanations about community development failed to motivate the average donor. Program people had a hard time believing that explanation because the nuances of their work motivated them personally.

Then came a test of everyone's beliefs. The direct-mail department sent out two appeals. One was an old appeal highlighting feeding programs. It showed a girl holding an empty bowl. It was short and simple, and it had consistently brought in more donations that any other appeal. "Empty bowl" was the gold standard of direct mail. The second appeal was a new one that highlighted the "teach a man to fish" rather than the "feed a man a fish" approach. It was attractively designed but long and described the program department's passions—community-development projects, sustainability, and self-help—in layperson's language. The appeals were different, but both emphasized the agency's low overhead and strong reputation, which research had shown were important to donors once they felt motivated to give.

Guess what? "Empty bowl" trounced the community-development appeal when the dollars were counted. Why? People gave to our organization because they wanted to feel they made an immediate difference in response to a real person's acute need. For the vast majority of donors, that was the reward they sought. Filling a child's empty bowl is a powerful idea. People cared about the feeding programs first, the farming programs second. The second appeal might have been a good message for foundations or government donors, but it wasn't interesting to the individuals who typically contributed. Nice reward, wrong audience.

People in the program department didn't like what they called the "dumbing down" of their complex work. But this wasn't about smart versus dumb; it was about different personal passions. The direct-mail results weren't a rejection of the organization's values; they were simply a reflection of the audience's. The audience's motivations, not ours, determine marketing success.

Rewards Are Better Than Those of the Competition

We spoke in previous chapters about the competition we face from everyone and everything prompting our audiences to do something other than take our action. That competition provides our audiences with a set of rewards. When we offer a reward, we need to think competitively.

➤ Our reward needs to be better than the rewards our audience gets from the status quo.

The Truth antismoking campaign, which encourages teenagers to fight against tobacco companies seeking to manipulate them, was masterful in this way. For many young people, smoking offers the reward of rebellion. The Truth campaign decided to offer the same reward—rebellion—but did a better job of positioning it. Its teen spokespeople were essentially saying to their peers, "We'll give you a better way to be rebellious and cool than by smoking. You can picket the tobacco headquarters, crank-call their public-relations executives, get on television, and meet cool people if you choose our way." To a sixteen-year-old, that sounds more rebellious than lighting up a Camel.

We can also face competition from psychological, social, and cultural mind-sets. Perhaps the action we want our audience members to take flies in the face of what they believe or have been told in the past. We need to convince them that the reward we offer is worth the cost of acting differently. Or we need to show them that being different has its own rewards. Taco Bell tells us to "think outside the bun." This tactic can work well with causes that have an edgy identity. A group of women in Tasmania, Australia, who wanted to raise money while promoting a happy image of aging put out a calendar with photos of nearly nude older women called "Bare to Be Different." The so-called Naked Grannies from Tasmania

turned cultural mind-sets on their heads with witty, tasteful photos—
for example, of nude women seated around a table playing cards
(the cards were strategically positioned to prevent us from seeing
too much). In so doing, they showed that having fun and being attractive are rewards for women of any age.

An opposite approach also works. We can make our audience
believe that taking our action isn't so radical by highlighting people like them who are doing it. The Ad Council and DDB Chicago's
spot promoting the Library of Congress's child-oriented Web site
took a gleefully ironic approach to this concept by showing children trying to play cards, sports, and other games with cardboard
cutouts of world historical figures. The tagline: "There's a better way
to have fun with history. Log on. Play around. Learn something."
The ad is effective because it makes a radical idea for kids—surfing
the net to learn about history—seem normal by juxtaposing it with
a decidedly abnormal way to "have fun with history."

Rewards Are Credible

Lastly, the reward we offer needs to be credible.

> If we make promises, especially bold ones, we need to support
> them. We don't need to quantify every reward or produce sci-
> entific evidence for every point we propose. We simply need
> to show that the action we ask for is feasible and the reward
> we offer is possible.

Facts and figures are one approach to sounding reliable, but the
problem is that they are quickly forgotten. Also, a lot of people
don't trust them. We need to make statistics as personal as possible
so they will be remembered and believed. The average person won't
recall how many pounds of nitrates run off into a river or the con-
centration of E. coli in parts per million in an aquifer, but they will
remember the poop in the tap water.

A slew of psychological studies have shown that vivid personal stories are incredibly convincing, far more so than quantifiable statistics. I make many decisions about the products I buy, the books I read, and the places I go based on recommendations from people I respect. If people tell me they had a good experience, I am likely to be persuaded that I will too. Those recommendations can come in the form of word of mouth, formal testimonials (like quotes on a book jacket), or written or visual success stories about people like me (like a story about someone who lost weight). If I read reviews and reliability reports on a new lawn mower, I may decide to buy a certain brand. But if my neighbor tells me his brother bought that brand and had a bad experience, I'll likely latch onto that story and change my mind, even though the new information I obtained was based on only one person's experience.

Often, the person who offers the testimonial or stars in the success story we use is as important as the story itself. The right messengers lend great credibility to our claims. Therefore, we should choose messengers who are known or respected by our audience or their immediate peers. The private sector uses this tactic skillfully. "Four out of five dentists recommend our toothpaste" is a common example of the use of an authoritative messenger. Peer messengers can be equally powerful; if we put our message for teenagers in the mouth of a teenager, we have made it far more credible than if we had used an adult. For example, the National Cancer Institute developed a nutrition-education campaign for specific ethnic groups such as Native Americans, Native Hawaiians, and Vietnamese. One message was that turning back to traditional ethnic foods was an excellent way to improve nutrition. Respected health providers and teachers from these groups served as campaign leaders and helped shape the messages, which tapped into cultural traditions to increase their appeal. The campaign combined a strong messenger and message to show its audience that "this is for us because this is where we came from."

We can also add credibility to our message by convincing our audience it can take action without too much effort and fuss. If an action seems like a big undertaking, that perception will undermine the idea that rewards are attainable. For this reason a lot of private-sector advertising has the word *easy* in it. It's also why people love remote controls and drive-through windows. We don't want to have to work too hard to get what we want.

Another approach is showing our audience members that many people like them are taking the action. Social psychologists and marketing experts talk about the power of "social norms" or "social proof."

> Social proof is the powerful idea that if we believe everyone
> is acting in a certain way, we're likely to act that way too.
> We're conformists by nature, and we take our cues about how
> to think and what to do from those around us.

According to the social psychologist Elliot Aronson, the more insecure we are and the more respected or similar the people around us, the more we are influenced by them.[2] Social norms fuel entire industries. Would the fashion world be able to motivate us to buy a narrower tie or a longer skirt this year if we didn't care what people think? Social norms were certainly part of the appeal of the Truth campaign. They are also the theory behind campaigns on college campuses to reduce binge drinking by convincing students that most of their peers drink less frequently and more moderately than they believe. The idea is to redefine students' perceptions of normal drinking in order to reduce pressure on them to conform to that standard. But research from the Harvard School of Public Health College Alcohol Study suggests this approach isn't working well. First, it implicitly acknowledges that some people (even if it's not the majority) are drinking a lot, a message that undermines the idea that young people should drink less. Second, student drinkers are more likely to be influenced by their friends' habits than by an abstract idea of what a faceless, "average student" imbibes. We look for social proof from the people who seem similar to us, so this approach works only if the audience feels close to the people held up as peers. An abstract idea of the "average peer drinker" is not a person, and it can't compete with the friend standing next to you.

Dwayne Proctor, a communications scientist at the Robert Wood Johnson Foundation who has studied alcohol ads and their effect on young people, says that research confirms the persuasive power of a familiar human face. "In beer ads, you don't actually see people sip from the bottle because of alcohol advertising regulations, but whether viewers witness drinking or not may not matter if they see the actors as 'familiar peers' who are drinking. They may identify with them and use the ad as a de facto demonstration of the appropriate use of the product. Ads that are only about the product with no people in it may mitigate this sense of identification."[3] Just as a friend provides social proof that an "average peer drinker" cannot compete with, a young person holding a beer is far more influential than the bottle alone.

POSITIVE VERSUS NEGATIVE REWARDS

We've focused in this chapter on rewards that bring our audience positive benefits, but it is also possible to use a negative approach. We discussed this concept in Chapter Two: we can raise the cost of not taking action by emphasizing the negative consequences of the status quo.

Going negative should be done with the utmost caution because selling works better than scolding. Shame, fear, and finger-wagging are overused and may alienate people. Threatening dire consequences of not taking action is motivating only when there is an immediate, personal sense of danger for an audience and a specific and feasible recommendation for taking evasive action. Without a way to deal with the fear instilled, people will be overwhelmed and scared away.

Some early campaigns to combat the spread of AIDS in Thailand were based on fear tactics, with widely publicized pictures of people in the advanced stages of the disease who were painfully thin and suffering from Kaposi's sarcoma. This fear tactic was intended to deter risky sexual behavior, but that idea was eclipsed by the stronger stigmatization of the disease. The campaign made people so fearful of HIV and AIDS that families started banishing members with HIV or AIDS from their homes. They had nowhere to go. It was a terrible unintended consequence of using the emotion of fear.

Mothers Against Drunk Driving succeeds with its message because we believe that getting behind the wheel drunk can have immediate, personal, value-based consequences. We could kill a mom's son or daughter tonight, and no one wants to do that. It's not that hard to call a cab or to use a designated driver instead, and so we act to avoid a tragedy. In another example, the Campaign for Tobacco-Free Kids ran an ad with photos of senators and, in the headline, asked them by name whether they were going to stand up for kids against Big Tobacco. The slogan was "Tobacco vs. Kids. Where America draws the line." For politicians, the political cost of not voting for restrictions on marketing tobacco to children was high. "Standing with America's kids" looked more attractive, and so the negative reward created a good benefit exchange.

Less effective than this antismoking campaign would be a campaign that promoted healthier eating by telling me a high-fat diet increases my risk of heart attack or stroke. That negative reward is not immediate because eating bacon may take years to kill me if it does at all. It's not personal because it's a general, abstract danger across a population. And it's not based in my values because I don't lie awake at night worrying about my cholesterol. The message sounds like a pesky aunt tsk-tsking me. The thought of changing my whole diet seems like a lot of work. So I will shut out the message.

HOW TO USE ROBIN HOOD RULE 6

Let's now go through some steps for identifying a good audience reward for taking action. At the end of this exercise we want to instill one concept: if our audiences take the action we're asking for, then they'll get a reward they truly want. That benefit exchange will then become the heart of our marketing message, which we'll create in the next chapter. Finding the one reward our audience truly wants—and that we can honestly offer—is not easy, so we're going to spend more time on this idea than on any other in the book. In addition, I'm going to use one example throughout these steps to show how the process works.

To make our own task seem easier, I'll select the hardest actions for which I've ever had to devise rewards. They are best introduced by an old riddle. The person who makes it doesn't need it, the person who buys it doesn't want it, and the person who uses it doesn't know it. What is it? The answer is a coffin, and as the riddle suggests, it's a complicated product. No one is eager to buy one, and its rewards are limited. We don't want to die, so the hardest products to sell are those that call attention to our own mortality.

In this section, we'll see how it's possible to identify a reward for anything—even actions related to death and dying. I worked with two successful organizations that met this challenge: Aging with Dignity and the Center to Advance Palliative Care; both are funded by the Robert Wood Johnson Foundation and were created to ensure that people receive the medical care they want when they are seriously ill or dying. Aging with Dignity, a nonprofit organization based in Florida, was promoting its well-written, accessible, and legally recognized advance directive (also called a living will). This document, which they called Five Wishes, allowed people to take two actions: to specify the medical care they wanted if unable to speak for themselves and to name a health care agent to make medical decisions for them if necessary. Aging with Dignity had a great product, and the need for Five Wishes was great. As the tragic case of Terri Schiavo would later dramatize, when people do not make a written record of their wishes or name a health care agent, family members—and even judges and politicians—are left to struggle over a patient's desires.

The second client, the Center to Advance Palliative Care, provided training and resources to help hospitals start palliative-care programs for their seriously ill and dying patients. Palliative care is specialized medical care that focuses on helping patients and families determine the type of care they want; these programs coordinate the treatment and support patients receive in the hospital and provide state-of-the-art management of pain, symptoms, and stress. Like Aging with Dignity, the Center to Advance Palliative Care had a great product—high-quality technical assistance. The need for palliative care in hospitals is great. Numerous studies show that despite the high caliber of medical care in the United States, too many hospital patients suffer from treatable pain and symptoms. Comfort measures are not a special focus of most institutions. In addition, patients' care is fragmented, and they don't have the kind of communication they want with their doctors. Palliative programs effectively address these problems, greatly improving quality of care and patient satisfaction while helping hospitals to run efficiently.

Two great products, but one big barrier: the rewards they bring happen when people are near death, and death does not seem like much of a reward. Let's find out how these organizations faced that challenge, and how we can shape the right rewards for our audiences.

1. Revisit Our Audience

The first step in creating a winning benefit exchange is to remind ourselves of our audience members' characteristics and their values. We should write those characteristics and values down for each of our audience segments and hang them on the wall because that information is a reality check: it reminds us that our issue is not our audiences' focus. Audience members have their own lives and their own priorities.

Now let's return to the actions we want our audiences to take. Make sure the actions we've got in mind are feasible and so concrete that we could film them. Don't be tempted to settle for actions that are intangible, like "raising awareness," or vague, like "support our cause." Make the actions specific.

Now review our audience members' current actions, which we should know from our audience research. Are they sitting on the sofa eating bonbons and watching *America's Top Model*? Going online and giving $10 to a charity that's not ours? Running a factory that dumps waste into a community's river? Listening to CDs instead of attending the symphony? These are all competitive actions, and they constitute our audiences' ingrained status quo.

Let's try this step on our two examples. Aging with Dignity wanted to reach people who do not have living wills. What are they like? They do not want to think about death, talk about death, or focus on a product associated with death, even if it's needed. American culture celebrates youth, Botox, and medical miracles, and few are willing to contemplate the limitations of these things. We wanted these audience members to fill out a living will by sitting down with their loved ones and doctor and discussing how they wanted to live and die, but people delay taking these steps. Having a life-threatening illness seems far in the distant future to most people, and so creating a living will lacks a sense of immediacy or personal relevance.

What about the Center to Advance Palliative Care's audience? Most hospitals did not have a palliative-care program and did not think they needed one. They believed the care they provided to their sickest patients was adequate, and so the cost of establishing palliative programs was not worth it. Doctors viewed palliative care as comfort measures only for the dying and resisted referring patients unless they were clearly on the verge of death. They didn't want to stop curative care or lose control over their patients. Patients thought palliative care meant giving up treatment of their disease. Although these were all misconceptions—in fact, palliative care is supportive care that can be provided at any point in an illness— they were strongly held beliefs. They raised the perceived price of palliative care so high that the benefits didn't seem worthwhile.

For both organizations, their audiences' perspectives left them with two alternatives. They could urge people to face their own mortality, thus resigning themselves to always being associated with unpleasant thoughts of death and dying. Or they could stake out a new association through a creative combination of the right audience, action, and reward.

2. Select Audience Values That Connect with the Desired Action and Frame a Benefit Exchange

Keeping in mind the values of each of our audiences, we can now link our agenda to our audiences. Can we offer a reward our audiences are seeking? Can we connect to certain audience segments better than to others because their values are more closely aligned with our action and cause?

Aging with Dignity knew most people were reluctant to fill out their own living will, but many people wanted their family members to do it. Baby boomers were worried about their parents' health but found it difficult to ask their parents about the kind of medical care they would want if they ever became so ill they could not speak for themselves. Adult children needed a way to have a conversation with their parents. Aging with Dignity believed that this audience would find a value in a living will that would start that difficult conversation. Five Wishes was designed to do a lot of the talking for them. It had an introduction listing benefits Aging with Dignity knew people liked about living wills: they help people retain control over their health care, ensure their wishes are followed, and avoid burdening loved ones with guessing a person's preferences. It then presented a series of questions to guide decisions about care.

By choosing to appeal to the values of boomers and their relationships with their parents, Aging with Dignity had begun the crucial process of reframing its product and creating strong rewards for using it. It was no longer a document requiring someone to face death. It was a conversation between son or daughter and parent. By asking a parent to fill out Five Wishes with them, adult children got the immediate reward of an easy way to broach a tough topic and, more important, they could feel good about themselves as a daughter or son now rather than feeling guilty later.

But Aging with Dignity recognized that offering to fill out the document with parents, while easier than starting a conversation cold, was still hard. When was the right moment, and what were the right words? We addressed this sizable barrier head-on by leading people through the process of asking someone to complete a living will and executing the document. A package of materials explained how to give a copy of Five Wishes to a family member, ways to talk about it, how to encourage someone to complete it, and how to raise the topic with doctors. We included testimonials from people who had talked to family members and others who had completed living wills to show that the process worked. The materials had several positive results. They helped the boomer audience believe they could have this conversation with their parents by making the reward not only immediate and personal but also credible. These audience members became effective messengers for the living-will message, thus increasing the likelihood that the parents would complete one. In the process, boomers were also likely to fill out their own living wills. They did not want their parents to ask, "Why do you want me to fill this out if you aren't doing it for yourself?"

The Center to Advance Palliative Care faced a similar challenge. Like Five Wishes, its product—palliative care—was often brushed aside as irrelevant until someone was at the brink of death. It offered good rewards for several of its audiences—relief from pain and suffering, better doctor-patient communication, and high patient and family satisfaction—but the perceived cost of that reward (dealing with death) seemed unreasonably high to each audience.

In order for patients, doctors, and hospitals to want it, palliative care needed to be repositioned as rewarding because it was an essential part of high-quality care throughout the course of treatment and not the end of the medical road.

We decided to emphasize the qualities of palliative care that patients, doctors, and hospitals wanted and not use terms like *dying* and *end of life*. We identified the benefits each audience wanted, the rewards we could promise, and the barriers we should remove to motivate each audience to take a specific action. For patients, the action was asking for palliative care. For physicians, it was requesting a consultation. For hospitals, it was starting a palliative-care program. Through these actions, the Center to Advance Palliative Care could achieve its goals of increasing the number of programs in hospitals and ensuring that more patients would receive access to this care than in the past.

For patients, we showed that palliative care brought the rewards of relief from pain and symptoms, improved communication with the people treating them, and increased coordination among the many physicians working on their care—all without having to give up curative or life-prolonging treatment. Palliative care started shifting from being the care no one wants to need to being the care everyone deserves.

For physicians, palliative-care consultations saved the precious commodity of time because the palliative-care team dealt with the management of complex pain and symptoms and held meetings with patients and families—without the physician having to give up control over the patient or a curative-treatment plan. A palliative-care program at the University of Alabama summed up these benefits beautifully in a brochure that featured a pager relaying a flurry of pages from patients needing immediate attention for pain or with questions about their care. The message: Got pages? Call for a palliative-care consultation.

For hospitals, palliative programs improved the quality of care, boosted patient and family satisfaction, and provided less fragmented, more streamlined care to very sick patients—all while lowering, not raising, the costs of care. We developed materials giving evidence of these benefits, including charts and tables that showed administrators the positive financial impact of palliative-care programs. As a result, more and more hospitals turned to the Center to Advance Palliative Care for technical assistance to start programs. Their work and efforts by like-minded advocates contributed to a doubling of the number of palliative-care programs in just three years.

It may sound as though the solution for the Center to Advance Palliative Care and for Aging with Dignity was to simply deny any connection to death. This is not the case. The solution was to offer a compelling reward—and then to show audiences that embracing death was not a prerequisite to getting that reward.

3. Test the Benefit Exchange

Once we've identified a reward for taking action, we have the benefit exchange. Write down a benefit exchange for each audience. Now test it. Is the reward we're promising immediate? Is it personal? Does it reflect audience values? Is it better than the status quo? Are our claims credible? If we fail on any of those fronts, we need to make adjustments. In our examples, the rewards of understanding a parent's wishes for care or easing patient pain met those criteria. Both organizations had good success with the benefit exchanges they created.

But Aging with Dignity began to wonder whether it could increase the immediacy of, personal relevance of, and connection to its product by reaching out to a new audience: the human resource departments of big companies and organizations. Increasingly, those departments were offering various kinds of employee assistance. One rapidly growing area was elder care. Many employees wanted help with aging or ill parents—in fact, these were the very same boomers Five Wishes was reaching individually through its current marketing approach. Companies were responding by offering long-term-care insurance for family members and other elder-care benefits.

The companies were willing to help for several reasons: their employees were asking for assistance, it was good for employee relations, and it was good business because offering such benefits seemed to increase productivity and reduce employee absences on account of sick parents.

The problem for human resource professionals was that such programs were expensive and not always feasible to provide. These professionals were looking for a way to offer help with these issues, but without too much investment. We did some research with this audience to test the living-will concept. The benefits that appealed to them were that providing living wills to employees showed that the employer cared about this issue and wanted to help, yet it was not expensive ($1 per copy for companies that ordered the documents in bulk), and it gave employees the peace of mind of knowing their parents' wishes in the event of serious illness. It was a good, affordable tool for elder care, and employers were interested in providing it.

But just like the boomers, human resource professionals weren't sure how to raise the topic and distribute the document. It seemed like a fairly personal, sensitive issue for the workplace. They wanted to provide Five Wishes, but they also wanted it to be easy. So we developed Five Wishes at Work, a kit that included all the material needed to provide the document to employees. The package was developed to look polished, unemotional, and businesslike in order to send the message to human resource professionals that it belonged in the office. The appearance of our message helped lend it credibility. The package included a brochure providing an overview of the program from the perspective of company management; it explained why Five Wishes at Work was good business practice and quoted business leaders who had distributed the document at their companies. To help human resource departments overcome the barrier of starting the conversation with employees, we included a variety of ideas of how to announce that Five Wishes was available at the workplace, including brown-bag lunches and newsletter announcements. We included a video that could be shown to employees at information sessions; it explained the whole program and answered typical questions. In addition, we included a sample article for company newsletters and an e-mail announcement for staff. Also in the packet were the materials we'd developed to help people discuss Five Wishes with family members and doctors, as well as an order form for additional copies. We made everything as easy as possible to lower the barriers and increase the rewards of offering Five Wishes at Work.

In these materials, Five Wishes at Work was positioned as similar to the other kinds of benefits employers provide—life insurance, health insurance, and pension planning—yet it was inexpensive and took little staff time. As with Five Wishes, the living will was positioned away from death and dying. Five Wishes at Work was instead "an easy way to help your employees plan for the unexpected." We emphasized this message—which tapped directly into the audience's values—in a series of articles we successfully placed in all the major newsletters and magazines for human resource professionals.

That message worked. Employers such as the U.S. Department of State, the National Football League Players Association, and MTV signed onto the program. Thousands of employees used the document for family members and themselves. With companies as the messengers for living wills, filling them out came to be perceived less as a scary prospect to be pushed out of our thoughts and more of a responsible and necessary part of health care planning. More than seven thousand companies and organizations now distribute Five Wishes.

Then, in early 2005, an event provided an acute sense of immediacy for that program and living wills in general. The case of brain-damaged Terri Schiavo dominated the news, as her husband, her parents, and Congress battled over the removal of her feeding tube. The constant media attention on their contentious legal fight was an example of how events in the marketplace can profoundly affect a cause. Watching politicians, activists, lawyers, and family members argue over Schiavo's fate made many people think about life and death and how they would want their own families to act if they were in a state like Schiavo's. The case brought a sense of immediacy to the concept of creating a living will and naming a health care agent. The public spectacle of her death showed the cost of not having a living will and health care agent: losing control of one of the most personal medical decisions. Paul Malley, the director of Aging with Dignity, was interviewed in the media nearly every day. He said the tragedy of the Schiavo story was that no one could agree on what her wishes might have been. This heartrending situation, he said, can be avoided if we make our preferences clear to those around us. This message resonated deeply with people. Before the Schiavo story, the organization distributed about fifty living wills per day. That number leaped to over six thousand, and in the one month the nation was absorbed with the case more than three hundred thousand copies of Five Wishes were ordered. This experience showed that creating a solid benefit exchange is vital, but equally important is being on the alert for new audiences, products, services, or current events that make the rewards we offer even more compelling. What is immediate and personal one day may be far more—or less—powerful over time, so we must be ready to adjust accordingly.

CONCLUSION

The one concept we should be sure to remember from this book is that of benefit exchange. We can't do our work without it. It's the difference between a marketing fortress solidly standing in bedrock and a fairy castle that stands only in Disneyland. All the components of a good reward can be summed up as follows: offer our audiences a reward they want right now. When we do that, we show our audience members that we know them well, accept them as they are, and want to give them a reward they like. That message is extremely powerful. What more could any of us hope for than to be seen, loved for who we are, and rewarded for what we do? The people who do accept, love, and reward us are the ones we will follow to the ends of the earth. The causes that do that for us are the ones that fully win our hearts and minds.

Interview
Selling Living Wills

Jim Towey is an unassuming yet intensely committed man. He pursues his causes with a businessman's logic and a zealot's passion, and the combination works. It's hard to imagine that a man who worked for Mother Teresa and who heads the White House's faith-based initiative doesn't have an urge to preach, but if he does, he never acts on it. He believes in benefit exchanges. He also believes in staying humble and has a disarming sense of humor and knack for self-deprecation.

Towey didn't set out to be a do-gooder, but an encounter with Mother Teresa changed his life. He visited her Calcutta home for the dying in 1985 as a political aide to Oregon Senator Mark Hatfield Jr. and the experience moved him to work with the poor. He left politics and volunteered in her soup kitchens and a hospice. He also handled her legal work. (Yes, even Mother Teresa had legal issues, as when a Tennessee coffee shop was asked to stop selling T-shirts supposedly showing her face on one of its cinnamon buns.) In the hospice, he sat with many dying people. "I saw so many bad deaths and feuds at the bedside that the spiritual imperative to me was to help people maintain their God-given dignity when they die," he says. After briefly returning to politics to head Florida's health and social service agency, he started Aging with Dignity, an organization described in this chapter. In 2002 he was named director of the White House Office of Faith-Based and Community Initiatives. Meanwhile, Aging with Dignity lives on; at the time of this writing, more than five million of the documents had been distributed since he launched the organization.

Q: As someone who felt a spiritual imperative to start your organization, did you find it difficult to think as a businessperson?

A: If you want to be effective, you have to. Everything you do is sales, whether it's an opinion or a product or a principle. When you're in the business of selling, you have to employ the most effective way to accomplish your goal. I see lots of different non-profits with different missions—to save the whales, feed the hungry, or spread culture and the arts. You have to temper the zeal of those missions with the sober reality of running a business that's going to prosper in a competitive environment. Charities work in a competitive environment and crowded marketplace competing for funds. You have to run a competent business, and there are lessons to learn from the for-profit community or anyone in the business of selling.

Q: So how did you sell living wills?

A: I started off with what I didn't want to do. I didn't want to talk about death and dying. I never used the "D" words, because they are, well, deadly to accomplishing something. That was important because I was around a lot of people in the end-of-life care community, and they all wanted to talk about making death a good experience. But the jury is already back on that: death is not good; that's why people cry at funerals. So we could not talk about end-of-life care and the challenges of planning for it and discussing it as death and dying. But we also couldn't do the equally stupid thing of coating the topic with a saccharine gloss as if it were about life and living. It's not a happy, upbeat thing. But we felt if we did it right, people would find that filling out a living will made them feel they'd done something truly worthwhile.

We named the document something uplifting—Five Wishes—to make it clear this was something beyond a person's last wishes. We designed it so that people could talk about wishes they were more comfortable talking about like comfort, dignity, how I want to be remembered, and little things I'd like done for me if I can't speak for myself. Those were the things that people did have opinions on and were willing to talk about—and then, oh yes, by the way, do you want ventilators and feeding tubes? If the discussion were only about whether or not you plug me into a machine, who in their right mind wants to talk about that? That's why so few Americans ever have that discussion— and even the ones who have signed a living will haven't talked about it to anyone.

Q: What were the most valuable things you learned in starting Aging with Dignity?

A: It was a learning process. People look at Five Wishes and say, "Wow, there's the most-used advanced directive in the country." But in truth, we had more of the Ben & Jerry's model. I started Aging with Dignity out of my wallet. We made something in our kitchen and said, "This is good!" So the first thing we did right was we started small. Nonprofits tend to think we need to grow because our size is a measure of our success. But plenty of small nonprofits succeed by sticking to their mission and establishing a solid financial base that doesn't entail a lot of risk.

Second, if you don't have a sensible plan of action for convincing people to act, you're not going to succeed. You have to connect with people in a way that gets their attention and motivates them to want to change.

Third, we got a lot of professional help because there's good expertise out there. We had physicians, nurses, lawyers, and marketers all giving us guidance.

Fourth, the last thing I'd say is that small groups should read the signs of the times. It's possible your organization may no longer have a purpose. If that's the case, then turn the lights off and shut down. Don't try to perpetuate yourself. We were prepared to close if Five Wishes didn't take off and our message didn't resonate. I think you have to be. You have to give yourself the freedom to fail—and if that happens, everyone should shake hands and go on to other work. This idea of sustaining an organization in perpetuity is often a dream of nonprofits. But once you accomplish your mission, you ought to shut down.

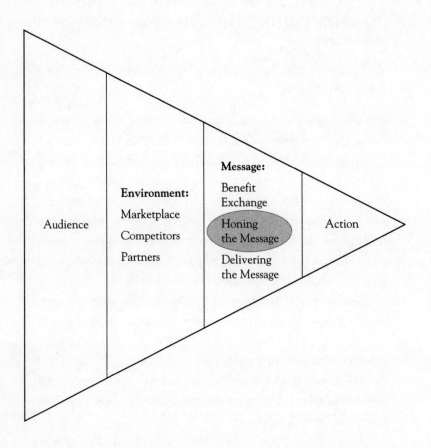

7

Sharpening the Arrow's Point

The Four Things Your Message Must Do

WHAT THIS CHAPTER SAYS

- A message precisely and concisely conveys everything we want an audience to think, feel, and do.

- Messages should establish a Connection, promise a Reward, inspire Action, and stick in Memory. We can remember those criteria as CRAM.

- To apply the principles in this chapter: We have to be able to CRAM with our audiences in three ways: through one-way communication, two-way communication, and the "third way" of communication— storytelling.

- One-way communication, which involves transmitting our message through traditional marketing outreach, should always CRAM in the most essential parts of a message.

- We also need to master two-way communication, conversation, so well that we can CRAM our message into the time it takes to ride an elevator to the top of a small building.

- Stories can illuminate one of the elements of a message, or they can convey all four with color, texture, images, emotion, and meaning.

BECAUSE I'M WORTH IT.

The devotee of L'Oréal beauty products stares at us from the television screen, her hair voluptuous and her smile sly. She buys L'Oréal for one simple reason: "Because I'm worth it." Celebrities from actress-model Andie MacDowell to Kyan Douglas from *Queer Eye for the Straight Guy* have uttered those words on behalf of L'Oréal, to great effect. The memorable mantra of the beauty giant constantly reminds us that we are worthy of luxury and indulgence. The approach elevates our ego while positioning L'Oréal as a delicious reward. We are placed up on a pedestal next to L'Oréal products, where we can feel unapologetically deserving of attention. We buy the products because we're worth it.

"Because I'm worth it" is not just a slogan, it's a message. That's what we're going to create in this chapter: a message that effectively communicates the reward we are offering in return for audience action.

➤ A message precisely and concisely conveys everything we want an audience to think, feel, and do. It is where the rubber of the benefit exchange hits the road of communication.

A message can be expressed in many different ways, but whether it's being communicated in a slogan or on a television show or by a giant inflatable condom, it should always have the same four elements: a connection, a reward, an action, and a memory. In the case of "I'm worth it," the benefit exchange (the reward and the action) is that if we buy L'Oréal products, we get to feel rightfully indulged. L'Oréal's shampoo may not be the most expensive, effective, or chemically advanced. It may not be best for curly hair. That doesn't matter. The reward is not that our hair will look better; it is that our ego will be burnished. We are exalted, special, and worthy of being put on a pedestal, right beside a drug-store hair product. Hallmark uses a twist on the same idea in its slogan, which tells us that our friends and family deserve a place on that pedestal alongside us: buy Hallmark "when you care enough to send the very best."

We're going to remember the benefit exchange with letters: *R* for *reward* and A for *action*. Surrounding this RA of reward and action like a gilded frame are the other two elements of a message. They attractively set off the benefit exchange within. One element pulls us in with a sense of personal *connection*. The other reinforces the benefit exchange by making it stick in our *memory*. Think of the connection as our entry point—it gets attention so our audience will notice the benefit exchange. Memory is our exit point— it ensures that people will not forget the benefit exchange after they come into contact with it. If we assign a C to connection and an M to memory and position them around our reward and action as entry and exit points, we get a useful mnemonic device: C[RA]M. We should cram it into our minds because it ensures that messages pass the quality test. "Because I'm worth it" CRAMs in all the elements. It's a masterful framing of a benefit exchange because we connect with the direct, personal appeal to our ego by beautiful spokespeople, and we remember the slogan.

Robin Hood Rule 7

Messages should establish a Connection, promise a Reward, inspire Action, and stick in Memory. CRAM is the key to getting our distracted audience attracted to our cause above all others.

In this chapter, we focus on each of the four crucial aspects of every marketing message. We'll transform the research and data we've gathered—about our marketplace, our audience, and our rewards—into a compelling message. We'll then CRAM this incisive, aerodynamic message into our marketing arrow. We owe such a message to our audience and our cause because we're both "worth it."

CRAMING IN PRACTICE

In one of my workshops in Ukraine, two different organizations funded by the Institute for Sustainable Communities tried CRAM-ing: an organization helping battered women and a community group trying to improve the quality of living in a small city. Members of the domestic-violence group wanted to focus on mothers who were being beaten by their husbands. They wanted the mothers to call the local women's shelter for help the next time they were hurt. The community group wanted adults living in certain neighborhoods to pay 5 UAH (about $1 at the time) to support the organization's cleanup projects.

The domestic-violence organization was having trouble with the core of its message: the benefit exchange. It wanted to tell battered women that they should seek help in order to protect their children and family. The reward—protecting the family—was a good one, but the organization's audience associated that reward with not seeking help. Many battered women accepted violence as part of everyday life, and to them seeking help seemed like a selfish act that would tear apart their family. How could the organization show that the way to protect children was to seek help rather than to avoid it?

The answer was in the way the benefit exchange was framed. The organization needed to connect with battered women so they would believe that their family's well-being required action against domestic violence. The organization decided it would use the voice of a child, so important to mothers, to convey the idea that domestic violence hurts the child as much as the mother. After fifteen minutes of brainstorming, a young woman who'd been quiet the whole day raised her hand and offered a memorable line: "Momma, when he hits you, it makes me black and blue." She suggested a child's drawing of a boy or girl looking sad and bruised, along with a positive call to action: "We can help. Call this toll-free number to protect your child and yourself."

The message connected with the target audience of mothers emotionally, through the voice of children they wanted to protect. It then redefined the reward mothers thought they were receiving through inaction and showed that action was the only sure way to protect their children. It was presented in a memorable way, through the drawings of children. It also used the principles of effective packaging by setting a sympathetic mood, tapping into a psychological opening, and using an effective messenger. We'll talk about these principles in the next chapter.

We then turned to the community group trying to convince people to pay $1 for their cleanup program. It had taken a long time for the group to focus on a specific action. Most of its past communications had been about the importance of joining a community group, the role and responsibility of citizens, and the group's meetings and activities. But the action the group wanted people to take wasn't clear. When we asked the group members to specifically define the desired action, they said they wanted people to show up, pay their $1 dues, and become members. What tangible, personal reward did they get for paying? The community group began talking about a cleanup project in a high-rise housing development where, because of irregular trash collection, unsightly, unsanitary piles of garbage were everywhere. The playgrounds were filthy. The group would be able to use dues from residents to hire a private contractor to pick up the trash and paint the playground. So the group had the beginnings of a benefit exchange: join our group for $1 and get a clean neighborhood and well-tended playground that will make the apartment complex feel like a true home.

The group members liked the benefit exchange but worried about the $1. They knew their audience did not want to pay for a service that a government agency was supposed be providing with their tax money. It was the government's job, not theirs, and so even $1 was too much to pay. We talked about that cost at length, and people shared a litany of stories about the incompetence of the government and acute skepticism about the possibility of developing a sense of community after decades of Soviet rule. People just didn't trust the government. Someone offered a Soviet-era joke illustrating this cynicism:

> COMMUNIST PARTY BOSS: How is the potato crop this year?
> PEASANT: There are so many potatoes that if we piled them all up they would form a pyramid stretching up to meet the feet of God.
> PARTY BOSS: There is no God.
> PEASANT: There are no potatoes either.

People living in the trash-strewn neighborhoods the community group wanted to clean up were dissatisfied with the status quo but distrusted any solutions. How could we use this fact without sounding as though we were pushing yet another collective concept that would yield no potatoes?

We decided the problem was not so much the reward as our strategy in presenting it. As with the domestic-violence example, we needed a strong, memorable connection to frame the benefit exchange. The group decided to forge the connection in two ways: by focusing on a real-life success story so people would connect with the promise being made and by being disarmingly honest and transparent about the price of realizing that promise: $1.

Private-sector marketers often turn negatives into positives by similarly admitting the downsides of their product while making those drawbacks seem like a small price to pay. Listerine makes mouthwash that tastes like medicine. Scope came along and took advantage of Listerine's negative feature of taste and positioned itself as a tastier alternative. But then Listerine came back and made the argument that its product was the more effective, so the bad taste was a small price to pay. Listerine even made fun of itself, showing a man using Listerine for thirty seconds and making painful faces as he tries to endure the experience. But meanwhile he's killing all those germs that cause bad breath because Listerine is real medicine. The bad taste is a relative bargain because we get better results—according to Listerine.

The members of the community group followed this example by asking up front for people to pay the price. They didn't hide the cost of the action any more than Listerine tried to downplay its bad taste. Honesty was a creative way to forge a connection with the audience. They didn't say, "Join our group" without admitting that the action came with a price. Instead, they showed that the price was a bargain for the result. The group members decided that when they packaged the message, they would show pictures of a neighborhood that had been cleaned up as an incentive to take action. They wanted the audience to think, "I will finally get the clean neighborhood I always dreamed of because it really is possible—this other neighborhood looks great."

Members of the group sketched out a flyer with before-and-after shots of the neighborhood that had been cleaned up. Underneath, they inserted the message: "How much for a new neighborhood? Only 5 UAH." The call to action said, "Don't wait for the government to do it. Pay 5 UAH to join us, and we'll clean up the place." This language sounds transactional and business-oriented, which has the advantage of lessening the negative associations with collectivization and communism and strengthening the connection with the audience. The group made a bold and memorable claim, and it backed it up with evidence. This strategy worked; the group successfully recruited new members.

WAYS WE CRAM

Once we have a sense of how to CRAM with our audiences, we have to be able to do so in three ways: through one-way communication, two-way communication, and the "third way" of communication: storytelling.

One-way communication is the most familiar to marketers. One-way communication means one person is doing the talking. We are engaging in one-way communication when we transmit our message to our audience through traditional marketing outreach like a slogan or brochure or advertising campaign. We engage in one-way communication all the time, and we usually try to consciously CRAM a message into it. We create a message, package it, and—if we've done our job right—our audiences receive it and take action in response.

In two-way communication we personally interact with our audience members in some type of conversation. Perhaps they've come into our office or we've met them at the bus stop or they've called our toll-free number. Two-way communication is often one-on-one, but it can also be with a group of people—for example, in a meeting with constituents or in a question-and-answer session following a speech. Although we communicate this way all the time, we may forget that every conversation is an opportunity to CRAM. We need to consciously seek to connect, provide a reward, inspire action, and stay in the memory of our audiences every time we interact with them.

The third way of communicating occurs when we tell a story. We could classify storytelling as a one-way communication, but that doesn't do it justice. When one person tells another person a story, the two people are transported together outside the present moment, to another time and place. They are living an experience together as one person recounts what happened and another imagines it in his or her mind. Stories can be part of one-way communication or two-way communication. I could talk about the time I hiked in the rainforest in Madagascar, or we could have a conversation about what it's like to hike in Madagascar, swapping tales. Either way, stories add a powerful element to communication. A story can CRAM an entire message or part of a message. Or it may be a way to connect so we can deliver the rest of a message in another way. Stories work well in all these ways, so we should use them as much as we can, as consciously as we can, always with our message in mind.

Let's explore some examples of how CRAMing works for these types of communication.

One-Way Communication: The Slogan

Mark Twain has been quoted as saying, "I didn't have time to write a short letter, so I wrote a long one instead." Communicating our message succinctly is hard, like expressing *Huckleberry Finn* in haiku form. Let's take the shortest form of one-way communication—slogans and taglines—as an example of how much can be CRAMed into a few words.

➤ One-way communication, even if it's as short as a slogan, should CRAM in the most essential parts of a message. If we don't CRAM in substance, we're wasting our words.

Let's look at three corporate slogans from carmakers by way of illustration. Volkswagen has used the slogan "Drivers wanted," which conveys a great deal in two words. It tells me that if I get a Volkswagen, I get the best driving experience because Volkswagen is the brand that focuses on me as a driver. If we are part of the VW market, we likely feel a sense of connection and reward, and we're likely to remember the slogan. We won't necessarily rush out and buy a car because of the slogan, but the slogan serves a purpose in that it nicely echoes and reinforces the many other marketing methods that VW uses.

Honda has used the slogan "The power of dreams." I have owned three Hondas and loved them all, but this slogan does not speak to me. In fact, it is so generic it could be applied equally to Microsoft, Barbie dolls, and the Ford Foundation.

➤ If we can take our slogan and place it next to another organization's name with no problem, then we have a problem.

Oldsmobile's infamous slogan, "This is not your father's Oldsmobile," was more a commentary about the disastrous brand problems that Oldsmobile was facing at the time than an effective sales tool to forge a connection with a new audience. It told us the kind of car Oldsmobile was trying hard not to be, rather than the kind of car it was. A slogan that is a transparent attempt to save a floundering organization is not a good one.

Let's look at some slogans from major nonprofit organizations. The American Red Cross, one of the most successful organizations at fundraising, has the tagline "Together, we can save a life." Although it is somewhat generic, in six words the slogan accomplishes a lot. It manages to connect with the organization's audience, show why it's relevant to them, convey the essence of its work, offer a vivid, concrete reward, ask for action, and express the sense of urgency that is so central to the identity of the American Red Cross. The Make-a-Wish Foundation tagline also CRAMs in a lot: "Share the power of a wish."

Other taglines or slogans, especially those for good causes, tend to be more inwardly focused. There is the "we're the biggest or best" slogan, as in "Ducks Unlimited: World Leader in Wetlands Conservation." There is the "why we do it" slogan, as in "CARE: Where the end of poverty begins." And there is the "who we are" slogan, as in AmeriCare's "Humanitarian lifeline to the world" or in "Alliance for the Chesapeake Bay: The voice of the bay." These approaches make sense if the element that the slogan emphasizes is the most important for audiences to hear. It may not be possible to convey every attribute of an organization, so we should convey the most essential. If the audience cares about other characteristics more, then it's time to rethink the few words chosen. We know we have the right words if our audience is likely to think: "Exactly. That's for me."

Two-Way Communication: CRAMing in the Elevator

Imagine we are on an elevator and another passenger steps on. Can we CRAM in our entire message in a conversation that lasts just as long as it takes to get to another floor?

➤ We need to master the two-way communication of a conversation so that we can CRAM our message into the time it takes to ride an elevator to the top of a small building.

For example, I worked with a clothing designer who ran a social enterprise—a workshop for disadvantaged women. The women learned to design and make high-end children's and women's clothes, which were then sold in a small boutique called Happy Endings. The styles were romantic and inspired by fairy tales, and they sold well.

Whenever the clothing designer gets on an elevator and sees a woman dressed with a hint of the style she markets, she CRAMs. She starts by complimenting the woman on an article of her clothing or how she wears it in order to establish a connection. We all like receiving thoughtful, sincere compliments, and we're usually willing to listen to the person who delivers them. Once she pays the compliment, she pauses so the woman in the elevator can thank her or, more likely, offer a self-deprecating comment. "This old thing? Oh, thanks." Then she explains why she noticed the item. "I'm a clothing designer and run a boutique that sells a similar style of clothing, so when I see romantic elements in someone's dress, I'm always inspired."

At that point, she stops and lets the other person respond again. That's because a good elevator conversation is a two-way conversation, not a monologue. Nearly every time, the woman she compliments then asks about the boutique or its name. She has a quick response that rolls the reward, action, and memorable image together succinctly: "It's called Happy Endings because our stitching is done by women in need whom we've hired and specially trained. Our customers love it because they can indulge in some beautiful clothes while giving someone else a Happy Ending. It's shopping without guilt!" She hands over a business card when she gets to the phrase "shopping without guilt." Her cards double as a sales tool because they feature a four-color picture of her designs on one side and her name and store information on the other. Her parting words are usually, "Have a great day" (or "Nice to meet you"), "and come visit us some time."

In half a minute or so, the designer connects with her target audience members, offers them the reward of shopping without guilt, asks them to visit her shop, and leaves them a memorable shop name and business card that sum up her cause in two words. She is essentially saying, "I have something very special to offer you, because I like your style. Come to me because you're worth it." The designer has practiced this spiel many, many times so that she can deliver it effortlessly, anywhere, in the form of a friendly conversation. She has different variations. For longer encounters measured in minutes, not seconds, she is ready to tell one of several moving stories about women who have been helped by her organization. This kind of information is always at the top of her mind, ready to go.

It's one thing to CRAM in one-way communication; it's much harder in a conversation. Unless we're extremely fast on our feet, it's difficult to CRAM with confidence and calm if we haven't rehearsed several versions, many times. Effective communicators from good causes have thoroughly practiced two-way communication so they have a short, spontaneous-sounding sell to build into conversations anywhere—at a cocktail party, on the sidelines of a professional conference, or on adjacent treadmills at the gym. Practice CRAMing in two-way communication until it becomes second nature.

The Third Way: Stories

Every good cause needs a collection of good stories—success stories, human-interest stories, short examples, and so on.

⟫⟶ Stories can illuminate one of the elements of a message, or they can convey all four with color, texture, images, emotion, and meaning. Good stories draw us in emotionally and capture our interest.

I once was asked to prepare a speech that the executive of a large aid agency was to deliver to an alliance of farmers, and I knew I needed to start it with such a story. Good speeches always start with stories because stories connect with people, and they convey a message—or aspect of a message—as a shared experience. I struggled to decide which story to tell. We wanted the audience to see how the U.S. government's overseas food-aid program benefited not only U.S. farmers by buying their crops but also the aid agency and thousands of people in need. We wanted audience members to call their representatives in the House and Senate to oppose any cuts to the government program. A good story would reveal and reinforce those messages in some way.

I spent long hours reading through the agency's library of personal accounts from people who had been helped by the organization over the years. Finally, I found the story of a farmer whose life had been ruined by war but who then received food aid that allowed his family to rebuild their lives and reclaim their farm. The speech opened with that story because it CRAMed completely. It created a series of emotional connections: between farmers and the people whom their food eventually reached, between farmers and the food-aid program, and between the organization and farmers. Through one farmer's experience, it made it clear that the overseas food-aid program not only brought financial rewards to the people in the audience but also saved the lives of people like them. And it was full of memorable details. After the audience members arrived home, it was probably the only part of the speech they remembered.

That story CRAMed in an entire message. Those are my favorite kinds of stories. In other cases, we need several stories to CRAM a message, or one story to open the mind to hearing our message. A correspondent for the *New York Times* once told me about the day he'd spent at an aid agency's workshop where land-mine victims were being fitted with prostheses. He'd remarked to the workshop director that he didn't see any prostheses for children there. "Children don't survive when they step on a land mine," he was told. That fact stuck with him, and, after hearing it, I found that an image of rows of artificial arms and legs—adult size only— was permanently lodged in my mind. That image makes me ready to hear an anti-land-mine message. It makes me want the reward and sense of connection that comes from sparing someone from losing a limb or, unimaginably worse, a child.

Sometimes, one detail tells a whole story or many stories. When I arrived in Ukraine, I saw one of these telling details. Under the arch of a centuries-old church, a stooped old woman crouched with an outstretched cup for spare change. The cup was from McDonald's. What a story: although the fall of communism and the rise of capitalism has benefited many, pensioners have lost much. Their safety nets gone, many are left on the sidelines, begging for scraps in a society that in their eyes has lost all predictability and has changed beyond recognition.

HOW TO USE ROBIN HOOD RULE 7

1. Write Down the Values for Each Audience and the Benefit Exchange

In this step we review—once again—our knowledge of the people we want to reach and the reward we should offer. This review may feel redundant, but that is not bad. It is so easy to lose track of our audiences' perspectives that we have to constantly remind ourselves of their states of mind in order to stay on track. It's also easy to forget that our audiences probably think quite differently from each other. We need a different message for each audience, complete with a unique connection, reward, action, and memory. Don't be tempted to avoid the work of creating messages for individual audiences by generating one big message with a little CRAM for everyone. Such a monstrosity is about as attractive as building a Tudor house with Greek columns and Frank Lloyd Wright windows. Who would want to buy it? In trying to please everyone, we please no one at all.

Now that we have a vivid, color snapshot of the audience, we insert ourselves into that picture.

2. Forge a Connection

Let's pretend we're standing next to a few of the members of our audience at the bus stop, trying to get their attention without seeming like a scary stranger. They are lost in their own thoughts, and we want to make a polite mental interruption. Do we turn to them and start lecturing them on how they should live their life? Do we launch into a monologue about ourselves? Not unless we want to attract the wrong kind of attention. A better way to start a conversation is to establish our psychological connection. We might simply nod hello and flash our winning smile. We might tell them we love their mohair sweater or red hair or Burberry umbrella. We might point out that we are wearing the same watch. We might ask them where they're headed, only to discover we're neighbors. We might say they look familiar and try to figure out how we know each other. We might comment on the weather or commiserate about how the bus is always late. Most of us make these kinds of comments at one time or another to people we don't know because we're social animals by nature. We have a natural tendency to reach out and find common ground with those around us.

In messaging we need to extend those bus stop skills to our cause's audiences so we can get their attention. We need to connect in the same way, but on a bigger scale. Why? Remember our Times Square analogy: in this day and age, everyone is busy, bombarded with messages, and overloaded with options. People have to process information and make decisions faster than ever, and if they don't feel a connection that creates a pause long enough for them to consider what we're saying, they won't even notice us.

Think back to the bus stop comments. They show several ways we can forge connections. One is through simply being friendly or flattering, with a smile or compliment like "nice coat." Another way is through mirroring: "Hey, we have the same watch!" If we appear familiar to people—for instance, if we speak, dress, or act similarly—they warm to us faster than they would if we were dissimilar. We can connect through shared experience: "I know your face—I think we went to the same elementary school!" A common feeling can also be a powerful connector: "Gosh, it's cold!" or "Don't you hate the way this bus is always late?"

Consider how different corporations and causes connect in these ways. The L'Oréal campaign connects with a combination of flattering the ego and recognizing a common emotional yearning for indulgence. A sense of possibility and hope draws us in. Consider an opposite approach to connecting with feelings. Mothers Against Drunk Driving connects on the common ground of sadness over a lost life. Think about how we can connect with our audiences in a similar way. What would we say at the bus stop? What would we say in a brochure? On the elevator? Choose the connection most likely to capture their interest.

3. Make It Memorable

Once we have some kind of connection, we have the entry point we need for offering our benefit exchange. Now we need to apply the other end of our frame so that the benefit exchange sticks there for a while. We don't want simply to make an impression; we want to make a lasting impression. Making the benefit exchange memorable completes the word CRAM, and it completes our message.

What makes something memorable? It's memorable if it's different. We don't remember every minute of our daily commute to work; we remember the one time a chicken truck overturned on the beltway. "Because I'm worth it" is such a bald-faced statement of entitlement, it stands out. It's different because it's extreme. Memorable things are also catchy. "Because I'm worth it" is a catchy phrase, easy to remember and use, and for that reason it's entered our lexicon. If we Google it, we find it used in other contexts by everyone from preachers to authors to bloggers.

Things are also more memorable if they are personal, specific, and contain a human element. Do we remember the total number of people who died in the 2004 tsunami or the story of the woman clinging to her child in a tree for hours? To get back to our skin-deep example, a consumer wouldn't remember how many millions of people use L'Oréal if the company said so. L'Oréal says, "Because I'm worth it" and not "Because lots of women and men who use cosmetics are worth it" for a reason. Their slogan is more personal and more memorable.

A word of caution: memorable elements should always be closely tied to our cause. Think of all the advertisements that were so funny or memorable that we told a friend about them, but when asked what product the ad was for, we were not sure. We don't just need a memorable idea or picture; we need an idea or picture that makes our cause memorable.

4. Practice CRAMing the Message

Now that we have the four elements of our message, try to condense them down to a slogan and an elevator conversation. Then, most important, start looking for stories that convey our message. Most good causes have a lot of good stories, but they may have trouble capturing them. Train front-line staff to relay the successes they hear about or witness. They should write them on paper or, even better, input them into a "story bank" that resides on the organization's computer server. If anyone shares a positive story about our cause, we should write it down immediately and ask that person to tell others. If we provide services of any kind, we can leave a section open for written comments on our evaluation forms. The bad comments can help us improve our services; the good ones are marketing material.

In writing a good story, keep in mind that, in addition to delivering our core message, it should have a minimum of three elements: a compelling protagonist, a conflict to overcome, and a clear meaning at the end that helps us look forward. We want people to identify with the characters we're talking about, and we want them to understand the importance of our cause for those individuals. We want those hearing the story to feel compelled to take action.

If you doubt the power of a story, think about the last time you gave money to a good cause. I'm willing to bet a free copy of this book that a story was behind your gift. I donated to an organization helping children in Sierra Leone after I read in the *Washington Post* a moving story about children who'd had their hands and arms amputated in war. They'd visited the United States to get prosthetic limbs, and their stories—and the pictures—compelled me to act. I also gave money to a cause in Saint Louis after hearing a radio report about a single mother's struggle to keep her children in school. And I gave to the victims of Hurricane Katrina—not because of the overwhelming scope of the disaster but because of the stories of families who'd lost everything to floodwaters and who'd had to wait far too long for help.

CONCLUSION

Now that we can CRAM for each audience, we should never leave home without those messages. Slogans, elevator conversations, and stories bring an important intentionality to our communications. We are always communicating some point, and it should be the right point for the right person. In every form of communication we undertake, we should know the message we need to communicate and why we need to do so. (We discuss how and when to deliver our message in the next chapter.) When we CRAM our message for people, we convey respect for who they are. We show them that we believe they are worth our attention, not just our preaching. In turn, we increase the chances that they will take action because it's "worth it." CRAMing doesn't just sell shampoo; it sells a good cause.

Interview
A Good Man Talks About Storytelling

Andy Goodman was born with a name for advancing good causes, but he took some wide-ranging steps in his career before he settled on such work. He worked in advertising. He founded and ran the American Comedy Network, an international radio syndication company. And then he worked as a television writer, spending three seasons writing and coproducing *Dinosaurs* and cowriting the pilot episode of *The Nanny.* Around that time, he began to get the feeling he describes as Is this all there is? He says, "It was fun and lucrative, but at the end of the day it was hard to look in the mirror and say, 'This is making a big difference.'" He was about to join *The Nanny* staff full time when a letter changed the course of his career. An old friend sent him a job posting for an executive director of an environmental media association. The job, which involved working with the film and TV industries to incorporate environmental messages into their work, seemed the perfect way to apply his diverse background in advertising, radio, and television and in using the media and to put that experience to work for a good cause. "I realized my career didn't look like a clear path, but I had to touch each of those bases to come to that point." He spent five years at the Environmental Media Association before becoming an independent communications consultant. He now helps good causes of all kinds communicate effectively. He has a special interest in storytelling as a communications tool and wrote the book *Why Bad Ads Happen to Good Causes*.

Q: What intrigues you about storytelling?

A: When I went to write for TV, the first job I got was on *Dinosaurs*. I'll never forget sitting down with Michael Jacobs, the executive producer of the show, who said to me, "It's great if you're funny and can write jokes, but there are a million guys who can write jokes. Our show is twenty-two stories a year. Breaking a story, now that's tough. If you can break stories, you can make it." That advice always rang in my ears. Robert McKee, famed for his scriptwriting course, bases his teaching on the theory that it's all about the story. If you don't have a good story, you've got nothing.

Most things are reduced to the set of stories that certain people agree are true. Stories define a person, a company, a movement, a culture, or a nation. You as an individual are the sum of the stories that you tell about yourself. Whenever you are in a new situation or meet a new person, you tell stories about yourself, your spouse, your family, and your interests. And, for them, that's who you are. You are that set of stories, and you reinforce to yourself your own sense of identity in telling those stories.

Storytelling has real communications value. There's a Gary Larson cartoon about what dogs hear when we speak to them: "Blah, blah, blah, Ginger. Blah, Ginger, blah, blah, blah." The dog hears only its name. Human beings are similar. We hear, "Blah, blah, blah, blah, and then yesterday I . . . ," and we get the cue a story is about to begin.

Q: Why is storytelling important to good causes, and why don't we do more of it?

A: There is a basic prejudice against storytelling among good causes. It's considered to be the softer side of communication, and it's anecdotal by definition. We think of it as what we do before work, after work, or at lunch, but it's not the kind of sound science, data, or hard research that gets you a grant from a foundation or the government. Also, because it's so pervasive in everyday life and throughout history, it's taken for granted.

We have to remember that human beings by nature, acculturation, and thousands of years of evolution are always looking for the story in what you're saying. They are looking for those narrative elements that tell them, "Ah, it's this person, trying to achieve this thing through time, running into these problems. Now I understand!" If we can identify the set of stories that tells where we came from, what our contribution to the world is, and how we're making a difference, all communications problems tend to go away.

Q: What are the challenges to telling our stories?

A: I think there are two challenges: we're either too far away from our stories or too close to them. Your cause may have to dig to get to the program people who are out on the street every day. Then you have to get those people to come out of the weeds, step back, and see some basic human things happening that can become stories. Don't fall into the trap of looking for the ultimate story that sums up everything a cause has ever done. It's very hard for any one story to be the ultimate tale that prompts the world to fall in love with you. I ask for a set of stories. I say, "What are the various points you'd make about your organization in a lecture? Each point should have a story." Perhaps one story makes all the points, but that is very rare.

Q: How do you collect and use stories as a way to deliver a message?

A: There are many, many good success stories about stories. Environmental Defense is an organization that is more than three decades old, with 260 employees and regional offices all over the United States. As an organization, it tended to tell the same small set of stories over and over again to show what it was all about. I worked with staff members at a retreat for two days pulling out their stories, and we generated eighty-seven. They weren't all success stories, but they characterized what it was like to work there, to make a difference, to care about the environment. The staff took the twelve best and put them in a booklet called *Staff-Told Tales*. They gave that booklet to potential donors and new staff members, board members, and so forth. They are essentially saying, "If you want to get to know us, read our stories." That's become a very effective tool for getting to know them—far better than an annual report or orientation or policy handbook. It's taken an organization that has a very strong orientation toward science and numbers and given them a strong grounding in storytelling as a basic way of communicating.

My advice is, figure out your core stories. Tell me the main points you want people to know about your organization and a story that illustrates each one. Tell me your how-we-got-started stories, your emblematic success stories, stories about when you fell short and what you learned, stories about where you're going. If you've got that down, your communications will be a lot simpler. People will remember you.

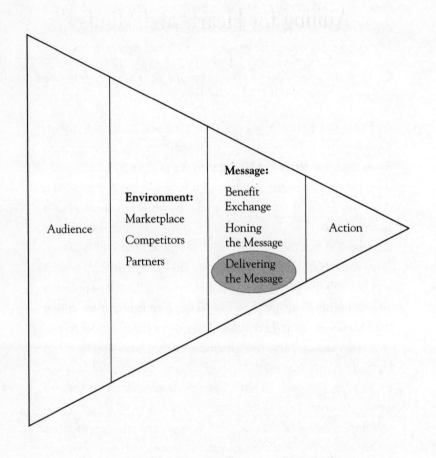

8

Aiming for Hearts and Minds

Take Your Message to Where Your Audiences Are

WHAT THIS CHAPTER SAYS

- Our message should be delivered to our audiences' precise physical, mental, and emotional locations.

- To apply the principles in this chapter, our strategic message needs four components: the right mood, messenger, moment, and channel.

- When choosing the mood, make sure it is consistent with the unique personality of the cause, the content of the message, and the specific audience's sense of self.

- We should place our message in the mouths of messengers from outside our cause.

- We need to identify open-minded moments, the times when our audience is most likely to want the reward we are offering and to be seeking the products or services we provide.

- Open-minded moments should then dictate the channels we choose, whether they are radio ads or e-mail campaigns.

- Test the mood, messenger, opening, and channel with audiences.

WELCOME TO MILLER TIME.

"Welcome to Miller Time," a slogan first broadcast over three decades ago, captured a mood and a moment we all understand. Miller Time is when the hard work of the day is done. We toss aside our lassos, our wrenches, or, less dramatically, our paperwork and seek some relaxation and indulgence. It's Miller Time, and we deserve a beer.

In this chapter, it's Miller Time because it's time to think like Miller Brewing. Miller's marketers knew just the moment when we were ready for their beer, and they named that time after themselves. They were onto a powerful concept: the best way of delivering a message and product is to make them arrive, in an attractive package, just at the moment our audience is most receptive to them. Let's steal that principle.

Robin Hood Rule 8

To get to audiences, go to where they are.

This principle is the final, critical piece of our arrowhead because it holds the key to ensuring that our one-way communication gets to its destination.

Our audiences shouldn't have to look for our message. It should be delivered to their precise physical, mental, and emotional location. Those spots may be far from our own coordinates, so we have to be ready to travel.

Our strategic message needs four components to make the trip to the threshold of our audiences' hearts and minds: the right mood, messenger, moment, and channel. Think of these four components as parts of a communications postal system. If we're sending a message, we need to choose the look and feel of the packaging (the mood), the mail handler who will take it on its way (our messenger), the right destination (the moment), and the best delivery vehicle (the channel, which could be anything from a TV commercial to an e-mail campaign). We need each component to prepare our arrow to get to where our audiences are.

Consider the components of Miller's message. The company's marketers chose to create for their product a distinctive mood that was fun, friendly, and fulfilling. Imagine you're the audience Miller is trying to reach. You can feel that mood instantly. It's been a long day, and now you're headed home or headed out, anticipating time with family, friends, or the TV with beer in hand. How do you feel? Relaxed? Relieved? Ready to have a good time? The television ad campaign reflected that unique and appealing mood and met us in that moment. Commercials showed blue-collar workers backslapping and drinking at the end of the day, and white-collar office workers celebrating an after-work softball victory at the bar. Miller invited us in: if you had the time, Miller had the beer.

The messengers in the ads were the people enjoying Miller Time. For beer drinkers, they were recognizable as "people like us." Miller Time was for everyone from the welder to the stock trader. We vicariously experienced a slice of the lives of the people in the ads, and we related their experiences to our own. In this case, the use of a peer messenger made us identify with the message. It was like discovering that the mail carrier in our communications postal system is a long-lost friend.

Miller Time is the moment when we're likely to buy a beer. Like Miller, most companies try to reach us in moments when we need their products, but Miller took that thinking to a new level by naming a time of day after a beer. Then they made it easy to get Miller moments by placing their promotional pieces and product everywhere we would think about buying a beverage: the convenience store, the bar, the ball game. They met the audience where the audience was, emotionally, mentally, and physically.

The last part of the delivery process is the channel. An ever-growing number of channels provides different ways to deliver our message. To name a few: advertisements or public-service announcements on TV or radio, brochures, newsletters, press conferences, events, speeches, personal meetings, canvassing, telemarketing, listservs, Web sites, signs and billboards, referral or word-of-mouth campaigns, performances, music videos, product samples, public relations, direct mail, sponsorships, and promotional items like magnets, buttons, and key rings. Miller used TV ads, but the beer maker also used many of these additional delivery vehicles. In bars, promotional clocks showed every hour as Miller Time.

Miller Time seemed to be everywhere and all the time, and that was the point. That's how Miller packaged and delivered one of the most memorable messages of the 1970s. Now let's look at each of the four components closely and think about how they apply to us and our cause today.

MOOD

The mood is the packaging that envelops the message. The packaging can be dressed up any number of ways: to appear funny, friendly, down to earth, comforting, harsh, hard-hitting, edgy, scary, shocking, sad, or sympathetic. This range of feeling can be expressed through pictures, words, music, or the quality of the materials.

➤ When choosing the mood, make sure it is consistent with the unique personality of the cause, the content of the message, and the audience's sense of self. Remember, different audiences require different messages, so the mood also must be tailored to fit each specific audience.

Water is one of the simplest substances on the planet. Yet many moods are used to advertise it, depending on the particular product and its audience. Perrier's advertising conveys a fun, zany, and retro tone with stylized and somewhat ironic images that perfectly fit its corporate identity as the "champagne of table water" and its upscale, urban audience. Coca Cola's Dasani and Pepsi's Aquafina water use humor in their advertising to convey a friendly, accessible mood. This down-to-earth mood makes sense for purified water that comes from a tap, not a spring, is packaged in plastic, and is sold to practical consumers at a relatively cheap price.

To illustrate the importance of selecting the right mood to market our cause, let's analyze two campaigns that were designed to encourage American adults to exercise. One was the facelift of the familiar food pyramid. In 2005, the U.S. Department of Agriculture removed the words and pictures that had been on the original pyramid and replaced them with vertical stripes and, on the left side of the diagram, a stick figure climbing stairs. The figure was meant to introduce the idea that exercise is as important as food choices for healthy living. The pyramid was labeled "Steps to a healthier you." What mood does the revised pyramid convey? The steps on the pyramid are so steep they make the idea of exercise seem daunting. The figure climbing the steps is a stylized stick figure, without hands or feet. Does that represent you? The rainbow colors radiating downward are attractive, but are they relevant? Is the action we are expected to take clear?

A drawback to the design was that the pyramid came alive only online, where users could enter an interactive Web site to find out which of twelve pyramids was right for them. The interactive site said what to eat, how much to eat, and how much to exercise—at least thirty minutes of moderate or vigorous activity per day. I learned that when exercising I have to elevate my heart rate; I am not allowed to count walking casually or doing light housework toward my daily allotment of physical activity. When I read the fine print, I learned that if I want to keep my current weight, I need to work out sixty to ninety minutes daily. But in other sections of the site, I was told to "have fun" and break up my required exercise time with simple activities like walking a dog or stretching while watching TV.

The mood online was mixed—stern and authoritative at some points, friendly and helpful at others. That's a problem. We are busy people without time for complexity. Messages need to be delivered quickly and clearly and to evoke an instantly appealing mood. Neither the pyramid alone nor the online experience—which took twenty minutes I might have spent being active rather than sedentary in front of the computer—conveyed a coherent and attractive mood. The main reason people give for not exercising or eating in a healthy way is that the prospect of changing their behavior seems too difficult and daunting. It doesn't "feel like" a task they can undertake. The pyramid did little to counter that perception; in fact, it may have reinforced it. I was left cold.

Around the same time the pyramid was released, the Ad Council and the U.S. Department of Health and Human Services launched public-service announcements to support their campaign against obesity. They employed an entirely different mood. In the television spots, people in various settings—a park, a grocery store, a basketball game—find abandoned body parts that had belonged to people who had taken small, incremental steps in order to lose weight.

In one spot, a perplexed-looking man wanders up to a representative at a lost-and-found booth holding two strange, jiggling blobs that he has discovered near some stairs. He hands them to the man at the booth and asks, "What are they?" The man responds, "Love handles. Lots of people lose them taking the stairs instead of the escalator." In another spot, two men operating a snowplow late at night stop when they see something odd in the road. They get out of the truck, and one man picks up two unidentified, flesh-colored objects. He looks bewildered. His coworker identifies them as someone's thunder thighs and concludes, "They must have lost them playing in the snow with their kids." At the end of each spot is a highly specific call to action tied to the benefit of losing love handles or thunder thighs. A long list of relatively easy ways to become active scrolls at the end of the ad and stops on the relevant action: "Take the stairs instead of the escalator" or "Play outside with your kids thirty minutes a day." A Web site is given for finding additional "small steps."

I then logged onto the Web site—although doing so was not necessary for understanding the message. The first statement I read was "We know that it's impossible for many people to make dramatic lifestyle changes. Instead, we want to help you learn ways that you can change small things about your life and see big results." A picture next to that statement showed a slightly chubby man standing on a bathroom scale smiling and holding up his pants because they are too big for him. The mood? Chummy, encouraging, and welcoming.

So did this mood pass the test? Was it consistent with the personality of the cause, the content of the message, and the audience's sense of self? The "small steps" campaign had a different personality from a typical governmental agency message because it was funny. It didn't tell its audience how to live, it made them laugh. It cut through the clutter. The tone—intensely personal, warm, and approachable—matched nicely with the "you really can do it" message and the audience's sense of self. It resonated with the mood of people who are overwhelmed by the idea of changing their lifestyles but who want to improve their looks and health.

This campaign and the food pyramid were both from governmental agencies, and they both were promoting exercise. Both used the idea of steps, developed images around the concept of steps, and launched an accompanying online campaign. But the similarities end there. The two approaches had completely different strategic messages for the action they promoted, as well as different packaging for their messages. The "small steps" campaign emphasized incremental change through humor, while the campaign promoting the "healthy steps" of the pyramid focused on ideal change and provided lots of information.

Remember our discussion about choosing appropriate actions. Health experts would argue that taking the stairs won't remove love handles; for that an hour on a stair machine is required. But that's a tough place to start, and we all have to start somewhere. Becoming active is a process, not an overnight transformation. The more appealing the first step in that process, the better. Ask yourself, Today, am I and my peers more likely to take the stairs or walk for an hour after designing our own food pyramids?

Let's take a smaller scale example because mood is especially important when we're face to face with our audiences. Imagine I'm appearing before the school board to advocate a position. Do I want to be the eccentric mom ranting about the school's shortcomings or the constructive mom describing the benefits of a specific policy change?

A constructive, nonscolding approach works better than the opposite approach nine times out of ten. Of course, I can't be everything to everyone, and if I am effective, my advocacy efforts are bound to irritate some people. But I am resigned to irritating those parties; my goal is not to annoy the audience I want to spur to action.

The mood need not always be lighthearted, fun, and funny. Although this approach is often effective, it is not appropriate for everyone or every topic. Sometimes it's better to be heart-warming rather than funny, or abrasive rather than welcoming. Greenpeace is never going to be warm and fuzzy, nor should it be. The goal is to create a mood that projects a suitable and appealing personality for the cause and connects with the intended audience.

MESSENGER

People listen to other people. They look to human beings, not corporations or causes, to communicate and connect with. Choosing the best people to act as our messengers is like selecting the right mood. It requires finding the best match with the cause, message, and audience. Obviously, our own staff, volunteers, or committee members are messengers for our cause. Whenever any of us talks about our work or the cause, we are delivering messages to someone. All of us, from the volunteer to the computer specialist to the board member, should be consistently delivering the right messages to the right audience. We should be reading from the same script.

→ We also should try to place our message in other people's mouths. Messengers from outside our cause may be better able to connect with our audience, and they make our promises far more credible than we do ourselves.

Which is more believable—my telling you this book is worth reading or a respected coworker's recommending it? If you were looking for the best product for your teeth, would you believe the advice of your dentist or a toothpaste manufacturer? If you're a teenager, would you trust the man in a suit or a friend on a skateboard?

Choosing the right messenger to deliver the message is as critical as the message itself. The right messengers lend extra punch; messengers deemed irrelevant or extremist get ignored. To return to our postal analogy, we will accept and open letters from people we know. The rest we assume is junk mail.

We need to turn back to our audience research to analyze who influences the people we want to reach. Whom do our audiences know, like, trust, and respect? Who do they believe has their best interests at heart (rather than a clear agenda or bias)? Influencers can include the following people.

- Authority figures or experts. If audience members usually make their decisions to act based on the recommendations of authorities or experts, then it makes sense to seek the endorsement of those figures. Companies might say "approved by pediatricians" for a child safety product or "rated best software" by a computer magazine. If a cause is trying to reach policymakers or academics, a well-regarded expert may be an important messenger; if the audience is teenagers, authority figures can be a negative.

- Opinion leaders. If audience members are swayed by certain individuals whom they like and respect, these individuals should be recruited to help deliver the message. Gatorade created a persuasive campaign for young people by being incredibly blatant about the use of the opinion leader Michael Jordan. "If I could be like Mike" captured the dream of being a high-flying basketball player and sold a sports drink in the process. Many companies choose well-known actors to hawk their products because the audience's familiarity with the celebrity and favorable associations with that person often translate into a positive emotional connection with the product. Tapping celebrities carries a calculated risk, but a well-known figure with personal links to an issue can do wonders for repositioning a cause or issue. Think of Betty Ford's and Liz Taylor's contributions to the destigmatization of substance abuse and AIDS, respectively. Fortunately, not all opinion leaders need to be celebrities. Respected figures in the community, church leaders, or a beloved teacher can have just as much star power with certain audiences as an A-list actor from Hollywood.

- Likable peers. Peers are excellent messengers when it's crucial for the audience to believe that people like them are taking the desired action. In Chapter Six we discussed the power of social proof; peer messengers are key to creating the sense that "people like me are doing it." For example, teenagers care about what other teenagers say. Because a peer can be such a powerful salesperson, it's worth investing significant effort in collecting and promoting testimonials, referrals, and stories from people who are similar to those we want to reach. Many ads for products marketed to teens feature other teens and are delivered in words, images, and sounds familiar to teens. They may employ a sarcastic tone or use an offbeat sense of humor to imply a teen messenger. The Truth antismoking campaign used teenagers as its leaders. If you're a cynic, you'll find it interesting that Philip Morris has poured much of its money into making parents its messengers to children with its "talk, they'll listen" anti-teen-smoking campaign. Meanwhile, its campaign for children implored, "Think. Don't smoke," with a decidedly authoritarian ring. It urged children to resist peer pressure—a tactic that has the interesting side effect of calling attention to those pressures.

• Inner circles. Friends and family are our inner circle and are often our biggest influencers. Having those closest to us encourage us to use a product greatly increases its appeal. The phone company MCI banked on the power of friends and family as the most persuasive spokespeople for long-distance service when it created the Friends and Family calling plan, which asked people to enroll their entire inner circles in MCI calling circles. The campaign worked well because it was hard for friends or family members to say no to saving their loved ones money. Similarly, grocery stores put products appealing to kids on the lowest shelves so children will ask their parent to buy them. Good causes can use the same principle, especially if family members or close friends can be convinced that an issue is vital to the health or welfare of a loved one. For example, if a group promoting health screenings discovers that wives are the ones who convince husbands to get checkups, those women are the best target for a message about men getting tested for colon cancer.

We may use these messengers in many different ways. We may include testimonials from key messengers in our materials. We may ask them to serve as formal spokespeople. Or we may simply choose language and images typical of the people who influence our audience. Regardless of the approach, the goal should be to amplify the cause's message by adding a whole choir of voices that can surround audiences where they live, work, and play.

MOMENT

The reason we don't see many ads for H&R Block tax-preparation services in October has to do with the principle of open-minded moments. October is not Miller Time for taxpayers.

> At open-minded moments our audience is most likely to want the reward we are offering and to seek the products or services we provide.

Tax preparation services are of interest to most of us before April 15, but in October, we have other things to worry about. For that reason H&R Block advertises heavily in early spring.

We all have small events or life changes that open us to certain messages. When I was buying a car, each model that I was considering suddenly seemed to be all over the highways. The number of Volvo and Honda sedans appeared to have doubled overnight. They'd been there before, but I didn't notice them because I wasn't in the market for a car. We tend to see only what we're looking for. Many people report a similar experience when they have children. After my first child was born, I noticed thousands of new things that had never before crossed into my frame of reference. I stopped to smile at other people's small children in the mall. I found myself reading the family column of the newspaper and engaging in long discussions with other parents about products like the Diaper Genie. When I held my newborn in my arms while watching TV in the middle of a tenth consecutive sleepless night, McDonald's ads about quality time with kids made me weepy. The exhaustion and exhilaration of being a new parent made everything look different. These examples show that open-minded moments, whenever or wherever they happen, are both psychological and physical.

➤ Open-minded moments occur when we are thinking about an action and are able to take it. We can have open-minded moments in certain places (at the bar), at certain times (during tax season), or in certain emotional states (new motherhood).

If we think of the mind as a camera, open-minded moments are the seconds when our mental shutter opens in response to a place, time, or emotional state. The aperture suddenly widens to let in light, and we focus on something specific. In that instant, we are open to an image or an idea or a word that falls within that frame of reference, and we grab it. "Hey—it's Miller Time—give me a beer!" Then, quick as a wink, the shutter closes. We stop noticing the beer ads and the beer. That moment of selective attention has passed, and we screen out what we don't need.

If we can predict when our audience's mental shutter will open—or if events occur that we know will cause that shutter to open—then we can show up for the photo shoot, thrust our offering into the picture, and succeed in being seen. This strategy is more efficient than trying to force off the lens cap and demand someone photograph us because we think our cause is beautiful. No matter how nicely we dress up, if our audience isn't looking for our message or finding it easy to take action, we stand a poor chance of getting noticed.

It's easy to forget this concept in the excitement of wanting to display our terrific strategic message everywhere. We want to believe our message is so convincing and our products or services are so compelling that the exact time or place we deliver them doesn't matter. Plenty of good causes skip over the concept of choosing the right moment and go straight to choosing the channel for communication.

They start organizing trainings, planning events, and deciding between a poster and a button without ever having thought about which is best suited to their audience's open-minded moments.

How can we predict those open-minded moments? If we have done our audience research, we should have an idea of when our audience is ready to hear our message, needs our benefits, or is able to take action. That's our moment, and that's where we need to take our message. We want to be right there when people are making the decision about whether they are going to take our action.

Look around and see how many companies are trying to reach us at all times of the day, whenever there is a better-than-even chance we may need their products. We see promotional pieces for tourist attractions, restaurants, and hotels in airports or read about them in in-flight magazines, right when we are thinking about how to spend time in a new city. In grocery stores, we see little blinking red boxes of coupons in many aisles. We are offered coupons next to a box of tissues in the paper aisle because that's the moment when we are deciding which brand to buy. We see posters advertising hair products at the beauty salon. The products are right there for purchase at the moment we are wondering how we are going to make our hair look exactly the way it does when we leave the salon. And we can't escape ads for Coca-Cola because they are everywhere. Their ubiquity is not surprising given that the company has famously said that its marketing goal is to always be within an arm's reach of desire. That means selling soda just about anywhere.

Choosing the right moment is especially important for good causes because we don't have the resources to plaster our message everywhere. We need to think in a radically different way than we do now. Instead of simply "getting our message out" or "distributing our materials" or "offering our training," we need to focus on promoting these products and services at the moment people want them.

Let's take some examples. In Washington, D.C., *Marketplace*, a radio show about business, is advertised on the back of city buses.

This is a wise place for a radio station to put its message because potential listeners, trapped in traffic on their way home, may be amenable to trying a new radio program. They see a message about the availability of entertaining, useful business news "for the rest of us" and instantly try the product by tuning in on their car radios. In Maryland, the Chesapeake Bay Foundation encouraged volunteers to spray-paint the message "Don't Dump—Chesapeake Bay Drainage" on storm drains. The stenciled message reminds people that rainwater and anything else that goes down storm drains is carried straight into local streams, rivers, and, eventually, the Chesapeake Bay. At the moment when someone is contemplating dumping a can of antifreeze into a storm drain, the stenciled warning is right there to deter the dumper.

A completely different organization half a world away—a small Ukrainian group trying to combat the sex-industry trafficking of young women—took a similar approach. The organization was working to warn young women about scams used to lure them into situations abroad where they would be sexually exploited. An advertisement promising high-paying work as a maid in Europe could be a front for a prostitution ring. A young woman might think she had found the opportunity of a lifetime, only to be forced into sex work upon entering another country. This organization decided it wanted to use its communications budget to be the last line of defense against young women being tricked into these schemes. Other groups were tackling the problem earlier in women's decision processes through education programs in schools and vocational training to help women find good work within the country. But not everyone received that education or training. The organization wanted to make sure that young women from its region who wanted to search for work in foreign countries were careful about their choices.

So the organization applied the principle of open-minded moments and asked, "When or where do women make the decision that sets them down this dangerous path? When or where would they be most receptive to our messages?" The answer was simple: when these women were reading the help-wanted sections of newspapers and job-notice boards. At that moment, when they were looking for an opportunity and holding out hope for improving their lives, they were at their most open and vulnerable.

The sex-trafficking industry also understood the importance of this moment, and it placed ads in these venues. The organization decided to do the same. It designed an advertisement that looked identical to the typical overseas employment ad. It had an attractive headline promising opportunity—"Employment Abroad"—and offered the benefits women were seeking, including high pay and good working conditions and terms. But in between each prominent headline and benefit was a line decoding the true meaning of the text. It revealed that the "high pay" could be your life, and the "terms" could be not returning home. At the bottom of the ad readers found the slogan "Learn to read between the lines—beware of misleading ads!" and the organization's hotline numbers. The organization placed the ad in the help-wanted section of local newspapers and on notice boards in communities. It was an inexpensive effort but highly effective because it got the right message and product (the hotline) to the right person at the right time. That's what open-minded moments are all about.

Some openings, like the one in this example, are predictable. Others come along and catch us by surprise. We should try to recognize unexpected openings when we see them because they are rare and fleeting. The tragic case of Terri Schiavo created a national open-minded moment on how we choose to live and die. Or think about the public health field in the wake of the anthrax attacks in 2001. At that time, people were openly thinking about how their government should be protecting their health. These were moments when causes like living wills or improvements to public health infrastructure got people's attention.

People who lobby on Capitol Hill or in state governments around the country are also aware of open-minded moments. In his landmark work on how issues find their way onto the federal government's agenda, the scholar John Kingdon talks about "policy windows."[1] Those are the moments of opportunity when everyone is suddenly focused on an issue because of political changes or a passing crisis. A policy window opens, and everyone who is ready thrusts forward their related cause or relevant proposal. Then the window slams shut again.

⟫⟶ Whether we visualize a window or a camera shutter, the image is clear: openings are short-lived. We need to see them coming and be ready with our message.

Network for Good, the leading Web site for donating to charity and volunteering, has powerful corporate partners that ensure we can take advantage of short-lived openings. When a major crisis or disaster occurs, our founding partners, AOL and Yahoo!, direct people to our site with "how to help" links. So in the aftermath of devastating Hurricane Katrina in 2005, people reading about the plight of the storm's victims or viewing pictures of the disaster online could instantly act on an urge to help with a few clicks of the mouse.

Ronald Reagan took advantage of an open-minded moment for political ends when he proclaimed "morning in America." His campaign knew a lot of people were longing for a sense of hope or a sense that the country was headed in the right direction, and he put a name to that feeling. He made his own Miller Time. Bill Clinton's campaign mantra, "It's the economy stupid," also responded to where the country was psychologically: in this case, people were worried about their wallets. For good measure, he tapped into Reagan's Miller Time when he said he was from "a place called Hope." Savvy politicians are good at seeing, naming, and branding open-minded national moments.

Finding an open-minded moment is tremendously powerful. When we act quickly to pin our solution to a sudden perceived problem or need, we can make great gains for our good cause. If we wait too long or fail to act, the opening will disappear, and we will be kicking ourselves for years to come.

MATCHING OPENINGS TO CHANNELS

Once we know the opportune moment to reach our audience, we can choose the channel. Do we need a brochure, a billboard, or a giant inflatable condom? We must know our openings before we answer that question because openings should always dictate channels.

➤ Think of the opening and the channel as the yin and yang of communications. Channels are the same old vehicles we always have to choose from, and they lack power without the yang of an opening, which increases the chance that our audience notices the message delivered. Together, the yin and yang create a coherent, powerful whole.

If we think back to our private-sector examples, we see the yin and yang of opening and channel matched precisely. When I fly into an airport and am looking for a place to visit or to eat at in a new city, a flyer is a good, portable message that I can stuff in my bag. At the grocery store, a dispenser next to a display of tissue that offers me fifty cents off is a good incentive to buy that brand. At the beauty salon, a poster on the ceiling advertising shampoo is the only thing I have to stare at when my hair is being washed, so I get the message.

The example of the help-wanted ad against sex trafficking also matched channel to opening effectively. Young women were thinking about work abroad when they read the help-wanted ads. To take advantage of that opening, the organization trying to stop human trafficking chose a small newspaper advertisement as a channel. Similarly, *Marketplace* reached its target audience with a bus ad because that best matched its opening.

Andy Goodman, the former television writer who spoke of storytelling in Chapter Seven, tells the story of two especially creative communications efforts involving a coaster and a hearse. They are also good examples of how openings dictate channels. Planned Parenthood in Vermont wanted to deliver a message encouraging condom use for young men. They considered the places where men were thinking about sex, and they decided bars were certainly one location. They chose a channel—coasters—that matched the opening. One side of the coaster read, "Don't Have Sex in the Dark," and the other gave information on AIDS and condom use, along with a toll-free number. Planned Parenthood convinced bar owners to distribute thousands of the coasters, and everyone who ordered a drink got the message placed right in front of them. Local television stations picked up the story.

Goodman also relates the story of sitting in bumper-to-bumper traffic on the Santa Monica Freeway one morning when he was working for a coalition of environmental groups. He suddenly saw in the agony of the morning commute an opening. Here was his target audience, captive in their cars and inhaling exhaust fumes. A few weeks later, he led a mock funeral procession of five hearses on the highway. He'd put billboards on the roof of each hearse with messages about air pollution in Southern California and, on the last hearse, the number of a toll-free line set up by the Environmental Protection Agency to record public comments. Morning radio and local evening news covered the spectacle, and calls spiked nearly 50 percent in a twenty-four-hour period.

There are several lessons here. The first is that openings make channels work. Second, thinking about openings can unleash new creativity in choosing channels. If channels are especially creative, they may even attract news coverage, which adds visibility for a message. Third, all these channels were inexpensive and highly efficient. The help-wanted ad, the coasters, and the hearses all together cost less than designing and printing a typical informational brochure, and they worked better.

⟫⟶ By putting our money and energy into reaching our audiences in open-minded moments, we ensure no precious resources are wasted on efforts that will go unnoticed.

At the beginning of this chapter, we ran through a laundry list of channels from advertisements to Web sites to promotional items.

⟫⟶ Many different channels can be used to deliver strong, well-packaged messages to an audience's location. In choosing the right combination, consider which will be most noticeable to each audience, most distinct from the competition, and most closely matched to each particular audience's open-minded moments.

AVOIDING CHANNEL PITFALLS

With those guidelines in mind, let's examine how good causes typically fall into traps in selecting and using channels. Here are some classic examples.

Using the "General-Public" Approach to Audiences

Because most good causes have limited resources, they have a desire to economize.

⟫⟶ Do not be tempted to try to save money by using one communication tool for all audiences.

IBM doesn't try to sell mainframe computers to me at the same time it's selling me a laptop. It would be a waste of time. Have a distinct audience in mind when choosing the channel and adapt the message to it. In writing a brochure, for example, have only one group of audience members in mind, show them why they should care, and tell them what they should do. Reading a bad brochure feels like listening to a dry lecture to six hundred people from all over the world, while reading a good brochure is like reading a letter someone sat down and wrote just for us.

Conveying Too Many Messages

Closely related to the pitfall of too many audiences is the pratfall of too many messages.

> The number of messages we use is inversely proportional to the number of messages our audience will remember. The more information we throw at them, the less they will retain.

In advertising especially, stick to one clear, unmistakable message and make it the headline. The most famous slogan of all time—"Just do it"—is not coincidentally one of the shortest and easiest to absorb. Decide on the one message needed to communicate in a channel and feature it prominently. Do not fear oversimplification. Once people support our cause, we can fill in the details if they want them.

Failing to CRAM

If we try to say too much, we may end up saying nothing at all.

> Be sure to communicate a strategic message in each chosen channel.

This warning may sound obvious, but a quick review of the average brochure, public-service announcement, or billboard shows how often good causes assume information alone will spur action. They fail to CRAM in a strategic message. In every communication, our audience should feel a sense of connection to the message, be easily able to identify a clear action and reward, and remember it later. Humor is often a way to CRAM quickly. The "small steps" campaign against obesity CRAMs this way. The ads offer a bold reward and a feasible action, and they connect that reward and action to the audience and make it stick in the memory through humor. There is something quite unforgettable about leftover love handles and abandoned thunder thighs.

Mismatching Channel and Opening

As noted previously in this chapter, good causes often invest significant resources in a channel without knowing whether it's the right match for an audience's open-minded moments. A well-intentioned cause may blunder into producing a fifty-page booklet on how to become more physically active for audiences who can't use a book—low-literacy groups, for example, or people whose chief barrier to exercise is a lack of time. Remember channel and opening go together like yin and yang.

➤ Go to where the audience is, psychologically and physically.

For example, visualize a doctor's office. A drug company advertising there tells us to ask our doctor about a new medication in many different ways. We may see a poster in the exam room. The doctor may use Post-it notes with the name of the medication on them. The doctor may even have free samples of the medication to distribute. The channels (posters, Post-it notes, samples) are all matched to the opening—when the patient and doctor are together, thinking about that patient's health. Good causes trying to reach physicians have done the same kinds of things. The Centers for Disease Control and Prevention (CDC) matched channel to opening when it wanted to encourage doctors to treat ulcers as an infectious disease rather than as a symptom of stress. It had been discovered that a bacteria that could be treated with antibiotics causes most ulcers. The CDC created physician fact sheets, waiting-room posters, and consumer brochures about the "good news infection"—a chronic condition that turned out to be curable.

Overrelying on One Channel, One Time

As the above example shows, even within one doctor's office, a message may need to be delivered in several different ways. Within a less confined space, more channels may be required. Although good causes aren't Coca-Cola, with its hundreds of millions of dollars to spend on marketing, we cannot settle on just one communication effort.

> We should use as many channels as we can afford to do well, and we should use them repeatedly. Most people hear a message many times in several different ways before they take action.

Even the smallest community group can communicate its message in more than one way. It can simultaneously post notices on telephone poles, put flyers on doorknobs, create a neighborhood e-mail list, and call people on the telephone.

Overinvesting in Traditional Channels

Because most causes have a brochure, newsletter, or elaborate Web site, we may be tempted to put a lot of resources into these channels. Keeping a newsletter or Web site fresh with new content is highly labor-intensive, so those channels are worth the effort only if they are the best way to reach our audience, and the audience is likely to read or use them often.

→ Good causes have limited resources, so consider alternative outreach vehicles that may have a strong impact but require less time and money.

We shouldn't think we have to use a certain channel just because it's the norm; in fact, if it's the norm, we want to choose a way to stand out from the crowd. Good causes use everything from computer games to wristbands to communicate. We can turn to our partners for advice about new channels and for help in using the channels they already have.

Designing Materials Poorly

Another common mistake is poor execution. A good message matched to the right channel can be rendered useless if it's in a brochure overstuffed with text or on a hard-to-read poster. Most of us aren't professional advertising people or designers, yet we must make decisions about design every day. We may even have to create our own materials. As a result our materials may lack creativity or polish. Sometimes we are too close to our topic to be able to think of original ways to convey our message. If we use outside designers, we may run into trouble if they see working for a good cause as a way to stretch their creative limits. Their agenda is to create interesting and different concepts and materials, a goal that is not necessarily the same as conveying our message cleanly and efficiently. To avoid off-the-mark efforts, prepare a creative brief for the designer. It's a document that profiles the audience and explains the message and packaging. It ensures that the design reinforces the message. Then look at the finished products and ask, Will audiences have to work hard to get the message? If they will, make the materials easier and more enjoyable to digest.

>>>——→   Plain and accessible is better than fancy and inscrutable.

Being Inconsistent

Good writers have a clear voice, and they stick to that voice because it makes their work unique and authentic. Good causes also need to be consistently true to the voice they choose for outreach.

>>>——→   Each communication with an audience should have the same look, feel, and message.

Inconsistent colors, morphing logos, or changing messages dilute efforts to communicate. It's hard enough to break through the clutter and repeatedly deliver a message; having the message or product look different each time is like starting over with each communication. The cumulative effect is lost. If we take the name off our various outreach vehicles, can we tell they are from the same group or organization? Many companies have style guides to ensure that everything from the size of their logo to the quality of the paper they use to the "feel" of outreach vehicles is consistent. Develop some rules of thumb and stick to them.

Designing by Committee, Not Audience

Everyone has an opinion, and when a lot of people with strong opinions contribute to a product, it ends up looking like Frankenstein. Because good causes often operate by consensus, many materials are designed by committee. In the process, they lose their coherence and the audience may be forgotten.

➤   It is hard to circumvent the consensus process, but try to convince colleagues that the tie-breaking opinion in design should be that of the audience.

Our audience research—and the reactions we obtain to materials when we test them—should trump one colleague's distaste for the color yellow or love of a pet phrase. We can finesse this situation quite effectively by praising the opinion of the person in question, whether a board member or a volunteer, and then depersonalizing the situation by invoking the audience. Shrug and say, "I agree with you, putting that quote from Aristotle in the original Greek on the cover is a terrific idea. What a shame our audience just doesn't get it, and what a pity we have to stick to what they can understand."

Not Tracking Results

Lastly, many causes—and many companies, for that matter—use channels without monitoring which are reaping the best results.

➤   If one channel isn't working, change channels or adjust the message and packaging used.

We'll cover this point further in Chapter Ten, but for now, remember that it's useful to track whether the message is being delivered. UPS and FedEx allow us to go online to see when our packages arrive. We can do the same by asking people who take action how they came to make their decision.

HOW TO USE ROBIN HOOD RULE 8

1. Map the "Postal System"

In Chapter Seven, we completed a message; now we want to determine how and when to convey it. Let's diagram the postal system for delivering the message. Draw a table or chart with space for the packaging (mood), the mail handler (messenger), the right destination (moment), and the best delivery vehicle (channel).

2. Set the Mood

Start with the mood. What adjectives come to mind when we think of the personality of our cause? Write them down. Then write down the tone of the message: Is it inspirational, tough, encouraging, stern, or funny? Now write down some adjectives our audiences might use to describe themselves when they are involved in our issue or are close to taking action. We now have three groups of adjectives. Look for terms common to the different sets of descriptors. Is there any overlap? Does a certain mood emerge? The goal is to set the mood that best conveys the essence of our messages while remaining true to ourselves and appealing to our audience.

3. Choose the Messengers

What types of people do we picture saying our message and conveying our mood? For each of the audiences, what combination of moods or messengers would be appealing? We have many choices of messengers: authorities or experts, opinion leaders, likable peers, family and friends. Once we have some good candidates, think about whether they can deliver our messages. Can they provide testimonials? Would they be able or willing to act as spokespeople? Or are we better off just using their language or images to indirectly reflect their endorsement or approval?

4. Identify the Opening

Now determine the places, times, or states of mind in which or during which our audiences will be most receptive. From our audience research, we should have an idea of the circumstances under which our audience is ready to hear our message, needs our benefits, or is able to take action. Who are audience members with at open-minded moments, and what are they thinking and doing? We want to reach them at those moments, rather than plastering our message everywhere. Read the newspaper and watch the news with an eye toward openings. Observe audiences going about their business and visualize when they might need to hear from us. Think about what we've learned about them and their marketplace. Identify the places or times when they make key decisions.

Then take a page from Miller's playbook and own those moments. Shape them according to the cause. The help-wanted campaign made its own Miller Time by redefining a moment of (false) opportunity as a moment of revelation, a moment for unveiling the truth—and thus a time to call a toll-free number.

5. Choose the Channels

Openings dictate channels; so the last step in devising our campaign is to find the vehicles of communication that are most convenient for reaching our audiences in their open-minded moments. Review channels that worked and those that didn't in the past and decide which should be eliminated, modified, or added. Look at partners' channels that could be appropriated. Develop a few wildly creative ideas for reaching audiences. Which channels would cut through the clutter? Revisit the list of pitfalls in this chapter in order to avoid common mistakes. The goal should be to create a list of all the channels that we can afford to do well. That is our starting point. The list should be fluid and not overly prescriptive over time. Marketers have to be opportunistic, and a new channel may be needed for an unexpected, open-minded moment caused by any event from sudden legislative action to breaking news (openings we explore in the next chapter).

6. Test the Message-Delivery System

Now that the message has a package, messenger, delivery time, and vehicle, we should find out whether our postal system works. Testing saves a lot of time and money because it catches flaws we can correct before we misdirect tons of mail. There are several ways to test. A small cause or group of volunteers can informally ask a few people from the target audience how they react to a logo, sign, or speech. Larger organizations can conduct systematic research through focus groups, intercept interviews, mass surveys, or small pilot programs. If possible, both small and large groups should try showing their material amid the competing messages the audience is likely to hear or see. If the vehicle is going to be an ad in a magazine or newsletter, show the ad alongside several other ads to see how audiences react to it in context. If it's a poster, put it on a wall beside other posters.

Remember, the goal is to test the message delivery with members of the target audience, not just friends and family. If the material has to go through gatekeepers to get to the audience, test it with them too. Will they be willing to pass on the message to the right people or to distribute our materials? By simply asking their opinion, we can increase their investment in our message and the degree to which they might support it.

> The point of testing is to learn whether the members of the audience got the essence of the strategic message, and if not, what message did they hear?

Did they feel a connection to the message or get the sense that "this is for me"? Which features drew them in and felt motivating, and which repelled them? Did the message stick in their minds as memorable? What was the best aspect and the worst aspect of the material? Did distracting details or strange images confuse them?

Remember that not every piece of feedback is valid. We don't want to change any part of the material until we've consistently heard people say they don't like it or don't understand it. One person's opinion may be just that. It's also advisable to solicit reactions to feedback from several different people besides ourselves. We all hear different messages according to our own perspective, and we need to take into account our own selective retention.

Every company and cause that has tested messages or run pilot programs has amusing and surprising stories of the lessons they learned. A new ecotourism company tested a logo on me and several other people. Above the company name was a stylized leaf, but that's not what any of us saw. We saw giant lips, like those in the Rolling Stones logo. The company thought it was communicating nature, and we thought it was selling sex, drugs, and rock 'n' roll. Disaster averted.

I was reminded of this gap between what we think we're saying and what is heard when I helped test some messages with a group of doctors. The goal was to encourage them to seek training in palliative care, which is the management of very ill patients' pain and symptoms. The messages created were based on testimonials from doctors who'd attended the training. They said, for example, "This training, in helping patients face life-threatening illness, brings the humanity back in medicine," and "This was why I went into medicine in the first place." When we presented these messages to doctors who hadn't had palliative-care training, the testimonials flopped. "That's Birkenstock medicine," remarked one scornful specialist. Said another, "I went into medicine to cure people, not hold their hands when they die." They were interested in the scientific basis for the training and new breakthroughs in pain and symptom management. Touchy-feely testimonials left them cold. Their feedback caused us to rethink our action and message. It made more sense to encourage them to call a "Birkenstock doc" specializing in palliative care for a patient consultation than to try to turn them into converts. Messages that emphasized the scientific-based, not psychosocial, benefits to patients resonated better than the testimonials.

CONCLUSION

Even with fabulous research in hand, we can have difficulty predicting our audiences' reactions. Look at the process of creating and delivering a message as highly iterative. We learn more and more as we go along, and as we do, we fine-tune our message and how we deliver it. There is no shame in changing course; in fact, adjustments in our direction are to be expected. We want to keep experimenting with the mix of mood, messenger, moment, and channel until we find the combination that works. That winning combination balances the marketing arrowhead and gives it the ability to find our audiences wherever they are, emotionally, physically, or mentally.

Achieving the balance is hard work, but it is well worth the effort because it greatly increases the chances that our message will sail directly into our audiences' minds at the exact moment they're ready for it. We want to keep plugging away until we get to the Miller Time of our issue. It's a great place to be.

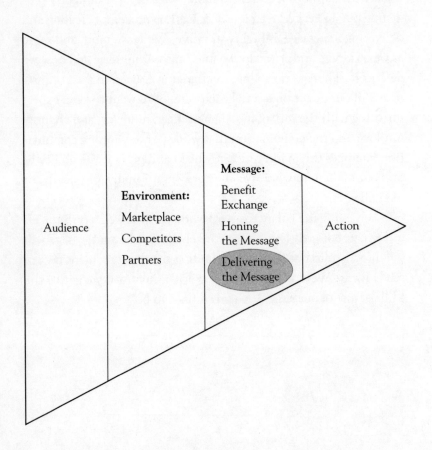

Audience

Environment:

Marketplace

Competitors

Partners

Message:

Benefit
Exchange

Honing
the Message

Delivering
the Message

Action

9

Robin Hood Media Savvy

Approach the Media as a Target Market

WHAT THIS CHAPTER SAYS

- We should treat the media like an audience.

- Most journalists face at least five challenges on a daily basis: they must become instant experts on a mind-boggling array of topics, they have to be fast, they need to be first, they are expected to be accurate, and they are required to tell an interesting story.

- If we understand the challenges and can help reporters cope, we gain a big media-relations advantage.

- To reach members of the media, we need to market to them on two levels. First, we need to establish some sort of psychological common ground with members of the media and offer them incentives for covering our story. Second, we need to sell the story.

- To apply the principles in this chapter: Focus on building solid relationships with a select group of journalists; then pitch them newsworthy stories that advance our cause.

Every chapter in this book has begun with a corporate marketing campaign, but this one will not for a good reason. If we want to truly understand the media and master the art of working with journalists, we should not look to the private sector. We should look to the members of the media themselves. When we enter the mindset of journalists—in the same way that we probe the hearts and minds of our other audiences—we gain the knowledge and insight we need to reach them effectively.

➤ We should treat the media like an audience. We need to learn what they are like, know their values, and identify the kinds of rewards they seek. Then we should appeal to them with that perspective in mind.

Robin Hood Rule 9

Approach the media as a target market, not as a mouthpiece for the message.

The need to market to the media just as we market to any other audience is a powerful yet commonly overlooked concept in media relations. I worked as a journalist for Reuters, Associated Press, and several newspapers, and, in that time, people seldom approached me with a sound understanding of the media or of my needs in covering a story. In fact, most media-relations people—whether they worked for a company or a nonprofit—simply called me up and asked whether I had received their press release or media kit. They viewed the media as a means of getting their message out, not as an audience with a mind of its own.

A small group of media-relations people got it. They built relationships with me and gave me newsworthy information. They contacted me when they didn't need anything to pass on interesting rumors and intelligence. I always took their calls, and I usually listened to them. By taking a similarly audience-centered approach, we too can raise our chances of being featured positively in the media and getting our message heard.

To approach members of the media as an audience, we apply all the marketing principles we've covered in this book. We must connect with them, offer them a benefit exchange, and make our message memorable (in other words, CRAM our message to them). We should then deliver that message in the right tone, at the right time, with the right messengers.

WHY MEDIA RELATIONS?

Although taking a marketing approach to media relations takes time, doing so is worth the investment of effort. The media can play a big role in calling attention to an issue, shaping public opinion, or motivating people to take action.

Consider a well-known analogy. A hiker is walking beside a rushing river and sees people drowning. He jumps in and starts pulling people out of the water one by one. After awhile he gets tired, but more drowning people keep tumbling down the river. Then he sees another hiker passing by and cries out for help. The other hiker looks over but keeps walking, and the first hiker desperately demands to know how he can refuse to help. The second hiker replies that he's going upstream to fix the broken dam that is sweeping people into the water in the first place. The moral is that every problem has immediate solutions ("downstream") as well as longer-term causes ("upstream"). For example, pollution may be contributing to children's asthma in urban areas. Managing the children's asthma attacks by providing them with inhalers is the pressing downstream concern. Upstream, the solution may be to require strict emissions standards for factories in order to clean up the air.

The biggest players in influencing or solving upstream problems are the media and elected officials. This chapter focuses on the media, although it's worth noting that marketing principles can be used also when lobbying political figures. (See Interview 1 at the end of this chapter.) It's worth investing effort in reaching the media with our messages so that we can raise our chances of participating in upstream solutions and gain attention and exposure we could not afford to buy in the form of advertising. We may even succeed in interesting the media in addressing our issue as a part of civic journalism. News outlets have covered race, poverty, and other issues in in-depth series in response to major news events; in the process they engage community members and good causes in the story and the public debates about the issues. Because we are a good cause and not a profit-motivated corporation, we have the potential to win over certain journalists and make them our allies in covering the problems we seek to solve. But to get to that level of exposure, we need to first understand members of the media.

UNDERSTANDING THE MEDIA

Perhaps because I've worked for both the media and nonprofits, I think members of the much-maligned media are not so different from people working on good causes.

‣→ Members of the media tend to be passionate, relentless people committed to what they perceive as a greater good: reporting information. That description—the passionate, relentless pursuit of a perceived greater good—should sound familiar. Many of us share those single-minded tendencies.

In addition, most members of the media are underpaid and underappreciated. They are not compensated like Sam Donaldson or Katie Couric. They work hard for little glory. We, too, know something of that level of commitment.

Let me humanize the media further. Although reporters' ideas of what is important, true, or untrue may not be the same as ours, members of the media usually perceive themselves as trying to fairly tell the story as they see it. Their corporate employers seek to reinforce that image, which is why most media conglomerates describe themselves as reliable centrists. CNN calls itself "the most trusted name in news," while Fox News has trademarked the phrase "fair and balanced."

Many people would not agree: in fact, the most common criticisms I hear of journalists are that they are lazy, sensationalistic, or sloppy. Why do we have that impression? Keep in mind the following.

Most journalists face at least five often competing challenges on a daily basis: they must become instant experts on a mind-boggling array of topics, they have to be fast, they need to be first, they are expected to be accurate, and, above all, they are required to tell an interesting story. These challenges are closely tied to the reporters' values and drive much of their behavior. If we understand the challenges and can help reporters cope, we gain a big media-relations advantage.

Let's take these challenges one at a time. The first is that the members of the media must become instant experts on many issues. When I worked for one wire service, I filed one to three stories a day, seven days a week. I covered everything from a plane crash to a coup d'état to the AIDS epidemic. I sometimes had as little as fifteen minutes to understand an airport's visual flight rules or the difference between the sound of mortar and rocket fire or the incidence of rural maternal-child HIV transmission. Beat reporters also face this challenge. For example, if a journalist covers crime regularly, she may know a lot about the topic, but if a shooting takes place at a school, she needs to gain enough of an understanding of school security and teenage social dynamics to tell a coherent story.

The second challenge is the enormous pressure to be fast. The twenty-four-hour news cycle has created real time pressures for journalists. They must constantly find and report fresh angles to a story. Related is a third challenge: most news organizations not only want their staff to be fast, they also want them to be first with a story. When I worked for wire services, my editors called the bureau soon after I filed big stories to inform me how many minutes and seconds my reporting was behind or ahead of competing news organizations.

The fourth challenge is the need to get the story right, which is often at odds with the pressure to get it fast and first and with the reality that the reporter may not intimately know the subject matter. No matter how thorough the journalist or how talented the editor, this pressure inevitably leads to mistakes. I'm not excusing inaccuracy, but I am pointing out that errors are often less about laziness and more about the challenges of reporting new information in haste.

The last and most important aspect we should understand about news reporting is the quality of the story. At the end of the day, to keep their jobs, members of the media need to tell a good story. As a result, they look hard for conflict, drama, and tension. Those are the aspects of a story that make a gripping novel, and they also get a story on the front page or at the top of the hour. Reporters want to find a protagonist, an antagonist, and an important stake so they can grab the attention of their audiences and sell their stories. If that requirement sounds familiar, it's because the media are CRAMing their stories just as we CRAM marketing messages. Remember, CRAMing means establishing a Connection with the audience, promising a Reward, inspiring Action, and sticking in the Memory. Members of the media have to find a way to make audiences feel connected to a story from the first or second sentence so people will take the action of reading, watching, or listening in return for the reward of information or entertainment. If their work is not compelling and memorable, reporters won't reach their audiences. Their outlets will be out of business. This is yet another natural overlap of journalism and the marketing of good causes: both require an ability to sell a story. When I was a foreign correspondent, I had to CRAM every story well because it's hard to get people far away to care about events unfolding in places like Laos or Madagascar. In marketing work, we also have to convince people to care—in our case, we want them to care about our cause.

This reality and the five challenges we've discussed shape reporters' goals: getting information quickly, out-competing rivals, and telling a good story well. When we understand these goals—and help reporters achieve them—we can begin building relationships with journalists and mastering the art of media relations.

SELLING A STORY

To reach members of the media, we need to market to them on two levels. The first level is establishing a relationship with the media: we need to find some sort of psychological common ground with members of the media and offer them incentives for covering our story. The second level is positioning the story we are trying to convince the media to cover. Think of the first as selling to the reporter and the second as selling the story.

Let's take an example. I once was asked to pitch a story to CNN International about a project to prevent HIV and AIDS in Thailand. That was a tough sell because the story wasn't new. In fact, it was the main health story coming out of Thailand, and every member of the media in Bangkok or visiting Bangkok had covered it. I needed to offer a compelling reason to the CNN correspondent to take an interest (in other words, I needed to sell the reporter), and I needed to prove I had material that would make the story of interest to international viewers (in other words, I needed to sell the story).

I had followed the work of one Bangkok-based CNN correspondent closely for some time. I noticed that he was especially interested in the increasing urbanization and industrialization of Thailand and often produced stories dramatizing the changing face of the country. He also had a sense of humor and often covered quirky angles to stories. Obviously, he also valued good visuals because television was his medium. Because he was a busy man based in traffic-choked Bangkok, I also figured that the closer those visuals were to his home base, the better. These observations told me that if I could frame the organization's AIDS work within the trend of urbanization, I could connect with his interests. Offering an uplifting or amusing visual element would make the story even more attractive for him to cover. In return for covering an AIDS project, he would get the reward of a unique story angle with minimal effort.

Fortunately, I had just the project to profile. My organization was working with garment manufacturers to offer HIV/AIDS education to young women from rural areas who had come to the Bangkok area to work in factories. The women were young, naïve, and away from home for the first time, and they were at high risk of contracting the virus. Through the program, they were asked to attend educational sessions during lunch hours, where they got instruction on preventing the disease and on using condoms. The sessions offered a nice visual for the story.

Then I thought about the story I wanted to tell and the message I wanted the viewers of CNN International to receive. The AIDS crisis in Southeast Asia was well known; in fact it was perhaps too well known. The fact that one apocalyptic story after another was emerging created a sense of helplessness and compassion fatigue in many people, including potential donors, around the world. A positive story showing how an aid agency was addressing the problem was a message more likely to motivate people to support the cause than another dire story.

→ The story we choose to sell should advance our mission. We don't simply want our name in the papers; we want the right message in our audiences' minds.

I pitched the story as a rare piece of good news, and, in order to create a sense of urgency, I emphasized to the reporter that the best footage would be at a training the following week. The correspondent liked my pitch, and he did the story, complete with footage of laughing young garment workers blowing up condoms like balloons and swatting them back and forth to each other. Prevention never looked so fun. The story broke through the clutter because it connected with people's need for some AIDS news that was uplifting and entertaining. It sent the message that supporting such efforts was a way to create good news, and it showed the impact of the project in a memorable way. It met my needs and the reporter's.

This process may sound time consuming, but consider the alternative. In the time it took to learn about the correspondent and shape the pitch, I could have sent out fifty press releases. But it is highly doubtful that any would have resulted in a favorable television story aired in dozens of countries. It's often wise to focus efforts on one influential outlet in this way because if the outlet covers the story, other outlets are likely to take its lead. Local press picked up on the CNN story.

Press conferences and media releases have their place, but they should never come at the expense of building solid relationships with a smaller group of members of the media. These relationships work because journalists need them as much as we do. The relationships that members of the media have with well-placed, well-informed people willing to trade information and able to help them meet the daily challenges of their job enable them to get good, accurate stories first.

As a journalist, I spoke with a few diplomatic sources several times a week; our trading gossip and facts served our mutual need to be informed of political developments. One person in particular proved especially valuable in providing information and quotes to be attributed to "diplomatic sources." On the evening of July 4, 1997, in Phnom Penh, I saw him at the American Embassy's Independence Day party, where the who's who of Cambodia was gathered. It was a rocky time for the country. Tensions had been escalating between the co–prime ministers, and the rumor mill was in overdrive with predictions of an imminent breakdown of the country's fragile coalition government. For political observers, this development was not altogether surprising. If you can imagine George W. Bush and Al Gore having resolved their election dispute by becoming co-presidents of the United States, then you can fathom the tenuous nature of Cambodia's government, which was born out of a UN-brokered compromise after disputed election results.

In fact, at the party, the royalist side of the government was conspicuously absent. Over the blare of Sousa marches, I quietly told the diplomat why only half the government was represented at the event. Co–Prime Minister Prince Norodom Ranariddh had abruptly left the country hours before, and rumors were flying that the other prime minister was poised to take sole power. My source provided an interesting nugget in return. "You see the general over there?" he asked me. "When I spoke with him just now, I said I would see him on the golf course tomorrow, like always. But he said no." The diplomat looked at me over his glasses. "He said he's busy tomorrow." Sure enough, the tanks rolled at dawn the next morning, and Co–Prime Minister Hun Sen seized sole power.

This is a dramatic example, but these exchanges typify relationships with the media. We don't have to give journalists the scoop of the year to have those exchanges. We simply need reasonably relevant, interesting information that meets the needs of the reporter and tells our story.

HOW TO USE ROBIN HOOD RULE 9

1. Decide Which Messages to Place in Which Media

Before we even start to court members of the media or to take their calls we want to decide which messages in which media would best advance our agenda. I can't emphasize this recommendation enough. Public-relations professionals, and I've been one, typically judge success by the number of times an organization is mentioned in the media. But this statistic is fairly meaningless if we have communication aims beyond name recognition. Getting our name in the media doesn't necessarily advance our agenda; getting our message in the media does. We want to selectively approach certain media and carefully craft the responses we give to media calls according to the message we want readers, viewers, or listeners to hear. We also need to remind ourselves to look for openings, the times when our audience is most likely to receive our message. Finding openings will help us prioritize our media targets. We then want to cultivate relationships with the reporters in those media and devise a strategy for handling incoming requests from key media.

2. Cultivate Relationships

We build relationships with members of the media by making their job easier. Remember that they need instant expertise and they want to be first with a good, accurate story. We want to help them on all those fronts. Providing such help requires that we become intimately familiar with the stories our priority media outlets cover and the work of key staff at these news organizations. We want to find out which staff members cover the issues important to us. We want to understand a reporter's individual needs, whether he or she is a science writer for *Time*, an executive editor at the *Topeka Capital-Journal*, a producer at Fox News, or a correspondent for *Living on Earth* on National Public Radio. Reporters have drastically different personalities, interests, and needs, and they attract different readers, listeners, or viewers. They aren't equally receptive to a story on global warming and one about a Kansas State football win. Know each reporter's style, interests, and favorite topics and create short profiles of them. When we interact with them, we can refer to their work and interests. Even jaded journalists are usually flattered to know someone has been following their reporting.

Then add to these profiles over time. Each time a member of the media calls, make a record of the kinds of questions they ask and the type of information they are seeking and file it away for future reference. Invite them to lunch and ask them about the stories they are following. Send them useful bits of information or propose desk-side briefings on topics they follow. Give them well-written fact sheets and background information on key issues that they can keep in their files and use when they need that kind of information. This interaction keeps us updated on reporters' needs while building relationships. It gives us the ability to strengthen our connection with them over time. If we offer them resources with no strings attached, they will likely feel favorably disposed toward us in the future.

3. Pitch Stories

As we build relationships with reporters, CRAMing them as an audience, we also need to be CRAMing specific stories. Public-relations people like to call the process of CRAMing "story pitching." Reporters ask three questions when they are evaluating a pitch: Why now, why is this news, and who cares? If a story is timely and newsworthy but irrelevant to their readers, they won't cover it. If it's newsworthy and relevant but lacks a sense of timeliness or is old, it's probably not going to make the cut. And if it's not newsworthy, it's not a story. Defining *newsworthy* is an incredibly subjective exercise. For *US Weekly*, the kind of sushi that actor Demi Moore ordered at Nobu is newsworthy. To the *New York Times*, it's not remotely interesting. We need to draw on our knowledge of the reporter and the outlet to know the stories that are news.

If we don't have a huge breaking news story—and usually we won't—we can devise other ways to make a story timely, newsworthy, and relevant. Here are some ideas:

- Provide an exclusive. If a media outlet gets an important story first, it may consider it big news because a scoop makes the station or publication look good.

- Make it different. A story that is new, novel, or original is news because it has what a journalist friend of mine calls the "gee whiz" factor, which lands stories on the front page or the top of the hour.

- Involve a big name. In our star-obsessed culture, the involvement of celebrities can add a "gee whiz" factor to a less interesting story.

- Be at the extreme. Any kind of superlative that can be claimed—first, biggest, smallest, oldest—can constitute a "gee whiz" factor.

- Play up the stakes. Most kinds of conflict or controversy are also news. The media love stories with a protagonist and an antagonist and the drama and emotion that they can bring to an issue.

- Be part of the solution. The media are often covering the negative impact of the issues we're seeking to address. We can position our cause as a rare "good news"

story because it's offering a promising solution to a
problem in the news.

- Put a face on the story. A compelling human-interest
angle of any kind is news because journalists are always
looking to put a human face on their stories.

- Make it local. A local angle on a national story is news
to media in our community.

- Provide pictures. A story with great visuals is always
news for television and print media.

4. Designate and Prepare Spokespeople

If we succeed in pitching a story—or if a reporter calls us about a
story—we need to be well-versed in handling interviews. Designate
a spokesperson and train everyone to refer all inquiries to him or
her. Anyone within our cause who comes into contact with the
media should be knowledgeable and trained in key messages and
handling interviews.

When it comes to interviews, remember to prepare, stay on
message, and stay in control. When we prepare ahead of time, we
know our messages, have thought of snappy words to express them,
and have made a list of interesting stories, examples, and analogies
that are suitable to our audience and that illustrate these points. In
the heat of an interview, it's easy to forget this supporting information. We want to compose a mental library that we bring into every
interview. Preparing in this way is easy enough if we have an interview scheduled in advance, but if a reporter calls us unexpectedly,
under deadline to write a story, we have less time for preparation.
Nonetheless, we want to give ourselves at least five minutes to collect our thoughts. Offer to call the reporter back immediately; then
take a few moments to write down the key messages to convey in

the context of the story and prepare some examples, statistics, or analogies that bring the messages to life.

The next requirement is to stay on message. We want to convey just one or two key ideas and not stray from them. State the "headline" idea simply and plainly from the start and reinforce it throughout the interview. Don't disguise it in jargon or highly complex language. Don't panic if the reporter is asking questions that stray from the message. We need to provide answers to media questions, but the answers don't have to exactly match the reporter's agenda. Public-relations people refer to "blocking and bridging," which means using certain phrases to steer the discussion to our message. For example, we can say:

- What's important to remember here is that . . .

- What that means in practice is that . . .

- That's a good point, and it gets back to the key issue, which is . . .

- Let me put that in perspective . . .

- The bottom line is . . .

- I have a story about that . . .

After a bridging statement, we can return to our key messages and illustrate them with colorful stories, examples, or analogies from our mental library. We can practice bridging by imagining the question we most fear being asked and devising an answer that includes a bridging statement.

Staying on message means staying in control and keeping our answers short and to the point. When I was a reporter, I would often use silence to get people off message. A person would answer a question, and I would wait. People feel a need to fill silence, and, by continuing to talk, they often reveal more than they wanted to. In an interview, we want to stop talking if we find ourselves going off message. We want to end our sentence or use bridging statements to go back to our main point.

We can also stay in control by sticking to what we know. If we don't know the answer to a question, we can just say so and offer to find the information. We should speculate only if we're comfortable having donors, supporters, partners, employees, and competitors read those ideas on the front page of the *New York Times*. After all, every remark is always on the record. We can't assume a statement is on background unless we have a long-standing, trusting relationship with a journalist. In interviews, I always imagine my words in print as I utter them. It keeps me alert and cautious.

CONCLUSION

We've covered a lot of "dos" in this chapter, so let's conclude with some "do not's." Avoid the following five media relations sins at all costs:

- Don't call up to ask, "Did you get or use my press release (fax, mailing)?" This is a sure-fire way to annoy journalists busy filing stories and meeting deadlines. Think up a good, newsworthy reason for a follow-up call or don't make one at all.

- Don't push a story that is a poor fit with the media outlet or the journalist. Next to the "Did you get my press release?" call, this is the greatest pet peeve of journalists. We want to research our media targets and tailor our messages to journalists so we capture their interest and don't waste their time.

- Don't write a press release that has no news or that hides the news. The *Washington Post* used to run an entry in the style section called "Annals of Puffery," which quoted the lamest, fluffiest press releases they received. Having our press release quoted in a column like that should be our worst nightmare. We should send press releases when we have real news and put that real news in the first paragraph. Don't make it hard to figure out.

• Don't abuse e-mail. Most reporters now prefer e-mail as a means of contact, but we need to keep some pointers in mind. Use a newsworthy, attention-grabbing subject line so the e-mail will get opened. Personalize the e-mail with the reporter's name. We don't want to put a huge list of reporters in the "to" section of our e-mail or else we'll look like we're sending spam. Keep the e-mail short and to the point, and do not attach files. Most journalists don't like attachments because they take time to open and can be hard to access. Imagine a journalist in a hotel room, waiting precious moments to download our PDF on his or her dial-up connection. Just paste the message or press release right into the e-mail.

• Don't get impatient. The art of media relations requires great stamina because we rarely land on the front page of the paper. Dealing with the media is an incremental process, built on long-term relationships and repeated CRAMing. For that reason it pays to have one person within a cause who is dedicated to media relations, even if those people are part-time volunteers. It's hard to create strong ties with members of the media without consistent personal contact. Just as in a good friendship, we need to stay informed, keep in touch, and cultivate the relationship.

Interview 1
Dating the Media and Playing Crazy Eights with Politicians

Serial monogamist James Browning fell in love with several careers before finding happiness as executive director of Common Cause Maryland and later as a lobbyist for the American Cancer Society. After graduating from college with majors in politics and writing, he worked on Jerry Brown's 1992 presidential bid and then in journalism and publishing in New York City. He turned to nonprofit work, managing a chapter of Recording for the Blind & Dyslexic. He studied creative writing and taught writing to undergraduates. In 2001, fed up with what he saw as government beholden to special-interest groups, he took up a long-held interest, working to reform the way political campaigns are financed. He returned to Common Cause, an organization he first worked for as an eighteen-year-old intern. He worked there four years before joining the American Cancer Society in late 2005.

In his advocacy of "clean elections," government accountability, and ethics reform for Common Cause in Maryland, Browning was frequently quoted in state and regional media. His research inspired an FBI investigation into illegal campaign contributions in Maryland that he credits with stalling the push for slot machines, even while surrounding states like Pennsylvania and West Virginia legalized them. He has exposed dozens of shell companies that exist only to make campaign contributions and skirt laws capping campaign contributions. Tall and angular, he was known for striding around the streets of Annapolis swigging an Odwalla.

Here he shares two of my favorite marketing analogies of all time: the dating game of media relations and the crazy eights of political persuasion.

Q: How is courting the media like dating?

A: We don't want to force things and try to go all the way on the first encounter. We want to establish trust and get a second date and a third. Calling a reporter and leaving three messages on voice mail about a press release sounds desperate. It's the kiss of death. Just as in dating, it's best not to chase someone and pull at their sleeve, but rather to build common ground over time.

One of the ways to do that is to start by planting a seed. I send out some interesting information or provide a great quote. It may not be used right away, but slowly it takes root. Routinely,

I'll put out a press release and it seems to sink like a stone. But then, six months later, a reporter will ask about the issue. I'll say, "Oh yes, we were looking into that last summer, but no one's picked up on the latest with that. If you're interested, I can pass along some details." I'm not the crazy person tugging at reporters' sleeves; I am more of a person doing them a favor. They feel the story is their own and their idea.

You don't want any blind dates. Before returning phone calls from reporters, I'll get on the Web and read everything they've written for the last month or so, to get on their wavelength. Dig up every article a journalist has written or TV story he or she has produced. Know the questions a reporter is likely to ask ahead of time and be ready to answer them in an interesting way. When gambling was before the Maryland legislature, I had in mind all the metaphors—going for broke, being dealt a bad hand, betting on a long shot. When the governor hired a racetrack executive to work on the issue, he claimed it was only to give him "general advice." I said that was like hiring John Glenn and then saying he's not there to help with your moon mission. When I talked about redistricting—one of the most complex and boring issues imaginable—I talked about the shapes of the districts. They looked like a crab, a barbell. I said the maps were so crazy that representatives would have to do crazy things just to be in touch with their constituents. They'd have to ride in a speedboat for an hour to get to people.

Some parts of the state tend to be more conservative or more liberal. I always kept that in mind when speaking to the press there. Common Cause opposed the legalization of slot machines in Maryland. Talking with someone in a conservative part of the state, I'd bring up religious leaders and their opposition to gambling. A liberal publication might be interested in studies of how gambling leads to increases in crime and drug use in minority neighborhoods and increases social inequities.

At the same time, I didn't want to sound overly rehearsed. Reporters, and politicians for that matter, know a canned message when they hear one. They are skeptics because they are used to being manipulated and lied to, all day long. Ernest Hemingway said in the *Paris Review*, "The most essential gift for a good writer is a built-in, shockproof shit detector." Great writers have that radar, and reporters and politicians do too.

Q: How is lobbying politicians like a game of crazy eights?

A: You play a card, the other side plays a card, and you play one back. The whole time you have to match the card that was played previously, by number or by suit. You need to establish a connection from the beginning. I start all conversations with politicians from a shared reference point. The next best strategy to being friends is having a common enemy or competitor. The feeling they should get is that we are on equal terms, even if our knowledge is unequal. When I worked at Common Cause, I was dealing with the Maryland legislature, which meets only three months a year and deals with three thousand bills. Chances are, the politicians I met had not read the bill or testimony I was concerned about, so I had to quickly make them care and put it into context. If you're dealing with a legislature, there is incredible variety in that group. There are people who like technical talk and big words, and there are others who will go to sleep with that style. You have to talk in a way that appeals to them.

I also had to recognize their political realities. One senator told me, "Look, I know you're examining how much money developers give campaigns, but you have to understand I've worked hard to get here so I can serve the people I'm fighting for. Without that money, I can't get elected and that's a disservice to the people I represent." She asked whom I was working for. I told her Common Cause. She said "No, I mean whom do you represent?" I said "I represent my six-month-old baby, whom I want to be able to breathe clean air and not have to keep inside down the road because of ozone levels in the air." For that twenty seconds, I had her attention. She understood, but she also wanted to stay in office.

At the same time you're connecting with politicians, you're playing to win. It's a balance between being friendly and charming but keeping a killer glint in your eye. Every day, politicians are told by lobbyists that if they don't vote a certain way, certain interests will back their opponents and they'll be destroyed. If you don't talk about political life and death, you don't get heard. If they are reminded of a critical newspaper story tracking a colleague's shady campaign contributions, they are more likely to listen than if you don't make the implied threat. They don't want that fate.

Interview 2
Get the Media's Attention

In fall 2000, communications professional Raphael Bemporad, whom we'll get to know better in Chapter Ten, had a small budget but big ideas for promoting the Do Something Kindness & Justice Challenge, an annual event sponsored by his then-employer, Do Something. Each year around Martin Luther King Jr. Day, the national nonprofit encouraged students in grades K–12 to perform acts of kindness and justice for the two weeks following the holiday in honor of Dr. King's memory. For the 2001 holiday, Do Something wanted to involve schools in all fifty states, get local and national media coverage of its event, and build public awareness of its programs. It had two celebrities to help meet the goal: Martin Luther King III and actor Andrew Shue of *Melrose Place*, who cofounded Do Something. Despite this advantage, though, Do Something was faced with the fact that securing media for a Martin Luther King Jr. Day event is very competitive.

Q: How did Do Something overcome the media competition?

A: In analyzing typical coverage of the day, we found that many stories, both national and local, ran on the Monday holiday, but the runup to the holiday garnered little coverage. Do Something took advantage of this opening by working to capture media attention early and often. Months before, the organization began signing up schools; sixteen thousand schools representing four million students agreed to participate. All teachers who signed up were asked to indicate whether they would be willing to be contacted by the media.

At the same time, Martin Luther King III promoted the event in conference calls with education reporters across the nation. We sent an op-ed by King and print public-service announcements to two hundred African American newspapers. Radio public-service announcements were delivered to urban stations and news-talk stations in the top fifty markets nationwide. In November, Ann Landers ran a letter exchange highlighting the opportunity the event presented for teachers.

In January, a full week before the holiday, King and Shue appeared at a school in New York where third and fourth graders were unveiling a mural featuring Dr. Martin Luther King Jr. and other heroes. In a moment perfect for television, the students took a pledge in front of cameras from the local station, promising to act kindly and justly; they then held hands and sang "We Shall Overcome." Afterward, reporters were invited to speak to the young students about the actions they were planning to take to fulfill their pledge.

Every network in New York City covered the story. To multiply that effect, we then sent out a video of the event via satellite to every television station in the country. To provide the ever-important local hook for the national story, in the top seventy-five markets, Do Something and its public-relations partner, Linden Alschuler and Kaplan, gave assignment editors the contact information for all the teachers in the market who were willing to talk to the media.

Q: What were the results?

A: The video feed led to 110 broadcast segments in sixty-four media markets reaching more than ten million viewers. The stories ran all weekend preceding the holiday, when there was no competition from events like marches and church services. The story worked because it had been made timely, unique, visual, local, and easy to run.

In the weeks after the holiday, Do Something chose the "Kindest School in the State" and the "Kindest Student in the State" based on stories submitted to its Web site. Every school was given a sample press release to use when the winners were recognized for their acts of kindness.

For $20,000, we ended up generating 150 million total impressions from print, radio, and television coverage, proving the incredible power of a visual, well-timed story.

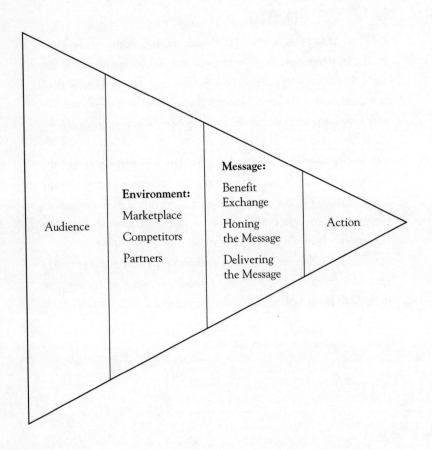

10

Letting Your Arrow Fly

*Execute Campaigns and
Assess Their Worth*

WHAT THIS CHAPTER SAYS

- A marketing campaign is a coordinated, concerted, multichannel effort to get certain people to take an action.

- To apply the principles in this chapter, focus on spurring one audience to a single action. Design a campaign backward from the actions a target audience should take.

- Deliver a message many times, over time, in many forms.

- Stake out a unique competitive position and reinforce a unique image while retaining the flexibility to seize unexpected opportunities.

- Test a campaign before, during, and after its execution.

- Don't forget to market internally. These marketing principles can require a radical reorientation for many good causes. We therefore need to apply the principles we've covered in this book to the people around us and show how our approach matches their priorities.

COME TO MARLBORO COUNTRY.

The Marlboro Man—the iconic centerpiece of one of the most enduring and effective marketing campaigns of all time—rounded up customers like none other. He built his brand into the best-selling cigarette in the world. Half a century after his launch, he's no longer seen in marketing campaigns, yet just a glance at the famous red-and-white logo that appeared with his face or a picture of a Western vista can bring him to mind.

From a public health standpoint we may revile the Marlboro Man, but from a marketing standpoint, we recognize and learn from his enduring success.[1] We can't survive with a white hat alone; we need the marketing prowess of the cowboy. He embodies the essentials of a strong marketing campaign, and our ability to use those elements in our own efforts will determine our ultimate success or failure.

⇒ Good marketing campaigns spell the difference between a lost cause, a noble fight, and a social movement.

A marketing campaign is a coordinated, concerted, multichannel effort to get certain people to take an action. It draws on all the principles we have covered in this book, and it incorporates the entire conceptual arrowhead. The Marlboro Man was the emblematic and most visible aspect of Philip Morris's campaign to get us to smoke their Marlboro brand. But advertising alone is not a marketing campaign. Philip Morris's marketing efforts also extended to how it designed the cigarettes and the packaging, made the cigarettes available to smokers, and set the price.

These broader efforts reflect seven universal principles of a successful marketing campaign. Let's steal them and name them for the movie whose brilliant soundtrack accompanied many of the early Marlboro Country ads: the Magnificent Seven. In this chapter, we discuss each of the Magnificent Seven. These seven principles summarize and synthesize all the ideas and audience-centered arrowheads we've generated in this book. We can turn them into an effective, orchestrated campaign that stretches our limited resources through a keen focus on audience and action.

Robin Hood Rule 10

Good marketing campaigns focus on spurring one audience to a single action.

Hang on to the white hat and grab the reins. It's time to harness Marlboro savvy for purposes more noble than selling cigarettes.

THE MAGNIFICENT SEVEN

1. A Campaign Should Be Designed by Beginning with the Desired Actions

This principle harkens back to our first chapter and the "just do it" approach. Marketing starts by defining a desired action for a specific audience within a marketplace and plans backward from there. That's why our marketing arrowhead has action at its tip. The marketing campaign's driving purpose is to prompt the action at the point of our arrow by making that action seem easy, desirable, and even fun. In Philip Morris's case, the desired action was straightforward: getting people to buy Marlboro cigarettes instead of another brand. The marketing campaign then showed people how making that choice was physically and psychologically feasible. The early cowboy ads claimed that the Marlboros "make it easy to change to a filter" because of their great taste and reasonable price.

2. A Campaign Must CRAM from the Perspective of the Target Audience

➤　Good campaigns are grounded in the perspective of the audience they are intended to reach.

As we discussed in Chapters Two, Six, and Seven, this audience perspective then becomes the basis for forging connections with the people we want to reach, offering them a compelling benefit exchange, and sticking in their memories.

Let's think of how the Marlboro campaign took its audience into account. Imagine we're back in the 1950s. Americans have been enjoying cigarettes for a long time without many worries, but now they are starting to hear about the bad health effects of smoking. The popular *Reader's Digest* already has called attention to the potential toll in an article in 1942, and in 1957, it will publish an article linking smoking to cancer. People who smoke are in a fix. They like their habit and they can't easily stop, even if they know it's bad for them. They begin wondering whether they can mitigate health risks by choosing a different cigarette. They begin to think about switching brands or using filters.

Philip Morris, the smallest of six major tobacco companies at the time, decides to launch its own filtered cigarette in response to this shift in popular opinion.[2] It wants to go after men who smoke but who are worried about the health effects. The cigarette maker decides to revive a defunct brand that faltered the decade before: Marlboro. (Marlboro was named after the street where Philip Morris's London factory was located—Marlborough.) The brand dates back to the 1920s, when Marlboro was billed as a refined, luxury product for the "elegant lady" who wanted a cigarette as "Mild as May."

Philip Morris has chosen an audience and added a filter to its product to meet the audience's needs, but now it has the marketing challenge of remaking the old "Mild as May" image for men of the

1950s. The company calls on legendary adman Leo Burnett to figure out how to handle this challenge. Burnett recognizes right away
the problem that the filter and the brand history present: the mak-
ings of a sissy combination that alienates the target market. Burnett
asks a copywriter for the most masculine symbol imaginable and gets
the reply, "A cowboy." Seizing on that answer, Burnett finds a picture of a cowboy and slaps on the slogan "Delivers the goods on flavor." Within twenty-four hours, the Marlboro Man is conceived,
created, and born. No research, but great instincts.

The Marlboro Man hits the Texas market in 1955 in a test, and
then goes national after early success in Texas with various tattooed,
rugged, and macho men who aren't cowboys, including fishermen
and guys who tinker with cars. "The filter doesn't get between you
and the flavor!" ads proclaim. Sales of the cigarettes grow incredibly fast. In 1957, the year *Reader's Digest* comes out with its second
article, Philip Morris is selling three times as many Marlboros each
day as it did in all of 1953.

The cigarette maker knew its audience, and it CRAMed accordingly. The male smoker was told he could get the perceived
benefit of lower health risk with filters yet not have to compromise
on flavor—or masculinity for that matter. The cowboy helped sell
that message by establishing a connection to the audience on a profound emotional level. In the increasingly complex United States,
he was the symbol of an ideal, simpler time, when a man was a man
and a smoke was a smoke. He evoked the qualities Americans
prided themselves on—freedom, individualism, open spaces, and
(ironically) fresh air. The cowboy, the ideas behind him, and the
accompanying images were also memorable because they were already part of Americans' collective memories. Philip Morris simply
appropriated the American West for its brand in the same way
Miller named Miller Time. Philip Morris and Miller took the expeditious route of naming memories already in their audiences' minds,
rather than creating new ones.

Marlboro Man creator Burnett, also known for the more benign figures of Tony the Tiger and the Jolly Green Giant, said ad writers, before they create copy, must be able to turn themselves into their customers and then say, "Here's what we've got. Here's what it will do for you. Here's how to get it." The Marlboro Man campaign reflected that thinking in a coordinated and consistent way across the marketing spectrum: with the formation of the product, in its advertising, through its reasonable price, and even in its packaging, which still features the original, individualistic red color.

3. A Campaign Must Be Inescapable

Good marketing campaigns are hard for the target audience to escape. Think of how many times and ways the Marlboro message has been conveyed over the years. The target audience can't help but take it in.

> To succeed marketing campaigns must deliver a message many times, over time, in many forms. A few ads do not constitute a campaign. We need to concentrate our marketing efforts, or they won't have an effect.

Unfortunately, most of us don't have huge marketing budgets at our disposal. We can't afford to target the general public, nor should we. We can do more with less and make our message inescapable by narrowing our audience and reaching them only when they are most receptive to our message. Recall the importance of market segmentation (Chapter Two) and open-minded moments (Chapter Eight). Marlboro targeted male smokers in a moment when they were worried about health risks and then repeated its message in many locations, from the mainstream media all the way to the point of purchase.

Repetition is key, but for some reason even experienced marketers seem reluctant to embrace it. We want continuity across the marketing campaign to create the consistent, steady drumbeat that is so essential to getting attention for our message. We should repeat the message in a similar way across the entire range of channels that we use. Don't be tempted to change a successful campaign out of boredom. It's highly unlikely that busy audiences daily bombarded with many different messages will share a feeling of overfamiliarity with the same old approach.

➤ If we have a strong, tested, audience-centered approach, we should stick with it so it has a chance of taking hold and producing an effect.

4. A Campaign Should Stake Out a Unique Competitive Position

Our marketing campaigns vie for attention with many other marketing campaigns, so we have to draw on the principles of competition from Chapter Four to make sure the campaign we create not only reinforces the unique competitive position we want to stake out but also stands out from other campaigns.

➤ The campaign should clearly reflect our unique selling proposition.

Marlboro's competitive position was "the manly filtered cigarette," which was solidly reinforced by the cowboy. The look and feel of the campaign was unique in its market.

As the individualistic cowboy shows, being competitive does not mean copying our competitors' moves, but rather differentiating ourselves from those competitors in the eyes of our audience members. It can be tempting to jump into "me too" marketing, as so many causes did when they created their own versions of the Lance Armstrong Foundation Live Strong yellow wristbands. But if we can't be the first, it's better to stake our own ground rather than to mimic the leader. We should be the campaigner leading the herd, not another cow in the crowd. If we find ourselves among the herd and we can't seem to break out, then we should partner with a leader. Good causes need allies to win their fight, and as we discussed in Chapter Five, unusual allies are sometimes the best friends we can make.

5. A Campaign Should Be Emblematic of the Cause and Extend the Brand

In making clear the competitive advantage of our product or service, the marketing campaign is defining our cause in the eyes of our audience. It is projecting who we are, what we do, and why our task is important. Therefore the campaign needs to be true to our cause.

⇒   A marketing campaign should be emblematic of our brand and reinforce it.

What do we mean by our brand? The Interview at the end of this chapter describes branding in detail, but the bottom line is that a brand is what we stand for in the hearts and minds of our audience. It's how people distinguish us from the rest of the crowd.

We have a brand whether we like it or not, and our audiences' every interaction with our cause has the potential to strengthen or weaken our brand. If we're doing a good job of branding, we are creating an increasingly solid relationship with our audience over the long term. Philip Morris's campaign defined a new brand. In replacing the old, feminine, "Mild as May" brand with a new, manly one, the company refined its product and captured a new place in people's hearts and minds.

6. A Campaign Must Be Flexible

Marketing campaigns are in sync with the marketplace, which shifts all the time, as we discovered in Chapter Three. Campaigns must be sensitive to those dynamics. If we fail to retain that flexibility, we may discover we're as irrelevant as a man in tights and clothes from another era (our beloved Robin Hood) running through Central Park.

➤ An opportunistic spirit, a keen sense of open-minded moments, and a willingness to change with the times make the difference between good and great campaigns.

The filtered Marlboro cigarette was a response to the marketplace. If Philip Morris had not changed its product, it would have eventually lost huge market share. *Reader's Digest* was talking about the health toll of smoking, and smokers were turning to filters. The company saw the writing on the wall. Once the brand was launched, the marketing campaign evolved over time in response to other marketplace forces. At first, the campaign featured not just cowboys but other rugged types. But because the cowboy resonated best, Philip Morris dropped the other characters. The company tapped many real-life cowboys to star in its ads over the years. Then it introduced Marlboro Country, with its sweeping Western vistas and Magnificent Seven soundtrack. Philip Morris expanded beyond Marlboro Reds to other products under the brand. It courted women. In this way the marketing campaign evolved while remaining consistent with its brand, and even though we no longer see the cowboy around these parts, Marlboro thrives.

➤ Good marketing campaigns are well planned, but they are also flexible. We want to always have one eye on the arrowhead and the other on the horizon. The most perfect plan on paper can be rendered useless if the world has changed while we've been busy refining it. Sometimes it's better to be ready than to be right.

7. A Campaign Should Be Tested Many Times

Good campaigns are tested before they happen, while they are happening, and after they happen.

Pretesting, or piloting, a first version of a campaign increases the chances that our final effort will resonate with its audience. The Marlboro Man was launched in Texas before it went national. Once a campaign is up and running, we should gauge whether it is working in order to make any necessary mid-course corrections. We need to set up a feedback loop that tells how we're doing. Then, after the campaign is over, we should assess which parts of it worked. We want to promote our success and learn from our failures. We need to be going back to our audiences over and over. We never want to stray too far from them. What are they thinking? How are they feeling? How are they reacting and why? By checking in with them, we can determine whether our campaign is moving us progressively closer to our marketing goal. That responsiveness to our audiences is key to retaining those we win over, as well as reaching new supporters.

We should approach evaluation with some caution however. We tend to conduct postmortem dissections of campaigns in order to try to discover which elements resulted in success. Was it the mass-media or the telemarketing piece or the distribution of brochures in doctors' offices? The problem with this dissection is we end up staring at a lot of cut up body parts. It's as though we're at an autopsy and are asking, "Which body part made this person live?" But we can't easily point to one sole part that by itself gives us breath and thoughts and motion. When we're dealing with human behavior, we face the same problem: it's hard to single out the one element that caused success or failure.

The question we want to answer in evaluation is not which part made the body on the table live, but rather how to keep the body alive in the first place. We want to view our campaign as a living, breathing creature that requires testing, tending, and care in order to thrive. Are there any congenital problems with our campaign that require surgery? Has a bone been broken? These problems we can understand and fix.

At the same time, we should be doing some checkups on ourselves. Are we consistent and on schedule? Is our team prepared and energized? Are we working toward the same goal? We can't easily keep our campaign in good health if we're under the weather ourselves.

CAMPAIGNING ON A SMALL SCALE

Let's take an example of the Magnificent Seven in action. This last example of the book is different from the others because it has to do with grassroots political organizing. I chose this example to emphasize how broadly useful the Magnificent Seven principles are. They are just as applicable to lobbying the town council or city government as they are to selling cigarettes, and they are just as useful on a local scale as they are in a global advertising campaign.

In Chapel Hill, North Carolina, in the 1990s, a group of citizens was unhappy with the stance of the majority of the town council on its policy toward growth and environmental issues. The citizens felt they weren't getting heard when they advocated for careful growth and preservation of green spaces, which they felt most voters preferred. They set goals: they wanted to raise their own profile in order to increase pressure on the town council to vote differently, and they wanted to galvanize popular support for more green-minded candidates in the next election. They had a clear marketing goal based on audience action—the first of the Magnificent Seven.

Diane Bloom, a leader of the group and not coincidentally a market-research expert, and her fellow activists decided to create a campaign. They felt that if done right, a campaign would bring several benefits: it would unite like-minded people under a shared brand, win increased attention to the issues, and mobilize citizens to vote for change. A campaign with one message would have a far greater impact than a group of individuals speaking about different aspects of the issue. "We began thinking of names . . . , and an early idea was 'Take Back the Town.' But we decided that was too negative. One of our members had just been to a car dealership and had seen a customer service slogan that said, 'Demand Better.' We liked that—it was a good umbrella name for a range of issues," Bloom says.[3] Demand Better was born.

To connect and CRAM with like-minded citizens (our second principle), the group decided to hold an event that would get the attention of the public and the local media. They organized a Demand Better march that would start at the downtown post office and proceed on a Sunday afternoon to the town hall. More than one hundred people agreed to participate, and the organizers contacted local media.

That Sunday afternoon, activist speakers surrounded by sign-carrying supporters stood on the post office steps and laid out the Demand Better stance on local development. Everyone wore Demand Better buttons. The organization also made good use of humor. Groups that had devised new lyrics to popular songs sang "Where has all the green space gone?" "Bring back community power to me," and "Walk on the wild side." Someone carried a coffin symbolizing lost green space. A dog was draped with a poster saying "Chapel Hill is going to the dogs." When they reached the town hall, the marchers arranged their signs inside the building and served refreshments. "We made it creative so people would notice, and we made it fun so people would want to participate," says Bloom. Not surprisingly, local television stations, radio stations, and newspapers liked the colorful approach and covered the highly photogenic and melodic event. A small group of activists were able to greatly amplify their message to the public and make it inescapable.

The group kept up the pressure, reflecting the third principle: be inescapable. The following day, the organizers attended the town-council meeting and pointed out that the town manager had thrown away their sign display, generating another news story. The council found that the public's right to due process had been violated and later passed an ordinance that permitted the display of banners and props in the town hall.

When the Demand Better group members spoke on a given issue to the council, they agreed to conclude their comments with a common call to action so the council, the public, and the press would hear the same message over and over. They also wore Demand Better buttons, as well as pins with the town logo with a

"NO" over it. "If you pass this, Chapel Hill as we know it will be gone" was the message. The orchestrated campaign reinforced the group's unique position in people's minds (the fourth principle) and extended the Demand Better brand over time (the fifth principle). The consistency of the message created the impression that many people were behind Demand Better, and the group was increasingly viewed as reflecting mainstream opinion.

As the group's work evolved, it began creating alternatives to town policy proposals. Group supporters were enlisted in developing alternative proposals for the council. "We didn't just want to be naysayers. We wanted certain proposals that we opposed off the table, but we always replaced them with our own proposals," says Bloom. That approach provided council members with an attractive political option. Rather than simply being lobbied to vote no, they were given a well-thought-out policy or development alternative. One of the first policies the group took on was a proposal to shorten the development review process by curtailing citizen involvement. Demand Better members recommended another option: an early concept review that preserved public participation. A modified version of this proposal was adopted by the council.

Flexibility and responsiveness to political developments (the sixth principle) ensured that Demand Better's agenda stayed before the town council. The close contact among the activists ensured that the campaign also stayed responsive to those it represented, reflecting the last principle of the Magnificent Seven. The group scored some key victories in regard to town policy and succeeded in the next election in adding new council members who reflected the group's priorities better than the previous council members.

INTERNAL MARKETING

For Demand Better, a key to success was its tireless efforts to keep all members united and in line with the same key messages. It is important not only to market to all our external audiences, including our target segments, our partners, and the media, which we've discussed at length, but also to market to those within our cause. But rallying everyone around the same marketing goal and approach can be difficult. Good causes typically make decisions within their consensus-reliant cultures by striking a compromise. For marketing, that is a disastrous approach. Good marketing campaigns are driven by the marketplace and the values of the target audiences, which are all outside—not inside—the cause. To paraphrase a famous phrase from corporate America, the audience is always right. Our audience, not our own compromise position, should determine our direction.

For many good causes, marketing can require a radical reorientation. Focusing on the audience can constitute a different way of doing business, and doing so will bother anyone invested in the status quo. So we need to apply all the principles we've covered in this book to the people around us. We can't tell them they should take a fresh approach to marketing because it's the right thing; we must show them how our approach matches their priorities.

Once we've won them over to our marketing approach, we can keep our internal audiences on our side over time in two ways. The first is by involving them in our marketing efforts. The more people feel they are a part of those efforts, the less likely they are to resist them. Be sure everyone from board members to front-line workers understands audience members and how to connect with them. Ask them to help in setting marketing goals. Keep them fully updated at every stage of a campaign. Be open about challenges and how they will be addressed, so they understand why changes are made. Get them involved in deciding how to reinforce the cause's brand through their own work.

The second approach is sharing credit for success. When determining marketing goals, set some interim goals to manage expectations and to ensure that there are early victories to collectively celebrate. It's hard to argue with success, especially if people feel they helped contribute to it. Internally promote every bit of progress, and recognize the people who made it possible. If we help people feel good about themselves, they will feel good about us.

HOW TO USE ROBIN HOOD RULE 10

1. Complete an Arrowhead for Each Audience

The first step in creating a marketing campaign is to synthesize the suggestions in the previous nine chapters by completing our marketing arrowhead. For each audience map the following:

- The specific action at the point of the arrowhead

- The audience values at the base of the arrowhead

- The environment surrounding the audience, including marketplace forces, competitors and our competitive positioning, and partnerships

- The message we want to deliver, including the benefit exchange, the CRAMed message, message packaging and delivery, and preferred channels and media targets

2. Check the Campaign Against the Magnificent Seven Principles

Once we have an arrowhead for each audience, we have all the essential elements of a marketing campaign. Double-check them against the seven principles in this chapter:

- Is there one specific and feasible action per audience?

- Are we CRAMing from the perspective of a well-defined audience?

- Is our campaign taking advantage of our audiences' open-minded moments and numerous channels so it is inescapable?

- Does our competitive position stand out in this environment?

- Are we reinforcing our brand identity?

- Does our campaign have enough flexibility to seize unexpected opportunities?

- Have we tested our campaign sufficiently and are we poised to measure its success?

3. Avoid the Three Great Sins of Marketing

Marketing campaigns that fail typically stumble in one or all of three areas. As we launch our marketing efforts, we want to avoid these common mistakes at all costs.

The first sin is falsely assuming that information results in action. It is the single deadliest and most common mistake in marketing good causes, and it's easy to make.

⫸⟶ It's tempting to assume that if people have information, they will act on it. But sadly, information doesn't prompt action.

Would Marlboro have become such a popular cigarette if Philip Morris had simply run an ad saying "here is a new cigarette and you should smoke it"? We know it wouldn't have, but when we are creating our own campaigns, we frequently assume that an appeal like that will work. We might assume that if we tell parents that it's important to read to their children, they will. Or we think that if we tell people eating more fruits and vegetables makes them healthier, they will change their diet. Or we imagine that if we tell people that exercise will make them lose weight, they will work out. Or if we tell people a lot of needy people require help, we assume they will give money.

Unfortunately, information does nothing on its own to inspire action. The problem is not a lack of desire. People want to be better parents, healthier eaters, or more generous givers. The problem isn't ignorance. People know that they need to read to their children, change their diets, exercise, or help others. The problem is, it always seems more difficult to change than to stick to business as usual. Good causes are forever in conflict with the status quo. To win this battle, we need first to create a personally compelling reason for taking action that is far better than the reward of sticking to the status quo. Second, we need to make it much easier to take action than to do nothing. In marketing terms, we need to improve our reward and lower our price. The examples of successful approaches throughout this book are not based on information dissemination; they stem from great rewards and feasible actions.

Think back to the Marlboro Man. Ads for antismoking causes mocked him for years by showing him as emphysemic, impotent, or ill with cancer. The ads were clever, but were they as effective in getting people to quit smoking as the Marlboro Man was in getting people to take up smoking? No, and not because smokers want to keep smoking—studies show that most want to quit. The problem is that it's so much harder to stop than it is to start. Only 2.5 percent of smokers successfully quit for good each year.

The second sin is forgetting that we're not the audience. In identifying those great rewards and feasible actions, we often fall back into another old pattern—seizing on the rewards and actions that appeal to us. We make decisions without consulting with our audiences. An action that seems rewarding to us or easy for us to accomplish is probably not rewarding or easy for our audiences. Every assumption we have should be suspect until we understand our audiences' mind-sets.

➤ We are not our target audience. When we assume our audience thinks the way we do, we are at odds with the principles of marketing. We must think like the people we want to reach if we want to succeed.

The third sin is treating marketing as an afterthought. Marketing, and its subset of communications, are often tacked on to a good cause's efforts at the last minute. For example, do-gooders may spend a lot of effort developing a strategic plan and then throw in a section about marketing at the end.

➤ In treating marketing as an afterthought, we deprive ourselves of the great benefits that marketing can bring to all our work. A marketing mind-set can help us design more effective projects, better meet the needs of people we want to help, win us more resources and support, and motivate people to act.

When we fail to incorporate marketing into the earliest stages of our work, we're often left to market a product or idea that is so far removed from our audiences' interests and reality that no amount of sales savvy can get people to buy. Money for marketing should be a part of every grant proposal and budget. If money is a problem, find a corporate sponsor or pro bono help. Stretch dollars by targeting audiences and reaching them in open-minded moments. Skimping on marketing means we will end up skimping on impact.

CONCLUSION

Marketing causes with corporate savvy is no longer a fringe pursuit but an accepted necessity in much of the nonprofit world. This approach is taught in business schools, and the American Marketing Association has even established a foundation devoted to building the marketing capacity of a range of good causes. All these efforts mean we can expect increased success. Our audience-focused, action-based approach will take our causes far. Anticipate and prepare for that success. Ask: Will we be ready if we generate high demand for the product we're selling or promoting? What steps will we take to meet the demand? Preparation is absolutely critical. If we fail to provide the product or service we promised, we'll be worse off than if we'd never gotten anyone interested in the first place.

At the same time that we're enjoying our accomplishments and their effects, though, we must stay humble. We can't forget that all of us have many options for spending the precious time we are given in this short life. Therefore we should feel an obligation to provide a very good case for why people should devote some of their life to taking the actions we're asking for. If we can't make that case competently and convincingly from their point of view, then we should leave people alone.

The people who have done the most to make the world a better place have been among the most humble to ever walk on this earth. They thought of others before they thought of themselves. There is great power in that practice. Each glimpse of the world beyond ourselves gives us a clearer vision into the actions that will change that world for the better. May you have many of those glimpses, much of that vision, and many victories in your pursuit of a greater good.

Interview
The Branding Solar System

Raphael Bemporad is a marketing strategist whose early love of philosophy serves him well in searching for the beliefs that shape an organization's brand. If philosophy—his undergraduate major—is the pursuit of understanding the universe, then branding in his eyes is the pursuit of understanding the universe of a good cause's identity. "Most people see communications as the sun and branding as an outlying planet, but branding should be the center of the solar system," he says. "It is how you stand out, build relationships, win loyalty, and inspire action." His firm, Bemporad Baranowski Marketing Group, counsels a wide range of corporations and causes in how to create and cultivate winning brands based on this holistic view.

Bemporad got his professional start working for a firebrand communicator in the political universe, Governor Ann Richards of Texas. After several years in the Texas political scene, he went on to manage communications for the national nonprofit Do Something before cofounding his own firm.

His business partner is Mitch Baranowski, whom he met when they were both teaching assistants for the same professor of utopian literature at the University of Texas at Austin. Their visionary professor may have inspired their lifelong pursuit of a greater good, but their approach is anything but idealistic. They believe in the proverbial reaching for the stars, but only if that hopeful grasp comes from solid grounding in an audience's reality.

Q: Branding is one of the more nebulous marketing concepts out there. How do you get a handle on your brand and shape it for the better?

A: At the end of the day, you will be able to stand for only one thing—if you're lucky—in the mind of your audience. That one idea is your brand. It needs to powerfully represent who you are and differentiate you from everyone else. It contains the unique message and image that meets the needs and aspirations of the audience and leads them to action.

When we help causes, we go through a series of steps to get to that one idea. We begin by asking a cross-section of stakeholders to articulate their vision in words—verbs and adjectives that describe who they are and what they want to accomplish. Then we think about all the key audiences who have the power to help the good cause fulfill that vision and ask what they want and what motivates them. We get to the benefit exchange. Next we figure out how to move that exchange forward in the context of various constraints, competitors, and the marketplace as a whole by putting these ideas in front of the audiences. If an organization has few resources, this step can be as simple as e-mailing a questionnaire or conducting a survey through surveymonkey.com. We ask: How would you describe this organization to someone else in one sentence and one word? How is it unique? How has it affected your life or that of others? What misconceptions do you perceive about the organization, and how can they be overcome?

Then we begin to piece together a clear idea of how to articulate an organization's unique value proposition. We create a branding brief that details the challenges, opportunities, and essence of what the organization is, what it does, what it believes, why it matters, and how a person can get involved with it. We look at the emotional and rational sides of the brand and create a platform with messages and supporting points. At the end, we also have a series of tagline options that sum up all of this in a phrase.

Q: So, from your perspective, branding is not simply a name or logo but rather the way others experience our marketing and everything that makes up the marketing arrowhead.

A: Yes. The brand is the substance of the arrow. It's the flint.

Q: How does branding work in practice?

A: We worked to rebrand an organization called the Center for a New American Dream, which was trying to promote the idea of acquiring quality in life rather than acquiring a large quantity of things. The Center had a range of programs that helped Americans live consciously, buy wisely, and take action in their communities. The way the Center expressed its mission was to ask Americans to resist the "more is better" mantra, and they stressed the costs of our consumption-based society—stress, pressure, debt, and bankruptcy. Even if people agreed with this mission, and a growing number of people did, it was expressed in way that created anxiety and stress rather than relief and inspiration.

To help break out of a negative frame, we asked the most active members how they benefited from the Center's programs, and they said the programs had helped them get more of what matters in life: more time with their children, more fairness in the marketplace, more beauty in their neighborhoods, and more fun with friends and loved ones. We used this insight to shift the message from "the costs of consumption" to "how to get more of what matters in life." Their newsletter, once called "Enough!" became "In Balance." The new logo has a highlighted "I" in "American," which visually emphasizes the "I dream" within "New American Dream." It conveys energy and life.

In short, we went from saying no to yes, from stop to start, and from less to more. With this approach, the organization has more than doubled its membership, from thirty thousand to over seventy-five thousand. When funders saw the new materials, the organization secured significant financial commitments right off the bat. A contest on the Web site to create a new slogan for their hybrid-vehicles campaign (with the prize being a Prius) got thirty-five thousand entries and more than three hundred thousand votes.

The new brand positioning helped resolve a problem that was holding the organization back. It was an incredibly intelligent, successful organization with programs that worked, but a disconnect existed between the language the organization used and the values it was trying to bring to life. "More of what matters" was a powerful, positive, clear, and compelling way to describe the organization's goals. The branding exercise wasn't about changing the organization but rather about elucidating the core of its uniqueness. The organization had the substance to back up that new slogan too. That's a law of branding: being authentic. You have to walk your talk or else your claims will make an impact but then fall apart soon after.

Q: What are the branding laws you advise good causes to follow to build a strong brand?

A: We've found that most successful organizations follow five laws of branding.

First is the law of the word. Own a word in the mind of your audience that differentiates your organization from all others. It must be a clear, simple word that no one else owns.

Second is the law of focus. The power of a brand is inversely proportional to its scope. Identify the one thing you do better than anyone else, and focus your brand on that unique value proposition.

Third is the law of leadership. Successful organizations are perceived as being the leaders at what they do. How can your organization be the first to develop a unique approach or service? What is the category in which you can uniquely claim leadership?

Fourth, as I mentioned, is the law of authenticity. Does your brand truly reflect who you are and what you do? Is it relevant to your clients and the community you serve? Authenticity is the proof behind your promise.

Fifth is the law of consistency. Trends come and go, but brands should stay the same. A brand cannot get into the mind of your audience unless it is communicated clearly and consistently over time.

NOTES

INTRODUCTION:
LOST IN SHERWOOD FOREST

1. P. K. Marmor, "Legends: The Robin Hood Pages," http://www.legends.dm.net/robinhood (accessed June 2005).

2. INDEPENDENT SECTOR, *Giving and Volunteering in the United States 2001* (Washington, D.C.: INDEPENDENT SECTOR, 2002).

3. INDEPENDENT SECTOR, *Employment in the Nonprofit Sector* (Washington, D.C.: INDEPENDENT SECTOR, 2004).

4. G. D. Wiebe, "Merchandising Commodities and Citizenship on Television," *Public Opinion Quarterly,* 1952, *15, 679–691.*

5. P. Kotler and G. Zaltman, "Social Marketing: An Approach to Planned Social Change," *Journal of Marketing,* 1971, *35*(7), 3–12.

CHAPTER ONE: THE HEART
OF ROBIN HOOD MARKETING

1. See http://www.nike.com/nikebiz/nikebiz.jhtml?page=4.

2. A good summary of the "Just do it" campaign is available from the Center for Applied Research, http://www.cfar.com/Documents/nikecmp.pdf (accessed June 2005).

3. E. Aronson, *The Social Animal* (New York: Worth, 2004), pp. 106–107. The study that Aronson cites was H. Zukier, "The Dilution Effect: The Role of the Correlation and the Dispersion of Predictor Variables in the Use of Nondiagnostic Information," *Journal of Personality and Social Psychology*, 1982, *43*, 1163–1174.

4. Aronson, *The Social Animal*; R. B. Cialdini, *Influence: Science and Practice* (Boston: Allyn & Bacon, 2001).

5. Cialdini, *Influence*, pp. 65–67.

6. P. Kotler, *Marketing Management* (Upper Saddle River, N.J.: Prentice Hall, 1994), p. xxv.

CHAPTER TWO: ROBIN HOOD RECONNAISSANCE

1. Aronson, *The Social Animal*; Cialdini, *Influence*.

2. Aronson, *The Social Animal*, p. 305.

3. P. K. Mitchell and others, *Social Marketing Lite* (Washington, D.C.: Academy for Educational Development, 2000).

4. D. Dorsey, "Positive Deviant," *Fast Company*, Dec. 2000, p. 284.

5. N. Weinreich, *Hands-On Social Marketing* (Thousand Oaks, Calif.: Sage, 1999).

6. The idea of the transformative nature of being seen and understood was discussed in Heinz Kohut's 1959 paper "Introspection, Empathy, and Psychoanalysis," presented at the Twenty-Fifth Anniversary Meeting of the Chicago Institute for Psychoanalysis. The description in this paragraph of how the psychiatrist elicits information from a patient is based on an interview with Professor Jeffry J. Andresen, M.D., Dallas.

CHAPTER THREE: THE VILLAGE SQUARE

1. M. Smith, *Wolves Eat Dogs* (New York: Simon & Schuster, 2004).

CHAPTER FOUR: ALL FOR ONE
AND ONE FOR ALL—WE WISH

1. The Gold Toe story here is based on a Gold Toe case study in *America's Greatest Brands 2004*, American Brands Council, http://www.superbrands.org/usa.

2. A. Ries and J. Trout, *Marketing Warfare* (New York: McGraw-Hill, 1997).

3. J. Levinson, *Guerrilla Marketing: Secrets for Making Big Profits from Your Small Business* (New York: Houghton Mifflin, 1998).

4. INDEPENDENT SECTOR and Urban Institute, *The New Nonprofit Almanac and Desk Reference* (San Francisco: Jossey-Bass, 2002).

5. D. La Piana, *Play to Win: The Nonprofit Guide to Competitive Strategy* (San Francisco: Jossey-Bass, 2005), p. 22.

6. Clausewitz.com, a Web site run by Chris Bassford, discusses the writings of the Prussian general with in-depth understanding, context, and nuance, including discussion of von Clausewitz's famous work *On War*.

7. Kotler, *Marketing Management*, p. 225.

8. Ibid.

9. Ibid.

10. A. Ries and L. Ries, *The Origin of Brands* (New York: HarperBusiness, 2004), pp. 172, 188.

11. M. Lagace, "Making Competitiveness a Lever for Good in Africa," *HBS Working Knowledge*, Feb. 28, 2005, http://hbswk.hbs.edu/item.jhtml?id=4664&t=globalization&nl=.

CHAPTER FIVE:
BUILDING A MERRY BAND

1. A. G. Breed, "Krispy Kreme: The Rise, Fall, Rise, and Fall of a Southern Icon," *Detroit News*, Jan. 22, 2005, http://www.detnews.com/2005/business/0501/22/business-66936.htm.

2. L. Grant, "Krispy Kreme Holes Up at Wal-Mart," *USA Today*, Sept. 16, 2003, http://www.usatoday.com/money/industries/food/ 2003–09–16-krispy_x.htm.

3. Quoted in ibid.

4. Interesting commentary on the Krispy Kreme and Wal-Mart alliance is available online at *Retail Wire*, http://www.retailwire.com/ Discussions/Sngl_Discussion.cfm/10542#poll.

5. J. E. Austin, *The Collaboration Challenge: How Nonprofits and Businesses Succeed Through Strategic Alliances* (San Francisco: Jossey-Bass, 2000), is an excellent resource for good causes that want to work with the private sector.

6. This discussion is drawn from the extensive discussion of Starbucks and CARE in ibid.

7. Personal interview with Paul Bloom, Apr. 22, 2005.

8. Ibid.

9. Personal interview with Mark Dessauer, June 11, 2005.

10. La Piana, *Play to Win*.

CHAPTER SIX: THE HEART OF THE GOOD ARCHER'S ARROW

1. Russ Alan Prince and Karen Maru File, *The Seven Faces of Philanthropy* (San Francisco: Jossey-Bass, 1994), groups many of the motivations for giving discussed in this chapter into seven profiles that mark major donors. The book may be useful to good causes seeking to tap into the values of philanthropists.

2. Aronson, *The Social Animal*, p. 66.

3. Personal interview with Dwayne Proctor, June 9, 2005.

CHAPTER EIGHT: AIMING FOR HEARTS AND MINDS

1. John Kingdon discusses this principle at length throughout his book *Agendas, Alternatives, and Public Policies* (New York: Longman, 2002).

CHAPTER TEN: LETTING
YOUR ARROW FLY

1. Two of the men featured in Marlboro campaigns died of lung cancer, and in the United States, the cigarette cowboys have been forced to ride into the sunset. But Marlboro cowboys continue to rope customers in other parts of the world, where they are still tolerated.

2. Many sources detail the making of the Marlboro Man, including National Public Radio, "Present at the Creation: The Marlboro Man," Oct. 21, 2002, http://www.npr.org/programs/morning/features/patc/marlboroman; R. Kluger, *Ashes to Ashes: America's Hundred-Year Cigarette War, the Public Health, and the Unabashed Triumph of Philip Morris* (New York: Knopf, 1996); and James A. Shaw's Web site, http://users.wclynx.com/theshaws/adsmarlboro.html.

3. Personal interview with Diane Bloom, May 28, 2005. All Bloom quotes in this chapter are from this interview.

THE AUTHOR

Katya Andresen is a marketing executive, writer, and mother of two daughters. She strives to apply Robin Hood Rules every day as vice president of marketing at Network for Good, the Internet's leading nonprofit charitable resource. Previously, she honed her skills in penetrating audiences' hearts and minds as a consultant and on staff at dozens of local, national, and international causes in the United States, Eastern Europe, and Africa. She traces her passion for helping good causes to the enormous need she witnessed overseas as a correspondent for Reuters News and Television, Associated Press, and several major U.S. newspapers. She lives in the Washington, D.C., area.